THE **BIG** BOOK OF **CHOCOLATE**

JENNIFER DONOVAN

THE **BIG** BOOK OF **CHOCOLATE**

365
DECADENT &
IRRESISTIBLE TREATS

DUNCAN BAIRD PUBLISHERS

LONDON

For my family: Kevin, Chris and James
The Big Book of Chocolate
Jennifer Donovan

First published in the United Kingdom
and Ireland in 2008 by
Duncan Baird Publishers Ltd
Sixth Floor
Castle House
75–76 Wells Street
London W1T 3QH

Conceived, created and designed by Duncan Baird Publishers

Managing Editor: Grace Cheetham
Editors: Alison Bolus, Judith More
Managing Designer: Manisha Patel
Design: Sharon Spencer
Studio Photography: William Lingwood
Photography Assistants: Jamie Bowering, Kate Malone, Rob Warren
Food Stylist: Bridget Sargeson
Assistant Food Stylists: Stella Sargeson, Jack Sargeson
Prop Stylist: Helen Trent

British Library Cataloguing-in-Publication Data:
A CIP record for this book is available from the British Library

ISBN: 978-1-84483-600-0

10 9 8 7 6 5 4 3 2 1

Typeset in DIN
Colour reproduction by Scanhouse, Malaysia
Printed in China by Imago

Publisher's note: While every care has been taken in compiling the recipes
for this book, Duncan Baird Publishers, or any other persons who have been
involved in working on this publication, cannot accept responsibility for any
errors or omissions, inadvertent or not, that may be found in the recipes
or text, nor for any problems that may arise as a result of preparing one of
these recipes. If you are pregnant or breastfeeding or have any special dietary
requirements or medical conditions, it is advisable to consult a medical
professional before following any of the recipes contained in this book.

UNLESS OTHERWISE STATED:
• Use large eggs
• Do not mix metric and imperial measurements
• 1 tsp = 5ml • 1 tbsp = 15ml • 1 cup = 250ml
• All recipes serve 4

CONTENTS

INTRODUCTION 6

BASIC RECIPES 12

CHAPTER 1

CHOCOLATE HEAVEN 14

CHAPTER 2

BAKING 66

CHAPTER 3

DESSERTS 142

CHAPTER 4

ICES 162

CHAPTER 5

CHOCOLATES & DRINKS 182

CHAPTER 6

SAUCES, FROSTINGS & ICINGS 202

INDEX 214

INTRODUCTION

There are few things in the world that evoke such intense emotions as chocolate. Silky, smooth and sensuous, chocolate has been around for centuries. It is thought to have been discovered in Mexico by the Aztec Indians, and then brought to Spain in the 16th century. It is believed that the Aztec Indians first used beans from the cacao tree to make a drink for royal occasions, and that the Spaniards made this bitter drink more palatable by adding cane sugar and spices such as cinnamon and vanilla. By the 17th century, drinking chocolate was fashionable throughout Europe, and by the 19th century chocolate to eat had been developed, and traditional hand-manufacturing methods for making chocolates gave way to mass production.

Today, chocolate has become more popular than ever. Gourmet chocolate boutiques cater for the growing passion for top-quality chocolate. Around the world, consumers are demanding better-sourced and higher-quality ingredients, so Fairtrade chocolate (where the cocoa beans have been sourced direct from farmers at prices that allow the farming communities to thrive and expand) and organic chocolate are both reaching a wider market.

This comprehensive book explains all you need to know about chocolate. It guides the home cook through a range of delicous chocolate recipes, from fabulous home-made cakes, brownies, ice creams, puddings and muffins to spectacular desserts and hand-made chocolates. Some of them will be familiar favourites, while others will provide some new and exciting ways to use chocolate.

As well as providing a wealth of simple-to-follow recipes, and briefly outlining the origins of chocolate, this book explains in simple terms the most common ingredients and methods used when cooking with chocolate – all designed to make the recipes even easier for you to reproduce at home.

WHAT IS CHOCOLATE?

Cocoa beans, from which chocolate is derived, are a product of the cacao tree. This is believed to have originated in the tropical areas of South America, although the exact location is a source of some dispute. A relatively delicate plant, the cacao tree needs protection from wind and a good amount of shade; it usually bears fruit in the fifth year of cultivation in natural conditions. Although there are around 20 different varieties of cacao plant, only three are widely used in the making of chocolate – Forastero, Crillo and Trinitero.

The fruit of the cacao plant, known as 'pods', contain between 20 and 50 cream-coloured beans, and it takes around 400 beans to make just 500g/1lb chocolate. The beans are fermented, dried, cleaned and roasted. Then the roasted beans are ground to produce a thick cacao liquor, or cacao mass, and finally pressed to extract the fat, known as cocoa butter.

Cacao liquor and cocoa butter are the essential ingredients of any chocolate product, and the amount included varies from around 25 per cent of the product's weight up to approximately 80 per cent, occasionally more. Other ingredients, including sugar, vanilla and milk, are added to the chocolate before it goes through the final processing stages. Generally, the sweeter the chocolate, the more sugar has been added and the less cacao liquor and cocoa butter it contains. The darker and more bitter the chocolate, the higher the cacao liquor and cocoa butter content; this is widely considered to be a superior chocolate. However, chocolate preferences vary between individuals, so it is best to experiment with what you have available to see which you prefer.

TYPES OF CHOCOLATE

There are a number of basic categories of chocolate. The first is dark chocolate, sometimes referred to as plain chocolate or couverture. This is designed for both eating and cooking. Look for chocolate with a high cocoa content (usually marked as a percentage on the label). Ideally, the percentage should be somewhere between 70 and 85 per cent, although it is important to remember what you are ultimately using it for. The most readily available chocolate tends to range between 60 and 70 per cent, which renders good results, though higher percentages do exist.

The recipes in this book have all been made from dark chocolate (where specified) with a cocoa butter content of 70 per cent. However, if you want to enjoy the best-quality chocolate straight from the packet, be aware that many people prefer the highest cocoa butter content they can find, which can be up to about 85 per cent. I prefer not to use a chocolate of that percentage for cooking as the result can often be too bitter for a chocolate sauce or cake, which requires a slightly sweeter finish.

Also commonly available is milk chocolate, which generally contains less than 3 per cent cocoa butter, and has sugar, milk powder and vanilla added. Milk chocolate is not as successful in baking and cooking as dark chocolate, but you can happily use it as a substitute in mousses, fillings, drinks and cookies, particularly if they are destined for children, who prefer the less bitter flavour. However, once again, for the tastiest results look for good-quality milk chocolate, as many manufacturers use vegetable oils, artificial flavours, fillers and milk solids in their products. Organic varieties of chocolate make a good choice here.

White chocolate is another widely available product, although it is technically not chocolate at all. This is because white chocolate does not contain cacao liquor, instead being made from cocoa butter, sugar, milk and vanilla. Although not a pure chocolate, white chocolate is still very popular and gives good results in cooking.

Cocoa powder and drinking chocolate are also derived from chocolate. 'Dutch-processed' cocoa, where the cocoa is treated with an alkali to give a slightly different flavour and a darker appearance, is considered to give the best taste. Cocoa powder is derived from the pressed cake that remains after most of the cocoa butter has been removed. It may have 10 per cent or more cocoa butter content. Most commercial drinking chocolate (which is designed to be made into a hot or cold drink) is usually made from a mixture of cocoa powder and sugar. Both cocoa powder and drinking chocolate have their uses in cooking, but, as with chocolate, the quality does vary, so experiment with the different brands and buy the best you can afford.

STORING CHOCOLATE

As a rough guide, chocolate will keep for a year if stored in the correct conditions. Store in a cool place – around 20°C (70°F) – and don't refrigerate it unless the temperature is very hot, as the moist environment of the refrigerator will shorten the life of the chocolate. Chocolate also absorbs the odours of foods stored around it, so be sure to keep it wrapped tightly in plastic film or in a container with a tight-fitting lid.

The white film sometimes found on chocolate that has been stored incorrectly is called a 'bloom'. This is caused by condensation that has melted the surface sugar on the chocolate, and although it will not taste or look as nice as chocolate in good condition, it can still be used for melting or baking.

COOK'S INGREDIENTS

Most of the ingredients used for the recipes in this book are widely available and are often very standard, but it is worth noting a few specific points.

Butter – all recipes, unless otherwise stated, use salted butter.

Eggs – large eggs are used in all the recipes. Some recipes contain raw eggs, which carry a slight risk of salmonella, and should therefore be served with care and not be given to small children, pregnant women or the elderly.

Flour – plain flour and self-raising flour are used throughout this book. Plain flour is also known as all-purpose flour. If you do not have any self-raising, and need to make some, simply add 1½ tsp baking powder and ½ tsp salt to every 125g/4¼oz/1 cup plain flour.

Gold leaf – this is an edible product and is most commonly available from specialist cake-decorating suppliers.

Leaf gelatine – this comes in solid sheets that you soak in cold water until they soften. They dissolve easily in very warm liquid. Where necessary, you can substitute powdered gelatine – 10g/¼oz will set around 500ml/17fl oz/2 cups liquid.

Sugar – caster sugar is used predominantly in the baking section of this book because its fine-grained quality gives the best results.

COOK'S TOOLS

You will not need much specialist equipment when working with chocolate. The recipes in this book use a standard range of kitchen utensils, including loose-bottomed spring-form cake tins and fluted tart tins in a variety of shapes and sizes. However, some items you may not already have do make the process that much easier.

Baking beans – these are ceramic beads that are used to weight a pastry case when baked 'blind', that is, without a filling.

Baking paper (sometimes called baking parchment) – this is used for lining tins and baking trays. It is better than greaseproof paper.

Double boiler – this consists of a saucepan fitted with a smaller pan on top. The base pan holds water, which is heated, while the ingredients sit in the top, away from direct contact with the heat. It is useful for heating and melting delicate ingredients such as chocolate and egg custards.

Electric hand mixer – this will enable you to beat and whisk ingredients with the minimum of effort. Alternatively, use a hand whisk or free-standing electric mixer (where applicable).

Food processor – use this to crush biscuits for crumb crusts and to bind cookie dough, among other culinary jobs.

Baking trays and tins – use nonstick bakeware where possible, ideally silicone, which is durable and flexible. Note that cake and flan tins come in various depths, and it is important to use the recommended depth to avoid having too much or too little filling. Choose tins with loose bottoms for ease.

COOKING TECHNIQUES

Using a bain marie – this French cookery term refers to a 'water bath'. You use this method to cook food in the oven very gently (often fragile dishes such as baked custards) and to prevent overcooking. You place the dish in which the food is cooked inside a larger vessel (sometimes with a cloth underneath to protect the base), which you then fill with water to come half way up the dish.

Melting chocolate – chocolate is a delicate product, and can burn easily. It melts best at temperatures between 40°C/104°F and 45°C/113°F. A double boiler is effective (see above), and prevents the chocolate from overheating, but you can also melt chocolate in a single saucepan directly on the stove over a very low heat, as long as you watch it closely and stir it gently. Alternatively, you can use a microwave oven. As the time needed will vary according to the amount of chocolate to be melted and the power of the oven, it's best to experiment to find out what works best for you. As a guide, use 30-second bursts until the chocolate has melted, stirring gently in between.

Tempering – this is a process involving the heating and cooling of chocolate at specific temperatures, which stabilizes the chocolate and gives it a shiny appearance. It also gives the chocolate a hard texture. Tempering is mainly used by professional chocolate makers, and can be done by hand or by machine. This process is not necessary for the recipes throughout this book.

FINISHING TOUCHES

Chocolate curls, leaves and piped shapes are simple to make and add a special touch to the final product.

Making chocolate curls – a simple way is to sweep a wide-bladed vegetable peeler over a block of chocolate. Keep the chocolate cool, or the curls will lose their shape. A slightly more complicated way is to spread melted chocolate over a marble slab, if you have one, or the back of a large metal baking tray. Leave to cool, and then slide a long-bladed knife along the surface of the chocolate to create a curl. This can take a little practice, but is very rewarding. You can use this technique with dark, milk or white chocolate, or a combination of two or more, which can look quite impressive.

Making chocolate leaves – simply brush melted chocolate on the back of a clean, well-defined leaf and chill. When cold, simply peel off the leaf, leaving a delicate imprint of veins on the chocolate.

Piping chocolate shapes and lines – you can pipe chocolate shapes with a fine nozzle on to baking paper – but don't make them too delicate, or they will fall apart. Chill, then lift off as required. You can also randomly pipe lines of dark and white chocolate quite densely over baking paper, then set aside to chill, and break off pieces as required. This is a simple and effective method of decorating ice creams, mousses and meringues.

BASIC RECIPES

Chocolate pastry cream
PREPARATION TIME 10 minutes   **COOKING TIME** 10 minutes   **MAKES** 500ml/17fl oz/2 cups

300ml/10½fl oz/1¼ cups milk
100g/3½oz dark chocolate,
   broken into pieces
1 tsp vanilla essence

2 egg yolks
2 tbsp caster sugar
2 tbsp plain flour

1   In a medium-sized saucepan, heat the milk and chocolate together over a low heat until the chocolate has just melted. Remove the saucepan from the heat and stir the mixture until smooth, then add the vanilla essence.
2   In a large bowl, whisk the egg yolks, sugar and flour, using a hand whisk, then whisk in the warm chocolate milk. Return the mixture to the saucepan and cook over a low heat until it thickens, stirring constantly with a wooden spoon. Continue cooking for 1 minute.
3   Pour the pastry cream into a clean bowl and cover with a circle of baking paper to prevent a skin forming while it cools.

Creamy thick chocolate custard
PREPARATION TIME 10 minutes   **COOKING TIME** 10 minutes   **MAKES** 750ml/26fl oz/3 cups

375ml/13fl oz/1½ cups milk
375ml/13fl oz/1½ cups double cream
8 egg yolks

150g/5½oz/⅔ cup caster sugar
2 tbsp cocoa powder
1 tsp vanilla essence

1   In a small saucepan, heat the milk and cream over a low heat, until just warm. In a large bowl, whisk the egg yolks, sugar and cocoa together, using a hand whisk, then whisk in the warm milk mixture. Return the mixture to the pan with the vanilla essence, and stir constantly with a wooden spoon until the mixture begins to thicken and coats the back of the spoon. Do not boil.
2   Transfer to a clean bowl and leave to cool completely.

Fresh caramel sauce
PREPARATION TIME 5 minutes   **COOKING TIME** 5 minutes   **MAKES** 500ml/17fl oz/2 cups

125g/4½oz/½ cup plus 2 tsp
   caster sugar

125g/4½oz butter, chopped
250ml/9fl oz/1 cup double cream

1   In a medium-sized saucepan, stir together the sugar and butter over a low heat until they melt, using a wooden spoon. Continue stirring gently until the mixture becomes a light caramel colour.
2   Remove the pan from the heat and add the cream (taking care not to burn your hand, as the sugar mixture will spatter), then return the pan to the heat and stir until well combined.
3   Pour the sauce into an airtight jar and set aside to cool completely before placing in the refrigerator. It will keep for 2–3 days.

Chocolate crumb crust

PREPARATION TIME 10 minutes   **COOKING TIME** 10 minutes   **MAKES** 1 x 23cm/9in crumb crust

250g/9oz digestive biscuits
2 tbsp cocoa powder

75g/2³⁄₄oz butter, melted

1   Preheat the oven to 200°C/400°F/gas 6.
2   Break up the biscuits roughly with your hands and then pulse them in a food processor (or place them in a plastic bag and crush with a rolling pin) until they are fine crumbs. Add the cocoa and melted butter, and pulse until the mixture is well combined.
3   Empty the mixture into a greased 23cm/9in spring-form cake tin, press it over the base and up the sides of the tin (according to the recipe), and bake in the hot oven for 10 minutes. Remove from the oven and leave the crust to cool completely before removing it from the tin.

Choux pastry

PREPARATION TIME 10 minutes   **COOKING TIME** 5 minutes   **MAKES** 6 large éclairs or 12 profiteroles

2 tsp caster sugar
60g/2¹⁄₄oz chilled butter, chopped

90g/3¹⁄₄oz/³⁄₄ cup plain flour, sifted
2 eggs, lightly beaten

1   In a medium-sized saucepan, combine the sugar, butter and 185ml/6fl oz/³⁄₄ cup water over a low heat, and stir constantly until the butter has just melted. Remove from the heat and add the flour all at once to the butter mixture, stirring well with a wooden spoon. (The mixture will form a thick dough.)
2   Return the saucepan to the heat and continue stirring for 1 minute, or until the dough comes away from the sides of the saucepan.
3   Remove the saucepan from the heat and beat in the eggs, using an electric hand mixer. For best results, use the dough while still warm.

Sweet shortcrust pastry

PREPARATION TIME 10 minutes, plus chilling   **COOKING TIME** 30–35 minutes
MAKES 1 x 23cm/9in pastry case or 4–6 individual pastry cases

250g/9oz/2 cups plain flour,
   plus extra for rolling out
3 tbsp icing sugar

150g/5¹⁄₂oz chilled butter, chopped
2 egg yolks

1   In a large bowl, combine the flour and icing sugar. Add the butter and rub it in with your fingertips until it forms small crumbs. (Alternatively, do this in a food processor, but work quickly or the pastry will be tough.) Work in the egg yolks and just enough of 2 tbsp iced water to form a dough, using a flat-bladed knife or spatula. Note that the less water you use, the more tender the pastry will be. Wrap the dough in plastic film and refrigerate for 15 minutes.
2   Preheat the oven to 180°C/350°F/gas 4. Roll out the pastry on a lightly floured surface to roughly 5mm/¹⁄₄in thick, to fit a 23cm/9in fluted loose-bottomed tart tin, 3–4cm/1¹⁄₂in deep. Place the pastry in the tin to form a pastry case, taking care not to stretch it, and trim around the edge.
3   Line the pastry case with baking paper and fill with baking beans. Cook in the hot oven for 20–25 minutes, then remove from the oven and gently lift out the paper and beans. Return the tin to the oven for a further 8–10 minutes, or until the pastry is dry and golden brown. (Alternatively, divide the pastry into 4 or 6 pieces and roll each one out to fit a 10cm/4in fluted loose-bottomed tart tin, 3–4cm/1¹⁄₂in deep, and cook for 10–12 minutes, then a further 5–7 minutes.)

VARIATION To make Chocolate Shortcrust Pastry, add 1 tbsp cocoa powder with the flour and cook the pastry until it is dry and dark brown.

CHAPTER 1

Chocolate Heaven

While chocolate cakes, bakes and desserts are, by their very nature, simply heavenly, sometimes the occasion calls for something just a little extra-special. The recipes in this chapter take chocolate that one step further. Perfect for a special celebration or when you just feel like being indulgent, this chapter's delicious desserts and sweet treats are the ultimate in chocolate bliss. From creamy cheesecakes such as Raspberry Ripple White Chocolate Cheesecake to whipped delights such as Chocolate Mousse Cake, Chocolate Roulade with Cinnamon Cream and Chocolate Pavlova, there is a recipe here to suit every taste. Most of the recipes included in this chapter can be prepared in advance, making cooking even more relaxing. For that very special celebration, you will also find a range of hot and cold soufflés. Despite their reputation, these are really simple to master and require only a speedy transfer from the oven to the table and a group of hungry friends or family! So, whatever the celebration (or your craving), there is sure to be a recipe here that will fit the bill perfectly.

001 Mocha marble cheesecake

PREPARATION TIME 25 minutes, plus chilling   **COOKING TIME** 40–45 minutes
MAKES 1 x 23cm/9in cheesecake

butter, for greasing
1 recipe quantity Chocolate Crumb
  Crust (see page 13)
300g/10¹/₂oz cream cheese, softened
200g/7oz ricotta cheese
200g/7oz/¹/₄ cup plus 2 tbsp
  caster sugar
3 tsp cornflour

3 eggs, lightly beaten
2 tsp vanilla essence
500ml/17fl oz/2 cups crème fraîche
250ml/9fl oz/1 cup double cream
2 tsp instant coffee granules
2 tbsp coffee liqueur
100g/3¹/₂oz dark chocolate,
  melted and left to cool

1   Preheat the oven to 170°C/325°F/gas 3. Grease a 23cm/9in spring-form cake
    tin with butter, and press the prepared chocolate crumb crust into the base.
2   In a large bowl, beat the cream cheese, ricotta and sugar together, using
    an electric hand mixer, until smooth. Add the cornflour, eggs and vanilla
    essence, and beat until just combined, then stir in the crème fraîche and cream.
    Divide the mixture evenly between 2 jugs. Blend the coffee, liqueur and melted
    chocolate into one half of the mixture, using the electric hand mixer, and leave
    the other half plain.
3   Pour both of the mixtures over the crumb crust base (use two hands and
    do this at the same time, if possible). Using a fork, swirl the mixtures together
    to create a marbled effect.
4   Bake in the hot oven for 40–45 minutes, or until the cheesecake is firm around
    the edges but still slightly wobbly in the middle. Remove from the oven and
    leave in the tin to cool completely.
5   Refrigerate the cheesecake for 2 hours or overnight, then remove from the tin.

002 Chilled chocolate cheesecake

PREPARATION TIME 25 minutes, plus chilling   **MAKES** 1 x 23cm/9in cheesecake

50g/1³/₄oz butter, softened,
  plus extra for greasing
1 recipe quantity Chocolate Crumb
  Crust (see page 13)
400g/14oz cream cheese, softened

2 eggs, lightly beaten
5 tbsp caster sugar
150g/5¹/₂oz dark chocolate,
  melted and left to cool
chocolate shavings, to scatter

1   Grease a 23cm/9in spring-form cake tin with butter, and press the prepared
    chocolate crumb crust into the base.
2   In a large bowl, beat the cream cheese, eggs, sugar, butter and melted
    chocolate together until the mixture is smooth and thick, using an electric hand
    mixer. Spoon the cheese mixture over the crumb crust base, and smooth the
    surface with a palette knife. Refrigerate the cheesecake for 2 hours or overnight.
3   Remove the cheesecake from the tin and scatter with chocolate shavings just
    before serving.

003 Chocolate sour cream cheesecake

PREPARATION TIME 20 minutes, plus chilling **COOKING TIME** 45–50 minutes
MAKES 1 x 23cm/9in cheesecake

butter, for greasing
1 recipe quantity Chocolate Crumb
    Crust (see page 13)
400g/14oz cream cheese, softened
200ml/7fl oz/³/₄ cup
    condensed milk

3 eggs, lightly beaten
250ml/9fl oz/1 cup sour cream
200g/7oz dark or milk chocolate,
    melted and left to cool
1 tsp vanilla essence

1   Preheat the oven to 180°C/350°F/gas 4. Grease a 23cm/9in spring-form cake
    tin with butter, and press the prepared chocolate crumb crust into the base.
2   In a large bowl, beat the cream cheese until light, using an electric hand mixer.
    Add the condensed milk, eggs, sour cream, melted chocolate and vanilla
    essence, and continue beating until well combined. Pour the mixture over the
    crumb crust base.
3   Bake in the hot oven for 45–50 minutes, or until the cheesecake is firm around
    the edges but still slightly wobbly in the middle. Remove from the oven and
    leave in the tin to cool completely.
4   Refrigerate the cheesecake for 2 hours or overnight, then remove from the tin.

004 Chocolate hazelnut cheesecake

PREPARATION TIME 20 minutes, plus chilling **COOKING TIME** 40–45 minutes
MAKES 1 x 23cm/9in cheesecake

butter, for greasing
1 recipe quantity Chocolate Crumb
    Crust (see page 13)
200g/7oz cream cheese, softened
250g/8oz ricotta cheese
100g/3¹/₂oz/¹/₃ cup plus 4 tsp
    caster sugar

2 egg yolks
2 tbsp chocolate hazelnut paste
200g/7oz dark or milk chocolate,
    melted and cooled
250ml/9fl oz/1 cup double cream,
    whipped to soft peaks

1   Preheat the oven to 180°C/350°F/gas 4. Grease a 23cm/9in spring-form cake
    tin with butter, and press the prepared chocolate crumb crust into the base.
2   In a large bowl, beat the cream cheese, ricotta and sugar together until smooth,
    using an electric hand mixer. Beat in the egg yolks and chocolate hazelnut paste
    until smooth, then stir in the melted chocolate and cream. Pour the mixture
    over the crumb crust base.
3   Bake in the hot oven for 40–45 minutes, or until the cheesecake is firm around
    the edges but still slightly wobbly in the middle. Remove from the oven and
    leave in the tin to cool completely.
4   Refrigerate the cheesecake for 2 hours or overnight, then remove from the tin.

005 Raspberry ripple white chocolate cheesecake

PREPARATION TIME 25 minutes, plus chilling   **COOKING TIME** 45–50 minutes
MAKES 1 x 23cm/9in cheesecake

butter, for greasing
1 recipe quantity Chocolate Crumb
  Crust (see page 13)
500g/1lb 2oz cream cheese, softened
200g/7oz/³/₄ cup plus 2 tbsp
  caster sugar
2 tbsp plain flour

4 eggs, lightly beaten
250g/9oz white chocolate,
  melted and left to cool
2 tsp vanilla essence
125ml/4fl oz/¹/₂ cup double cream
125g/4¹/₂ oz/1 cup
  raspberries, puréed

1   Preheat the oven to 180°C/350°F/gas 4. Grease a 23cm/9in spring-form cake
    tin with butter, and press the prepared chocolate crumb crust into the base.
2   In a large bowl, beat the cream cheese and sugar together until light and
    creamy, using an electric hand mixer. Add the flour, eggs, melted chocolate and
    vanilla essence, and beat until just combined. Stir in the cream. Gently swirl
    through the raspberry purée, using a wooden spoon and taking care not to over-
    mix. Pour the filling mixture over the crumb crust base.
3   Bake in the hot oven for 45–50 minutes, or until the cheesecake is firm around
    the edges but still slightly wobbly in the middle. Remove from the oven and
    leave in the tin to cool completely.
4   Refrigerate the cheesecake for 2 hours or overnight, then remove from the tin.

006 Chocolate & vanilla ripple cheesecake

PREPARATION TIME 20 minutes, plus chilling   **COOKING TIME** 40–45 minutes
MAKES 1 x 23cm/9in cheesecake

butter, for greasing
1 recipe quantity Chocolate Crumb
  Crust (see page 13)
500g/1lb 2oz cream cheese, softened
200g/7oz/³/₄ cup plus 2 tbsp
  caster sugar

2 eggs, lightly beaten
200ml/7fl oz/³/₄ cup double cream
150g/5¹/₂oz dark chocolate, melted
  and left to cool
1 tsp vanilla essence

1   Preheat the oven to 170°C/325°F/gas 3. Grease a 23cm/9in spring-form cake
    tin with butter, and press the prepared chocolate crumb crust into the base.
2   In a large bowl, beat the cream cheese and sugar together until smooth, using
    an electric hand mixer. Beat in the eggs, then gently stir in the cream. Divide the
    mixture evenly between 2 jugs. Stir the melted chocolate into one portion and
    the vanilla essence into the other. Pour the vanilla mixture over the crumb crust
    base and top with the chocolate one. Using a fork, swirl the two mixtures
    together gently to create a rippled effect.
3   Bake in the hot oven for 40–45 minutes, or until the cheesecake is firm around
    the edges but still slightly wobbly in the middle. Remove from the oven and
    leave in the tin to cool completely.
4   Refrigerate the cheesecake for 2 hours or overnight, then remove from the tin.

007 Mini white chocolate cheesecakes

PREPARATION TIME 30 minutes, plus chilling   **COOKING TIME** 20–25 minutes
MAKES 6 mini cheesecakes

butter, for greasing
½ recipe quantity Chocolate Crumb
   Crust (see page 13)
200g/7oz cream cheese, softened
5 tbsp caster sugar

1 egg, lightly beaten
125g/4½oz white chocolate,
   melted and left to cool
100ml/3½fl oz/⅓ cup double cream

1 Preheat the oven to 180°C/350°F/gas 4. Grease 6 holes of a large muffin tin
   with butter, and line each with a strip of baking paper, extending it up the sides.
   Divide the crumb crust mixture evenly between the holes and press down firmly
   to form the cheesecake bases.

2 In a large bowl, beat the cream cheese and sugar together until light and fluffy,
   using an electric hand mixer, then beat in the egg. Stir in the melted chocolate
   and cream, using a wooden spoon, then divide the mixture between the holes.

3 Bake in the hot oven for 20–25 minutes, or until the cheesecakes are just set
   and beginning to brown. Remove from the oven and leave in the tin to cool for
   15 minutes.

4 Remove the cheesecakes from the tin, using the strips of baking paper to
   help you, transfer to individual plates and leave to cool completely. Chill for
   1 hour before serving.

008 Chocolate mascarpone cheesecake

PREPARATION TIME 20 minutes, plus chilling   **COOKING TIME** 50–55 minutes
MAKES 1 x 23cm/9in cheesecake

butter, for greasing
1 recipe quantity Chocolate Crumb
   Crust (see page 13)
250g/9oz mascarpone cheese,
   softened
150g/5¹/₂oz dark chocolate,
   melted and left to cool

60g/2¹/₄oz/¹/₂ cup plus 1 tbsp
   ground almonds
3 eggs, separated
125ml/4fl oz/¹/₂ cup double cream,
   whipped to soft peaks
100g/3¹/₂oz/¹/₃ cup plus 4 tsp
   caster sugar

1   Preheat the oven to 170°C/325°F/gas 3. Grease a 23cm/9in spring-form cake
    tin with butter, and press the prepared chocolate crumb crust into the base.
2   In a large bowl, beat the mascarpone until light and creamy, using an electric
    hand mixer. Stir in the melted chocolate, ground almonds and egg yolks until
    just combined, using a wooden spoon, then gently fold in the cream. In a clean
    bowl, whisk the egg whites until soft peaks form, using an electric hand mixer.
    Gradually add the sugar, whisking until the mixture is stiff and glossy. Fold the
    whisked whites into the chocolate mixture, using a metal spoon, then pour the
    mixture over the crumb crust base.
3   Bake in the hot oven for 50–55 minutes, or until the cheesecake is firm around
    the edges but still slightly wobbly in the middle. Remove from the oven and
    leave in the tin to cool completely.
4   Refrigerate the cheesecake for 2 hours or overnight, then remove from the tin.

009 Chocolate-banana mascarpone cheesecake

PREPARATION TIME 20 minutes, plus chilling   **COOKING TIME** 45–50 minutes
MAKES 1 x 23cm/9in cheesecake

butter, for greasing
1 recipe quantity Chocolate Crumb
   Crust (see page 13)
250g/9oz mascarpone cheese,
   softened
100g/3¹/₂oz/¹/₂ cup plus 2 tsp
   soft brown sugar
3 eggs, lightly beaten

100g/3¹/₂oz dark or milk chocolate,
   melted and left to cool
2 large ripe bananas, mashed
2 tbsp cornflour
125ml/4fl oz/¹/₂ cup double cream
1 tbsp rum
1 tsp vanilla essence

1   Preheat the oven to 170°C/325°F/gas 3. Grease a 23cm/9in spring-form cake tin
    with butter, and press the prepared chocolate crumb crust into the base.
2   In a large bowl, beat the mascarpone and brown sugar together until creamy,
    using an electric hand mixer. Add the eggs, and beat until combined. Stir in the
    melted chocolate, bananas, cornflour, cream, rum and vanilla essence, using
    a wooden spoon, then pour the mixture over the crumb crust base.
3   Bake in the hot oven for 45–50 minutes, or until the cheesecake is firm around
    the edges but still slightly wobbly in the middle. Remove from the oven and
    leave in the tin to cool completely.
4   Refrigerate the cheesecake for 2 hours or overnight, then remove from the tin.

010 White chocolate cheesecake

PREPARATION TIME 20 minutes, plus chilling   **COOKING TIME** 40–45 minutes
MAKES 1 x 23cm/9in cheesecake

butter, for greasing
1 recipe quantity Chocolate Crumb
   Crust (see page 13)
200g/7oz cream cheese, softened
100g/3½oz/⅓ cup plus 4 tsp
   caster sugar

2 eggs, lightly beaten
200ml/7fl oz/¾ cup double cream
200g/7oz white chocolate,
   melted and left to cool

1   Preheat the oven to 170°C/325°F/gas 3. Grease a 23cm/9in spring-form cake
    tin with butter, and press the prepared chocolate crumb crust into the base.
2   In a large bowl, beat the cream cheese and sugar together until light and
    smooth, using an electric hand mixer. Add the eggs a little at a time. Stir in the
    cream and melted chocolate, then pour the mixture over the crumb crust base.
3   Bake in the hot oven for 40–45 minutes, or until the cheesecake is firm around
    the edges but still slightly wobbly in the middle. Remove from the oven and
    leave in the tin to cool completely.
4   Refrigerate the cheesecake for 2 hours or overnight, then remove from the tin.

011 White chocolate & blueberry cheesecake

PREPARATION TIME 25 minutes, plus chilling   **COOKING TIME** 45–50 minutes
MAKES 1 x 23cm/9in cheesecake

butter, for greasing
1 recipe quantity Chocolate Crumb
   Crust (see page 13)
400g/14oz cream cheese, softened
100g/3½oz/⅓ cup plus 4 tsp
   caster sugar
3 eggs, lightly beaten

2 egg yolks
1 tbsp plain flour
1 tsp vanilla essence
125ml/4fl oz/½ cup double cream
300g/10½oz white chocolate,
   melted and left to cool
225g/8oz/1½ cups blueberries

1   Preheat the oven to 170°C/325°F/gas 3. Grease a 23cm/9in spring-form cake
    tin with butter, and press the prepared chocolate crumb crust into the base.
2   In a large bowl, beat the cream cheese and sugar together until smooth, using
    an electric hand mixer. Add the eggs and yolks, flour and vanilla essence, and
    whisk until just combined. Stir in the cream and melted chocolate, using
    a wooden spoon, then fold in the blueberries. Pour the mixture over the crumb
    crust base.
3   Bake in the hot oven for 45–50 minutes, or until the cheesecake is firm around
    the edges but still slightly wobbly in the middle. Remove from the oven and
    leave in the tin to cool completely.
4   Refrigerate the cheesecake for 2 hours or overnight, then remove from the tin.

012   Strawberry, hazelnut & chocolate shortcakes

PREPARATION TIME 35 minutes, plus chilling   **COOKING TIME** 10–12 minutes

100g/3¹/₂oz butter, softened,
   plus extra for greasing
4 tbsp plain flour
2 tbsp rice flour
2 tbsp icing sugar, plus
   extra, sifted, for dusting
1 tbsp cocoa powder

2 tbsp roasted hazelnuts,
   finely chopped
1 recipe quantity Chocolate Pastry
   Cream (see page 12)
150g/5¹/₂oz/1 cup strawberries,
   hulled and sliced
75g/2³/₄oz dark chocolate,
   melted and left to cool

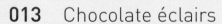

1   Preheat the oven to 180°C/350°F/gas 4. Grease a large baking tray with butter. In a large bowl, whisk the butter until light and creamy, using an electric hand mixer. Gently stir in the plain flour, rice flour, icing sugar, cocoa and hazelnuts until the mixture forms a dough.

2   Cover the dough with plastic film and refrigerate for 20 minutes. Roll it out on a floured surface to approximately 5mm/¹/₄in thick. Cut out 8 circles, using a large scone cutter, and prick each circle 3 or 4 times with a fork.

3   Place on the prepared baking tray and bake in the hot oven for 10–12 minutes, or until the shortcake rounds are golden brown. Remove from the oven and leave to cool on the tray for a few minutes. Transfer to a wire rack to cool completely.

4   When ready to serve, assemble the shortcakes. Place a shortcake round on each plate and spoon over a large dollop of chocolate pastry cream, plus some of the sliced strawberries. Drizzle over the melted chocolate, then cover with a second shortcake. Dust with icing sugar before serving.

013   Chocolate éclairs

PREPARATION TIME 40 minutes, plus chilling   **COOKING TIME** 20–25 minutes
MAKES 6 large éclairs

1 recipe quantity Choux Pastry
   (see page 13)
250ml/9fl oz/1 cup double cream,
   whipped to soft peaks

1 recipe quantity Dark Chocolate
   Ganache (see page 209)

1   Preheat the oven to 220°C/425°F/gas 7. Line a large baking tray with baking paper. Spoon the choux pastry into a piping bag with a plain 1cm/¹/₂in nozzle and pipe 6 x 13cm/5in pastry lengths on the baking tray. Sprinkle lightly with water.

2   Bake in the hot oven for 20–25 minutes, or until the éclairs are a deep golden brown. It is important to make sure that the middles are as dry as possible to achieve the best result.

3   Remove the éclairs from the oven and transfer to a wire rack. Pierce the base of each éclair with a small, sharp knife to make a tiny hole through which the steam can escape. Leave to cool completely, then split lengthways and, if any wet dough remains, scrape it out.

4   Using a piping bag with a 1cm/¹/₂in star or round nozzle, pipe the whipped cream into the middle of each éclair. Using a palette knife, smooth a layer of dark chocolate ganache along the top of each éclair. Refrigerate the éclairs for 30 minutes before serving.

014 Profiteroles with coffee cream & chocolate sauce

PREPARATION TIME 40 minutes   **COOKING TIME** 20–25 minutes   **MAKES** 12 profiteroles

1 recipe quantity Choux Pastry
  (see page 13)
250ml/9fl oz/1 cup double cream
2 tsp instant coffee granules

1 tbsp coffee liqueur
2 tbsp caster sugar
1 recipe quantity Rich Chocolate
  Sauce (see page 204)

1 Preheat the oven to 220°C/425°F/gas 7. Line a large baking tray with baking paper. Spoon 12 tablespoonfuls of the choux pastry on the baking tray. Sprinkle lightly with water.

2 Bake in the hot oven for 20–25 minutes, or until the profiteroles are a deep golden brown. It is important to make sure that the middles are as dry as possible to achieve the best result.

3 Remove the profiteroles from the oven and transfer to a wire rack. Pierce each profiterole with a small, sharp knife to make a tiny hole through which the steam can escape. Leave to cool completely, then split widthways and, if any wet dough remains, scrape it out.

4 For the filling, put the cream, coffee, liqueur and sugar in a bowl and whip to soft peaks, using an electric hand mixer. Spoon the creamy filling into the profiteroles. Place 3 profiteroles on each plate and pour over the chocolate sauce.

015 Strawberry profiteroles with chocolate sauce

PREPARATION TIME 25 minutes   **COOKING TIME** 20–25 minutes   **MAKES** 12 profiteroles

1 recipe quantity Choux Pastry
(see page 13)
1 recipe quantity Chocolate Pastry
Cream (see page 12)
1 tbsp strawberry liqueur

1–2 tbsp double cream (optional)
150g/5½oz/1 cup strawberries,
sliced
1 recipe quantity Rich Chocolate
Sauce (see page 204)

1   Preheat the oven to 220"C/425°F/gas 7. Line a large baking tray with baking
paper. Spoon 12 tablespoonfuls of the choux pastry on to the baking tray.
Sprinkle lightly with water.
2   Bake in the very hot oven for 20–25 minutes, or until the profiteroles are a
deep golden brown. It is important to make sure that the middles are as dry
as possible to achieve the best result.
3   Remove the profiteroles from the oven and transfer to a wire rack. Pierce each
profiterole with a small, sharp knife to make a tiny hole through which the
steam can escape. Leave to cool completely, then split widthways and, if any
wet dough remains, scrape it out.
4   For the filling, place the chocolate pastry cream and the liqueur in a bowl and
gently stir together, using a wooden spoon, adding a little double cream if it
is too thick. Fold in the strawberries, then spoon the filling into the profiteroles.
Place 3 profiteroles on each plate, and pour over the rich chocolate sauce.

016 Passionfruit profiteroles with white chocolate sauce

PREPARATION TIME 20 minutes   **COOKING TIME** 20–25 minutes   **MAKES** 12 profiteroles

1 recipe quantity Choux Pastry
(see page 13)
4 passionfruit
3 tbsp icing sugar, plus extra,
sifted, for dusting

250ml/9fl oz/1 cup double cream,
whipped to soft peaks
1 recipe quantity White Chocolate
Sauce (see page 206)

1   Preheat the oven to 220°C/425°F/gas 7. Line a large baking tray with baking
paper. Spoon 12 tablespoonfuls of the choux pastry on the baking tray. Sprinkle
lightly with water.
2   Bake in the very hot oven for 20–25 minutes, or until the profiteroles are a
deep golden brown. It is important to make sure that the middles are as dry
as possible to achieve the best result.
3   Remove the profiteroles from the oven and transfer to a wire rack. Pierce each
profiterole with a small, sharp knife to make a tiny hole through which the
steam can escape. Leave to cool completely, then split widthways and, if any
wet dough remains, scrape it out.
4   Remove the fruity pulp from the passionfruit and place in a bowl. Mix in the
icing sugar, using a wooden spoon, and fold it into the whipped cream. Spoon
the passionfruit cream into the profiteroles. Place 3 profiteroles on each plate,
and dust with icing sugar. Serve the white chocolate sauce separately.

017 Chocolate macadamia nut tart

PREPARATION TIME 40 minutes   **COOKING TIME** 1 hour   **MAKES** 1 x 23cm/9in tart

1 recipe quantity Chocolate
  Shortcrust Pastry (see page 13)
25g/1oz butter, chopped
25g/1oz dark chocolate,
  broken into pieces
2 eggs
5 tbsp caster sugar

200ml/7fl oz/³/₄ cup clear honey
1 tsp vanilla essence
200g/7oz/1¹/₄ cups macadamia nuts,
  roughly chopped
icing sugar, sifted, for dusting
  (optional)

1   Preheat the oven to 180°C/350°F/gas 4. Roll the pastry out on a lightly floured surface to around 5mm/¹/₄in thick, and ease into a 23cm/9in fluted, loose-bottomed flan tin, 3–4cm/1¹/₂in deep. Line the pastry case with baking paper and fill with baking beans. Bake in the hot oven for 20 minutes. Remove the paper and beans from the pastry case, and bake in the hot oven for a further 5–10 minutes, or until the pastry is dark brown.

2   For the filling, in a small saucepan, heat the butter and chocolate together over a low heat until just melted. Remove from the heat and set aside to cool. In a large bowl, beat the eggs and sugar together until light and creamy, using an electric hand mixer, then beat in the honey, chocolate mixture and the vanilla essence. Stir in the nuts, then pour the filling into the prepared pastry case, being careful not to overfill.

3   Bake in the hot oven for 30–35 minutes, or until the filling is just firm. Remove from the oven, and leave the tart in the tin to cool completely, then dust with icing sugar, if wanted.

018 Grasshopper pie

PREPARATION TIME 20 minutes, plus chilling   **COOKING TIME** 5 minutes
MAKES 1 x 23cm/9in pie

4 sheets leaf gelatine
2 tbsp crème de menthe liqueur
2 egg whites
3 tbsp plus 1 tsp caster sugar
250ml/9fl oz/1 cup double cream,
  whipped to soft peaks

100g/3¹/₂oz dark chocolate,
  melted and left to cool
3 tbsp mint leaves,
  finely chopped
1 Chocolate Crumb Crust, baked
  (see page 13)
3 tbsp dark chocolate, grated

1   In a large bowl, soak the gelatine sheets in cold water for 5–10 minutes until soft, then remove them and wring out any excess water.

2   In a small saucepan, heat the crème de menthe liqueur over a low heat, then add the soaked gelatine. Remove the pan from the heat and stir with a metal spoon until the gelatine is completely dissolved. Set aside to cool slightly.

3   In a large bowl, whisk the egg whites to soft peaks, using an electric hand mixer, then add the sugar gradually, whisking until stiff. Using a metal spoon, fold the whipped cream into the egg whites with the gelatine mixture, melted chocolate and mint leaves.

4   Pour the filling mixture into the chocolate crumb crust and smooth the top with a palette knife. Sprinkle over the grated chocolate. Refrigerate the pie for 2 hours, or until set, before serving.

019   Strawberry & chocolate mille-feuilles

PREPARATION TIME 45 minutes, plus cooling   **COOKING TIME** 20–25 minutes

375g/13oz ready-rolled puff pastry
2 tbsp milk
4 tsp caster sugar
250ml/9fl oz/1 cup double cream,
  whipped to soft peaks

150g/5½oz/1 cup strawberries,
  hulled and thinly sliced
100g/3½oz dark or milk chocolate,
  melted and left to cool
icing sugar, sifted, for dusting

1   Preheat the oven to 190°C/375°F/gas 5. Roll the pastry out on a lightly floured surface to 1cm/½in thick. Cut into 8 rectangles, each approximately 10 x 7cm/ 4 x 2¾in. Place the rectangles on a large baking tray, and lightly brush the top of each one with milk. Using a fork, prick the pastry in 5 or 6 places, then sprinkle with caster sugar.

2   Bake the rectangles in the hot oven for 20–25 minutes, or until the pastry has risen and is golden brown. Remove from the oven, and leave the rectangles on the baking tray to cool completely.

3   To assemble the mille-feuilles, place a rectangle on each plate and spread over a spoonful of whipped cream. Top the cream with one-eighth of the strawberries and drizzle over one-eighth of the melted chocolate. Repeat with a second set of layers – pastry, cream, strawberries and chocolate – then dust the mille-feuilles with icing sugar and serve immediately.

020   Chocolate custard mille-feuilles

PREPARATION TIME 45 minutes, plus cooling   **COOKING TIME** 20–25 minutes

375g/13oz ready-rolled puff pastry
2 tbsp milk
4 tsp caster sugar
1 recipe quantity Chocolate Pastry
  Cream (see page 12)

icing sugar, sifted, for dusting
1 recipe quantity Chocolate Rum
  Sauce (see page 206)

1   Preheat the oven to 190°C/375°F/gas 5. Roll the pastry out on a lightly floured surface to 1cm/½in thick. Cut into 8 rectangles, each approximately 11 x 5cm/ 4½ x 2in. Place the rectangles on a large baking tray, and lightly brush the top of each one with milk. Using a fork, prick the pastry in 5 or 6 places, then sprinkle with caster sugar.

2   Bake the rectangles in the hot oven for 20–25 minutes, or until the pastry has risen and is golden brown. Remove from the oven, and leave the rectangles on the baking tray to cool completely.

3   To assemble the mille-feuilles, place a rectangle on each plate and spread over a large spoonful of chocolate pastry cream (some will be left over). Place a second pastry layer on top of each mille-feuille, and dust with icing sugar. Serve with the chocolate rum sauce.

021 Chocolate nut bavarois

PREPARATION TIME 25 minutes, plus cooling and chilling   **COOKING TIME** 5 minutes

200ml/7fl oz/³/₄ cup milk
2 tbsp chocolate hazelnut paste
2 tbsp hazelnut liqueur
100g/3¹/₂oz dark or milk
   chocolate, broken into pieces
3 sheets leaf gelatine

4 egg yolks
3 tbsp plus 1 tsp caster sugar
250ml/9fl oz/1 cup double cream,
   whipped to soft peaks
chocolate curls, to sprinkle
   (optional)

1 In a medium-sized saucepan, heat the milk, chocolate hazelnut paste, liqueur
   and chocolate over a low heat until the chocolate has melted, stirring constantly
   with a wooden spoon. Remove from the heat and stir until smooth, then set
   aside to cool.
2 Meanwhile, soak the gelatine sheets in a bowl of cold water for 5–10 minutes
   until soft, then remove them, wring out any excess water and stir into the
   chocolate mixture until they dissolve. In a clean bowl, beat the egg yolks and
   sugar together, using a hand whisk, then gradually add to the cooled chocolate
   mixture. Pour into a clean bowl and set aside for approximately 1¹/₂ hours until
   cool and beginning to thicken.
3 Gently fold in the cream, using a metal spoon, then pour the mixture into
   a 500ml/17fl oz/2-cup capacity jelly mould. Refrigerate for 3 hours or overnight.
   Sprinkle with chocolate curls, if wanted, before serving.

022 Mocha bavarois

PREPARATION TIME 20 minutes, plus cooling and chilling   **COOKING TIME** 5 minutes

200ml/7fl oz/³/₄ cup milk
2 tsp instant coffee granules
125g/4¹/₂oz dark or milk
  chocolate, broken into pieces
3 sheets leaf gelatine

375ml/13fl oz/1¹/₂ cups double
  cream, whipped to soft peaks
chocolate-coated coffee beans,
  to decorate

1 In a medium-sized saucepan, heat the milk, coffee and chocolate together over a low heat until the chocolate has just melted. Remove from the heat and stir until smooth, using a wooden spoon.
2 Meanwhile, soak the gelatine sheets in a bowl of cold water for 5–10 minutes until soft, then remove them, wring out any excess water and stir into the mocha mixture until they dissolve. Pour into a clean bowl and set aside for approximately 1 hour until cool and beginning to thicken. Fold in two-thirds of the whipped cream using a metal spoon, and divide the mixture equally between 4 glasses. Refrigerate for 3 hours or overnight.
3 Top each glass with a spoonful of the remaining whipped cream and a few chocolate-covered coffee beans just before serving.

023 Dark chocolate orange bavarois

PREPARATION TIME 25 minutes, plus cooling and chilling   **COOKING TIME** 5 minutes

200ml/7fl oz/³/₄ cup milk
125g/4¹/₂oz dark chocolate,
  broken into pieces
2 tbsp orange liqueur
3 sheets leaf gelatine

zest of 1 orange, finely grated
375ml/13fl oz/1¹/₂ cups double
  cream, whipped to soft peaks
orange slices, to decorate

1 In a medium-sized saucepan, heat the milk, chocolate and orange liqueur together over a low heat until the chocolate has just melted. Remove from the heat and stir until smooth, using a wooden spoon.
2 Meanwhile, soak the gelatine sheets in a bowl of cold water for 5–10 minutes until soft, then remove them, wring out any excess water and stir into the chocolate mixture until they dissolve. Pour into a clean bowl and set aside for approximately 1 hour until cool and beginning to thicken.
3 Fold in the orange zest and two-thirds of the whipped cream using a metal spoon, and divide the mixture equally between 4 dishes. Refrigerate for 3 hours or overnight. Top each dish with a spoonful of the remaining whipped cream and decorate with orange slices just before serving.

024   Chocolate & coconut bavarois

PREPARATION TIME 35 minutes, plus cooling and chilling   **COOKING TIME** 5 minutes

100ml/3¹/₂fl oz/¹/₃ cup milk
100ml/3¹/₂fl oz/¹/₃ cup coconut cream
125g/4¹/₂oz dark or milk chocolate,
   broken into pieces
2 tbsp coconut liqueur

3 sheets leaf gelatine
375ml/13fl oz/1¹/₂ cups double
   cream, whipped to soft peaks
2 tbsp toasted coconut

1   In a medium-sized saucepan, heat the milk, coconut cream, chocolate and liqueur together over a low heat until the chocolate has just melted. Remove from the heat and stir until smooth, using a wooden spoon.
2   Meanwhile, soak the gelatine sheets in a bowl of cold water for 5–10 minutes until soft, then remove them, wring out any excess water and stir into the chocolate mixture until they dissolve. Pour into a clean bowl and set aside for approximately 1 hour until cool and beginning to thicken. Fold in two-thirds of the whipped cream using a metal spoon, and divide the mixture equally between 4 dishes. Refrigerate for 3 hours or overnight.
3   Top each dish with a spoonful of whipped cream and sprinkle with toasted coconut before serving.

025   White chocolate bavarois with blueberries

PREPARATION TIME 20 minutes, plus cooling and chilling   **COOKING TIME** 5 minutes

200ml/7fl oz/³/₄ cup milk
125g/4¹/₂oz white chocolate,
   broken into pieces
3 sheets leaf gelatine

250ml/9fl oz/1 cup double cream,
   whipped to soft peaks
150g/5¹/₂oz/1 cup blueberries

1   In a small saucepan, heat the milk and chocolate together over a low heat, until the chocolate has just melted. Remove from the heat and stir until smooth, using a wooden spoon.
2   Meanwhile, soak the gelatine sheets in a bowl of cold water for 5–10 minutes until soft, then remove them, wring out any excess water and stir into the chocolate mixture until they dissolve. Pour into a clean bowl and set aside for approximately 1 hour until cool and beginning to thicken.
3   Fold in the whipped cream, using a metal spoon, and divide the mixture equally between 4 dishes. Refrigerate for 3 hours or overnight. Top each dish with blueberries just before serving.

026 White chocolate panna cottas

PREPARATION TIME 15 minutes, plus cooling and chilling   **COOKING TIME** 5 minutes

3 sheets leaf gelatine
250ml/9fl oz/1 cup double cream
125ml/4fl oz/½ cup milk
100g/3½oz white chocolate,
   broken into pieces

2 tbsp caster sugar
1 tsp vanilla essence
125g/4½ oz/1 cup raspberries
2 tbsp icing sugar, sifted

1   Soak the gelatine sheets in a bowl of cold water for 5–10 minutes until soft.
2   In a small saucepan, heat the cream, milk, chocolate, sugar and vanilla essence
    together over a low heat until the chocolate has just melted. Remove from the
    heat and stir with a wooden spoon until smooth. Remove the gelatine from
    the water and wring out any excess. Drop the gelatine into the cream mixture
    and stir briefly until dissolved.
3   Divide the mixture evenly between 4 x 125ml/4fl oz/½-cup capacity moulds on
    a tray, and set aside to cool for approximately 30 minutes. Refrigerate the panna
    cottas for 3 hours or overnight.
4   In a blender, pulse the raspberries to a purée with the icing sugar to make a
    coulis. Dip the moulds briefly into hot water and run a sharp knife around the
    sides. Turn the panna cottas out on to 4 plates and serve with the coulis.

027 Coconut & white chocolate panna cottas

PREPARATION TIME 15 minutes, plus cooling and chilling   COOKING TIME 5 minutes

2 sheets leaf gelatine
300ml/10½fl oz/1¼ cups
    coconut cream
100ml/3½fl oz/⅓ cup milk
100g/3½oz white chocolate,
    broken into pieces

2 tbsp caster sugar
1 tbsp white rum
pieces of pineapple,
    for serving (optional)

1   Soak the gelatine sheets in a bowl of cold water for 5–10 minutes until soft.
2   In a large saucepan, mix the coconut cream, milk, chocolate and sugar together
    over a low heat until the chocolate has just melted. Remove from the heat.
    Remove the gelatine from the water and wring out any excess. Drop the gelatine
    into the cream mixture and stir briefly until dissolved. Stir in the rum.
3   Divide the mixture evenly between 4 x 125ml/4fl oz/½-cup capacity moulds on
    a tray and set aside to cool for approximately 30 minutes. Refrigerate the panna
    cottas for 3 hours or overnight.
4   Dip the moulds briefly into hot water and run a sharp knife around the sides.
    Turn the panna cottas out on to 4 plates, and serve with pieces of pineapple,
    if wanted.

028 Mocha panna cottas

PREPARATION TIME 20 minutes, plus cooling and chilling   COOKING TIME 5 minutes

3 sheets leaf gelatine
300ml/10½fl oz/1¼ cups double
    or single cream
200ml/7fl oz/¾ cup milk
3 tbsp plus 1 tsp caster sugar

100g/3½oz dark chocolate,
    broken into pieces
1 tsp instant coffee granules
1 tsp vanilla essence
berries, for serving (optional)

1   Soak the gelatine sheets in a bowl of cold water for 5–10 minutes until soft.
2   In a large saucepan, heat the cream, milk and sugar until it is just boiling, then
    add the chocolate, coffee and vanilla essence. Remove the gelatine from the
    water and wring out any excess. Drop the gelatine into the cream mixture and
    stir briefly until dissolved. Stir well until combined and the chocolate has just
    melted, using a wooden spoon.
3   Divide the mixture evenly between 4 x 125ml/4fl oz/½-cup capacity moulds on
    a tray and set aside to cool for approximately 30 minutes. Refrigerate the cooled
    panna cottas for 3 hours or overnight.
4   Dip the moulds briefly into hot water and run a sharp knife around the sides.
    Turn the panna cottas out on to 4 plates, and serve with berries, if using.

029 Quickest-ever dark chocolate mousse

PREPARATION TIME 10 minutes, plus chilling

2 egg whites
5 tbsp caster sugar
200g/7oz dark chocolate,
    melted and left to cool

250ml/9fl oz/1 cup double cream,
    whipped to soft peaks

1   In a large bowl, whisk the egg whites until soft peaks form, using an electric
    hand mixer. Add the sugar gradually while continuing to whisk until the whites
    are thick and shiny. Using a metal spoon, fold in the melted chocolate and cream.
2   Using a large spoon, divide the mousse between 4 dishes, and refrigerate for
    30 minutes before serving.

030 White chocolate & passionfruit mousse

PREPARATION TIME 20 minutes, plus chilling   **COOKING TIME** 5 minutes

200g/7oz white chocolate,
   broken into pieces

375ml/13fl oz/1½ cups double cream
3 ripe passionfruit

1   In a small saucepan, heat the chocolate and 100ml/3½fl oz/⅓ cup of the cream together over a low heat until the chocolate has just melted. Remove from the heat and stir with a wooden spoon until smooth. Set aside to cool.
2   Using a sharp knife, remove the pulp from the passionfruit. Whip the remaining cream until it forms soft peaks, using an electric hand mixer. In a large bowl, fold the fruit pulp into the chocolate mixture, using a metal spoon, along with the whipped cream.
3   Using a large spoon, divide the mousse between 4 dishes, and refrigerate for 30 minutes before serving.

031 Chocolate nougat mousse

PREPARATION TIME 10 minutes, plus chilling

2 egg whites
3 tbsp plus 1 tsp caster sugar
200g/7oz dark chocolate,
   melted and left to cool
1 tbsp hazelnut liqueur

150g/5½oz nougat pieces,
   finely chopped
250ml/9fl oz/1 cup double cream,
   whipped to soft peaks

1   In a large bowl, whisk the egg whites until soft peaks form, using an electric hand mixer. Add the sugar gradually, continuing to whisk until the whites are thick and shiny. Using a metal spoon, fold in the melted chocolate, liqueur, nougat and whipped cream, just until combined.
2   Using a large spoon, divide the mousse between 4 dishes, and refrigerate for 30 minutes before serving.

032 Coffee, chocolate & praline mousse

PREPARATION TIME 20 minutes, plus chilling   **COOKING TIME** 5 minutes

200g/7oz dark chocolate,
   broken into pieces
2 tsp instant coffee granules
1 tbsp hazelnut liqueur

4 tbsp chocolate hazelnut spread
3 eggs, separated
chocolate-coated coffee beans,
   for serving (optional)

1   In a medium-sized saucepan, heat the chocolate, coffee and liqueur together over a low heat until the chocolate has just melted. Remove from the heat and stir with a wooden spoon until smooth. Stir in the hazelnut spread, and leave to cool for 10 minutes. Stir in the egg yolks.
2   In a large bowl, whisk the egg whites until stiff, using an electric hand mixer, then fold into the chocolate mixture, using a metal spoon.
3   Using a large spoon, divide the mousse between 4 dishes and refrigerate for 30 minutes. Decorate with the chocolate coffee beans, if using, before serving.

033 Mocha rum mousse

PREPARATION TIME 20 minutes, plus chilling **COOKING TIME** 5 minutes

250g/9oz dark chocolate,
  broken into pieces
2 tsp instant coffee granules

4 eggs, separated
3 tbsp dark rum
chocolate, grated, for sprinkling

1 In a small saucepan, melt the chocolate over a low heat, stir in the coffee with a metal spoon, then set aside to cool. When cool, stir in the egg yolks and rum. In a large bowl, whisk the egg whites until stiff, using an electric hand mixer, and mix into the chocolate mixture until well combined.

2 Using a large spoon, divide the mixture between 4 dishes and sprinkle with grated chocolate. Refrigerate for 1 hour before serving.

034 Cappuccino mousse

PREPARATION TIME 20 minutes, plus chilling

200g/7oz dark chocolate,
  melted and left to cool
3 eggs, separated
1 tbsp coffee liqueur

125ml/4fl oz/$\frac{1}{2}$ cup double cream,
  whipped to soft peaks
2 tbsp drinking chocolate, sifted

1 In a large bowl, mix the melted chocolate and egg yolks together using a metal spoon, then stir in the liqueur. In a clean bowl, whisk the egg whites until stiff, using an electric hand mixer, and stir into the chocolate mixture until they are well combined.

2 Using a large spoon, divide the mixture evenly between 4 serving dishes and refrigerate for 1 hour. Just before serving, top each mousse with whipped cream and sprinkle over drinking chocolate.

035 Chocolate liqueur mousse with raisins

PREPARATION TIME 25 minutes, plus chilling **COOKING TIME** 5 minutes

60g/2$\frac{1}{4}$oz/$\frac{1}{2}$ cup raisins
3 tbsp orange liqueur
175g/6oz dark chocolate,
  broken into pieces
2 tbsp milk

2 egg whites
375ml/13fl oz/1$\frac{1}{2}$ cups
  double cream, whipped to
  soft peaks

1 Place the raisins in a small bowl and cover with the liqueur. Microwave the liqueur-soaked raisins for 1 minute, then set aside until cold.

2 In a small saucepan, heat the chocolate and milk together over a low heat until the chocolate has just melted. Remove from the heat and stir until smooth, using a wooden spoon.

3 In a large bowl, whisk the egg whites until stiff, using an electric hand mixer. Using a metal spoon, fold the whisked whites into the chocolate mixture with two-thirds of the whipped cream and the marinated raisins.

4 Using a large spoon, divide the mixture evenly between 4 dishes and chill for 1 hour before serving. Decorate each mousse with the remaining cream.

036 White chocolate mousse with raspberries

PREPARATION TIME 20 minutes, plus chilling   **COOKING TIME** 5 minutes

200g/7oz/1½ cups raspberries,
  plus extra for serving (optional)
150ml/5fl oz/⅔ cup milk
200g/7oz white chocolate,
  broken into pieces

1 tsp vanilla essence
2 sheets leaf gelatine
200ml/7fl oz/¾ cup double cream,
  whipped to soft peaks
chocolate curls, for decorating

1 Divide the raspberries evenly between 4 small glasses. In a small saucepan, heat the milk, white chocolate and vanilla essence over a low heat until the chocolate has just melted, stirring frequently with a wooden spoon.

2 In a small bowl, soak the gelatine in cold water until soft. Remove the gelatine from the bowl and squeeze out any excess water, then stir the gelatine into the chocolate milk until dissolved. Pour into a clean bowl, and set aside until cool and beginning to thicken. Fold the whipped cream into the chocolate mixture using a metal spoon, then spoon the resulting mousse over the raspberries in the glasses. Refrigerate for 3 hours or overnight.

3 Use the chocolate curls and the extra raspberries, if using, to decorate the top of each mousse.

037 Dark chocolate marquise

PREPARATION TIME 30 minutes, plus chilling   **COOKING TIME** 5 minutes   **SERVES** 4–6

450g/1lb dark chocolate,
  broken into pieces
100g/3¹/₂oz butter,
  chopped

250ml/9fl oz/1 cup double cream,
  whipped to soft peaks
berries, for serving (optional)

1 Line a 1.5-litre/52fl oz/6-cup capacity loaf tin with plastic film.
2 In a medium-sized saucepan, heat the chocolate and butter together over a low heat until the chocolate has just melted. Remove from the heat and stir until smooth, using a wooden spoon. Set aside to cool to room temperature. When cool, fold in the whipped cream using a metal spoon, then pour into the prepared loaf tin. Refrigerate the marquise for 3 hours or overnight.
3 When ready to serve, unmould the marquise from the tin and remove the plastic film around it. Dip a sharp knife in hot water to heat it, then cut the marquise into 1cm/¹/₂in slices and place on individual plates. Serve the marquise decorated with berries, if using.

038 Chocolate truffle dessert

PREPARATION TIME 15 minutes, plus chilling

125g/4¹/₂oz dark chocolate,
  melted and left to cool
125ml/4fl oz/¹/₂ cup Creamy Thick
Chocolate Custard (see page 12)

200ml/7fl oz/1 cup double cream,
  whipped to soft peaks
cocoa powder, sifted, for dusting

1 Line a baking tray with baking paper and place 4 small pastry rings on top.
2 In a large bowl, using a metal spoon, fold together the chocolate, custard and cream. Spoon the mixture evenly into the rings, cover with plastic film and refrigerate for 1 hour or overnight.
3 Remove the plastic film, then, using a spatula, slide the rings on to 4 plates. Loosen the rings with a sharp knife and lift them off the desserts. Dust each dessert with a little cocoa before serving.

039 White chocolate, blueberry and citrus pots

PREPARATION TIME 15 minutes, plus chilling

3 eggs, separated
125g/4¹/₂ oz white chocolate,
  melted and left to cool

125ml/4fl oz/¹/₂ cup double cream
zest of 1 lime, finely grated
150g/5¹/₂oz/1 cup blueberries

1 In a large bowl, beat the egg yolks into the melted chocolate, using an electric hand mixer. Using a wooden spoon, stir in the cream and lime zest.
2 In a clean bowl, whip the egg whites to soft peaks, using clean attachments for the electric hand mixer, then fold into the chocolate mixture with a metal spoon.
3 Divide the blueberries evenly between 4 glasses and pour over the chocolate mixture. Refrigerate for 2–3 hours before serving.

040 Strawberries romanoff with white chocolate

PREPARATION TIME 40 minutes, plus chilling

300g/10¹/₂oz/2 cups strawberries,
   hulled and sliced
2 tbsp orange liqueur
2 tbsp icing sugar

250ml/9fl oz/1 cup double cream
1 tbsp caster sugar
100g/3¹/₂oz white chocolate, melted
   and cooled

1   In a large bowl, stir together the strawberries, liqueur and icing sugar. Refrigerate the mixture for 30 minutes to allow the flavours to mingle.

2   In a clean bowl, whisk the double cream and caster sugar together to form soft peaks, using an electric hand mixer, then stir in the melted chocolate. Purée half of the strawberry mixture in a blender, then, using a metal spoon, gently fold it into the cream mixture with the remaining strawberries.

3   Divide the mixture evenly between 4 dishes.

041 Brandy snaps with chocolate cream

PREPARATION TIME 20 minutes   **COOKING TIME** 10–15 minutes   **MAKES** 8 filled brandy snaps

50g/1³/₄oz butter, chopped,
   plus extra for greasing
3 tbsp plus 1 tsp caster sugar
1¹/₂ tbsp golden syrup

4 tbsp plain flour
1 recipe quantity Chocolate Chantilly
   Cream (see page 208)

1   Preheat the oven to 190°C/375°F/gas 5. Grease 2 large baking trays with butter.

2   In a small saucepan, heat the butter, sugar and golden syrup over a low heat until the butter melts, then remove from the heat and stir in the flour, using a wooden spoon. Place 4 heaped teaspoonfuls of the mixture on each tray, leaving enough room around each spoonful for the biscuits to spread.

3   Bake in the hot oven for 6–8 minutes, or until the biscuits have spread and are golden. Remove from the oven and leave on the trays to cool for 1–2 minutes. Gently remove a biscuit from the tray with a large spatula. Working quickly, roll it around the handle of a wooden spoon, leaving it on the handle for a few minutes to set. Gently remove the set biscuit and leave it on a wire rack to cool completely. Repeat the rolling process with the rest of the biscuits.

4   When ready to serve, pipe some chocolate chantilly cream into the middle of each brandy snap.

042 Chocolate & chestnut mess

PREPARATION TIME 10 minutes

300ml/10¹/₂fl oz/1¹/₄ cups
   double cream
6 tbsp tinned, sweetened
   chestnut purée

125g/4¹/₂oz dark chocolate, grated
2 tbsp coffee liqueur
1 tbsp caster sugar
8 crispy-style meringues

1   In a large bowl, whip the cream and chestnut purée until the mixture is just beginning to thicken, using an electric hand mixer. Add 100g/3¹/₂oz of the grated chocolate, the liqueur and sugar and whip until the mixture is smooth and holds its shape lightly (taking care not to over-whip).
2   Put the meringues in a plastic bag, crush them lightly with a rolling pin, then empty them into the cream mixture and fold in, using a metal spoon.
3   Spoon the mixture into 4 dishes and sprinkle the remaining grated chocolate over the top.

043 White chocolate & raspberry Eton mess

PREPARATION TIME 10 minutes

300ml/10fl oz/1¹/₄ cups double cream
1 tbsp caster sugar
2 tbsp raspberry liqueur
8 crispy-style meringues

100g/3¹/₂oz/¹/₃ cup white chocolate,
   melted and left to cool
125g/4¹/₂oz/1 cup raspberries,
   lightly crushed

1   In a large bowl, whip the cream, sugar and liqueur together until the mixture just forms soft peaks, using an electric hand mixer.
2   Put the meringues in a plastic bag, crush them lightly with a rolling pin, then empty them into the cream mixture and mix together, using a wooden spoon. Fold in the melted chocolate and raspberries.
3   Spoon the mixture into 4 dishes and serve immediately.

044 Chocolate zabaglione

PREPARATION TIME 10 minutes   **COOKING TIME** 7–8 minutes

8 egg yolks
4 tbsp caster sugar
5 tbsp Marsala wine

100g/3¹/₂oz dark chocolate,
   melted and left to cool
4 sponge-finger biscuits

1   In a large, heatproof bowl, beat together the yolks, sugar and Marsala wine, using an electric hand mixer. Place the bowl over a pan of gently simmering water (making sure that the bowl does not touch the water or the eggs will scramble). Whisk vigorously until the mixture is frothy and just starting to thicken (this will take around 7–8 minutes), using a hand whisk.
2   Remove the bowl from the heat and beat in the melted chocolate, using an electric hand mixer.
3   Using a large spoon, divide the mixture evenly between 4 dishes. Serve immediately, accompanied by the sponge-finger biscuits.

045 Chilled chocolate zabaglione

PREPARATION TIME 20 minutes, plus chilling   **COOKING TIME** 7–8 minutes

5 egg yolks
4 tbsp caster sugar
5 tbsp Marsala wine
100g/3¹/₂oz/¹/₃ cup dark chocolate,
   melted and left to cool

250ml/9fl oz/1 cup double cream,
   whipped to soft peaks
chocolate, grated, to decorate
   (optional)

1   In a large, heatproof bowl, beat together the yolks, sugar and Marsala wine, using an electric hand mixer. Place the bowl over a pan of gently simmering water (making sure that the bowl does not touch the water or the eggs will scramble). Whisk vigorously until the mixture is frothy and just starting to thicken (this will take around 7–8 minutes), using a hand whisk.
2   Remove the bowl from the heat and pour the mixture into a large, clean bowl. Beat in the melted chocolate, using an electric hand mixer. Leave to cool and then refrigerate for 30 minutes, stirring occasionally.
3   Remove from the refrigerator and fold in the whipped cream, using a metal spoon. Using a large spoon, divide the mixture evenly between 4 dishes or tall glasses, and decorate each with a little grated chocolate, if using, before serving.

046 Zuccotto

PREPARATION TIME 25 minutes, plus chilling   **SERVES** 4–6

300g/10¹/₂oz plain butter or
   sponge cake
3 tbsp cherry liqueur
3 tbsp almond liqueur
500ml/17fl oz/2 cups double cream,
   whipped to soft peaks
100g/3¹/₂oz/³/₄ cup plus 1 tbsp
   icing sugar

150g/5¹/₂oz dark chocolate,
   roughly chopped
50g/2oz/¹/₃ cup roasted
   almonds, chopped
2 tbsp roasted hazelnuts, chopped
100g/3¹/₂oz/¹/₂ cup ready-to-eat
   figs, chopped
cocoa powder and icing sugar,
   sifted together, for dusting

1   Line a 1.5-litre/52fl oz/6-cup capacity pudding bowl with plastic film.
2   Cut the cake into 5mm/¹/₄in thin slices, then cut each slice in half to make triangles. Line the pudding bowl with the cake, cutting smaller pieces to fit any gaps. Reserve the remaining cake for the top. In a small bowl, combine the cherry and almond liqueurs, then use a pastry brush to brush it evenly over the cake.
3   In a large bowl, fold together the whipped cream, icing sugar, chocolate, almonds, hazelnuts and figs. Spoon this mixture into the middle of the cake-lined pudding bowl, then top with the remaining cake. Cover the bowl with plastic film then refrigerate for 3 hours or overnight.
4   When ready to serve, turn it out on to a serving plate. Dust the cocoa and icing sugar over the zuccotto before serving.

047 Individual berry & white chocolate trifles

PREPARATION TIME 25 minutes, plus chilling

100g/3¹/₂oz trifle sponges or
  plain cake, sliced
280g/10oz/2 cups mixed berries,
  e.g. strawberries, raspberries and
  blackberries
juice and zest of 1 orange
1 tbsp icing sugar

6 tbsp strawberry liqueur
1 recipe quantity Creamy Thick
  Chocolate Custard (see page 12)
100g/3¹/₂oz white chocolate,
  melted and left to cool
250ml/9fl oz/1 cup double cream,
  whipped to soft peaks

1 Break the trifle sponges or sliced cake into small pieces and divide them evenly between 4 tall glasses.
2 Slice the strawberries and combine them in a large bowl with the remaining berries. Pour over the orange juice, 1 tsp of orange zest, and the icing sugar and set aside for 15 minutes for the flavours to mingle.
3 Sprinkle the liqueur over the sponge bases. Divide the berries and their juice between the glasses, reserving 4 tbsp for decorating. Add a layer of creamy thick chocolate custard to each glass, then refrigerate the trifles for 2 hours or overnight.
4 Just before serving, fold the melted chocolate into the cream, using a metal spoon. Divide the chocolate cream between the glasses, spooning it over the berry layer. Decorate each glass with 1 tbsp of the reserved berries.

048 Fig, chocolate & Marsala trifle

PREPARATION TIME 20 minutes, plus chilling   SERVES 4–6

200g/7oz trifle sponges or
  plain cake, sliced
6 tbsp Marsala wine
8 ripe figs, sliced
100g/3¹/₂oz/³/₄ cup slivered
  almonds, roasted

150g/5¹/₂oz dark chocolate,
  chopped roughly
1 recipe quantity Creamy Thick
  Chocolate Custard (see page 12)
250ml/9fl oz/1 cup double cream,
  whipped to soft peaks
chocolate curls, for decorating

1 Place the trifle sponges or sliced cake in the base of a large serving bowl, and drizzle over the Marsala wine. Layer the sliced figs on top of the cake, and scatter over the slivered almonds and the chocolate. Spoon over the creamy thick chocolate custard in an even layer, then top with the cream.
2 Sprinkle the top of the custard with chocolate curls, then refrigerate the trifle for 2 hours before serving.

049   Black cherry trifle

PREPARATION TIME 30 minutes, plus chilling   **SERVES 4–6**

200g/7oz trifle sponges or
   plain cake, sliced
4 tbsp cherry brandy
400g/14oz/2 cups tinned cherries,
   drained, syrup reserved
1 recipe quantity Creamy Thick
   Chocolate Custard (see page 12)

250ml/9fl oz/1 cup double cream
2 tbsp caster sugar
100g/3½oz dark chocolate,
   melted and left to cool
6 ripe cherries

1   Place the trifle sponges or sliced cake into the base of a large serving bowl and
    sprinkle over the cherry brandy. Scatter the tinned cherries over the sponge
    base, along with 4 tbsp of the reserved syrup, then top with the creamy thick
    chocolate custard.
2   In a large bowl, whip the cream with the sugar until thick but not too stiff, using
    an electric hand mixer, then spread it over the custard in the bowl. Drizzle over
    half of the melted chocolate. Refrigerate the trifle for 2 hours or overnight.
3   Meanwhile, half-dip the cherries in the remaining melted chocolate, leave
    them to set on baking paper and then use to decorate the trifle.

050 Quick tiramisu with chocolate

PREPARATION TIME 10 minutes

200g/7oz mascarpone cheese, softened
2 egg yolks
100g/3¹/₂oz/³/₄ cup plus 1 tbsp icing sugar, sifted
200ml/7fl oz/1 cup double cream

100g/3¹/₂oz dark or plain chocolate, melted and left to cool
6 sponge-finger biscuits
125ml/4fl oz/¹/₂ cup strong coffee
4 tbsp Marsala wine
4 tbsp chocolate shavings

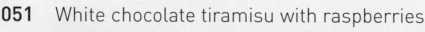

1 In a large bowl, beat the mascarpone, egg yolks and icing sugar together, using an electric hand mixer. Blend in the cream and melted chocolate.
2 Break the sponge-finger biscuits up into small pieces and divide them evenly between 4 dishes.
3 In a small jug, combine the coffee and Marsala wine and pour over the sponge mixture, then spoon over the mascarpone mixture. Top with the chocolate shavings before serving.

051 White chocolate tiramisu with raspberries

PREPARATION TIME 20 minutes, plus chilling   **SERVES** 4–6

2 eggs, separated, plus 3 yolks
100g/3¹/₂oz/¹/₃ cup plus 4 tsp caster sugar
250g/9oz mascarpone cheese, softened
100g/3¹/₂oz white chocolate, melted and left to cool

250ml/9fl oz/1 cup strong coffee
4 tbsp raspberry liqueur
10 sponge-finger biscuits
250g/9oz/2 cups raspberries
4 tbsp grated white and dark chocolate

1 In a large bowl, beat all the egg yolks and the sugar together until light and creamy, using an electric hand mixer. Blend in the mascarpone and melted chocolate until combined. In a clean bowl, whisk the egg whites until stiff but not dry, using clean attachments for the electric hand mixer, then, using a metal spoon, fold the whisked whites into the mascarpone mixture.
2 In a clean bowl, combine the coffee and liqueur and dip the sponge-finger biscuits into the mixture, allowing them to soak up some of the liquid.
3 Use the soaked biscuits to line the base of a serving dish approximately 28 x 18 x 6cm/11 x 7 x 2¹/₂in. Scatter over the raspberries in a layer, then pour over the mascarpone mixture and sprinkle with the grated chocolate. Refrigerate for 2 hours before serving.

052 Dark chocolate tiramisu

PREPARATION TIME 20 minutes, plus chilling   **SERVES** 4–6

2 eggs, separated, plus 3 yolks
100g/3¹/₂oz/¹/₃ cup plus 4 tsp
  caster sugar
250g/9oz mascarpone cheese,
  softened

100g/3¹/₂oz dark chocolate, melted
  and cooled, plus 4 tbsp grated
350ml/12fl oz/1¹/₂ cups strong coffee
4 tbsp Marsala wine
20 sponge-finger biscuits
2 tbsp cocoa powder, sifted

1   In a large bowl, beat all the egg yolks and the sugar together until light and
    creamy, using an electric hand mixer. Blend in the mascarpone and melted
    chocolate until combined. In a clean bowl, whisk the egg whites until stiff but
    not dry, using clean attachments for the electric hand mixer, then, using a
    metal spoon, fold the whisked whites into the mascarpone mixture.
2   In a clean bowl, combine the coffee and Marsala wine and dip the sponge-finger
    biscuits into the mixture, allowing them to soak up some of the liquid.
3   Use 10 of the soaked biscuits to line the base of a serving dish approximately
    28 x 18 x 6cm/11 x 7 x 2¹/₂in. Pour half the mascarpone mixture over the biscuit
    layer. Cover with the remaining biscuits, then the remaining mascarpone. Dust
    the top with cocoa and sprinkle over the grated chocolate. Refrigerate for 2
    hours before serving.

053 Chocolate meringue torte

PREPARATION TIME 30 minutes, plus cooling   COOKING TIME 50–60 minutes
MAKES 1 x 23cm/9in torte

5 egg whites
300g/10½oz/1⅓ cups caster sugar
2 tbsp cocoa powder, sifted
1 tsp vanilla essence

1 recipe quantity Chocolate Chantilly
  Cream (see page 208)
chocolate shavings or grated
  chocolate, to decorate

1 Preheat the oven to 140°C/275°F/gas 1. Draw a 23cm/9in circle on 2 sheets
   of baking paper, turn them over and use to line 2 baking trays.
2 In a large bowl, whisk the egg whites to soft peaks, using an electric hand
   mixer, then gradually whisk in the sugar until thick and glossy. Whisk in the
   cocoa and vanilla essence. Spoon on to the prepared trays and, using a palette
   knife, spread over the circles on the baking paper. Using a spatula, smooth
   the tops of the meringue rounds.
3 Bake in the warm oven for 50–60 minutes, or until crisp. Turn off the oven
   and leave the meringues in the oven on the trays to cool completely.
4 When the meringues are cold, remove them from the oven and carefully peel
   away the lining paper. Sandwich the two meringues together using two-thirds
   of the chocolate chantilly cream, place on a serving plate and spread the
   remaining cream on top. Decorate with chocolate shavings or grated
   chocolate before serving.

054 Chocolate roulade with cinnamon cream

PREPARATION TIME 25 minutes, plus cooling   COOKING TIME 10–12 minutes   SERVES 4–6

butter, for greasing
100g/3½oz/⅓ cup plus 4 tsp
  caster sugar
4 eggs, separated
200g/7oz dark chocolate,
  melted and left to cool

250ml/9fl oz/1 cup double
  or whipping cream
2 tbsp icing sugar, plus extra,
  sifted, for dusting
2 tsp cinnamon

1 Preheat the oven to 180°C/350°F/gas 4. Grease a 33 x 23cm/13 x 9in Swiss
   roll tin with butter, and line the base and sides with baking paper.
2 In a large bowl, beat the caster sugar and egg yolks together until thick and
   creamy, using an electric hand mixer, then stir in the melted chocolate, using
   a wooden spoon. In a clean bowl, whisk the egg whites until stiff but not dry,
   using clean attachments for the electric hand mixer, then gently fold into the
   chocolate mixture, using a metal spoon. Pour the mixture into the prepared tin
   and spread evenly, using a palette knife.
3 Bake in the hot oven for 10–12 minutes until just firm. Remove the roulade from
   the oven, leave to stand for 5 minutes, then turn it out on to a second piece of
   baking paper and remove the lining paper. Cut away any crisp edges, cover the
   roulade with a clean tea towel and leave to cool completely.
4 In a large bowl, whisk the cream, icing sugar and cinnamon together until soft
   peaks form, using an electric hand mixer, then spread over the roulade.
5 Using the paper to help you, but making sure that it does not get trapped inside
   the roulade, gradually roll up the roulade Swiss-roll style from a short end.
   Transfer carefully to a serving plate and dust with icing sugar before serving.

055 Passionfruit, white chocolate & strawberry meringue roulade

PREPARATION TIME 25 minutes, plus cooling **COOKING TIME** 15–18 minutes **SERVES** 4–6

melted butter, for greasing
4 egg whites
pinch salt
250g/9oz/1 cup plus 4 tsp
  caster sugar
250ml/9fl oz/1 cup double cream,
  whipped to soft peaks

150g/5^{1}/$_{2}$oz white chocolate,
  melted and left to cool
300g/10^{1}/$_{2}$oz/2 cups strawberries,
  hulled and sliced
4 passionfruit
icing sugar, sifted, for dusting

1 Preheat the oven to 170°C/325°F/gas 3. Line a 33 x 23cm/13 x 9in Swiss roll tin with baking paper, so that the paper hangs over the edge. Lightly grease the paper with melted butter.

2 In a large bowl, whisk the egg whites with the salt until soft peaks form, using an electric hand mixer, then gradually add the sugar and continue whisking until stiff. Spread the meringue mixture over the prepared tin, using a palette knife.

3 Bake in the hot oven for 15–18 minutes, or until the surface is crisp. Remove from the oven and leave to cool completely in the tin.

4 Turn the roulade out on to a large piece of baking paper and peel off the lining paper. In a large bowl, fold the cream and melted chocolate together, using a metal spoon. Using a palette knife, spread the cream mixture evenly over the roulade, then cover with the strawberries. Remove the pulp from the passionfruit, using a sharp knife, and scatter it over the strawberries.

5 Using the paper to help you, but making sure that it does not get trapped inside the roulade, gradually roll up the meringue Swiss-roll style from a short end. Transfer carefully to a serving plate and dust with icing sugar before serving.

056 Raspberry & chocolate meringue roulade

PREPARATION TIME 20 minutes, plus cooling **COOKING TIME** 15–18 minutes **SERVES** 4–6

melted butter, for greasing
4 egg whites
pinch salt
250g/9oz/1 cup plus 4 tsp
  caster sugar

2 tbsp cocoa powder
250ml/9fl oz/1 cup double cream,
  whipped to soft peaks
250g/9oz/2 cups raspberries
icing sugar, sifted, for dusting

1 Preheat the oven to 170°C/325°F/gas 3. Line a 33 x 23cm/13 x 9in Swiss roll tin with baking paper, so that the paper hangs over the edge. Lightly grease the paper with the melted butter.

2 In a large bowl, whisk the egg whites with the salt, using an electric hand mixer, until soft peaks form, then gradually add the sugar and continue whisking until stiff. Lastly, whisk in the cocoa until just combined. Spread the meringue mixture over the prepared tin, using a palette knife.

3 Bake in the hot oven for 15–18 minutes, or until the surface is crisp. Remove from the oven and leave to cool completely in the tin.

4 Turn the roulade out on to a large piece of baking paper and peel off the lining paper. Cover the roulade with the whipped cream, spreading it over evenly with a palette knife, then scatter with the raspberries.

5 Using the paper to help you, but making sure that it does not get trapped inside the roulade, gradually roll up the meringue Swiss roll style from a short end. Transfer carefully to a serving plate and dust with icing sugar before serving.

057 Chocolate pavlova

PREPARATION TIME 20 minutes, plus cooling **COOKING TIME** 70 minutes **SERVES** 4–6

4 egg whites
250g/9oz/1 cup plus 4 tsp
   caster sugar
2 tsp cornflour
1 tsp white vinegar

50g/1³/₄oz dark chocolate, grated
1 recipe quantity Chocolate Chantilly
   Cream (see page 208)
50g/1³/₄oz dark or milk chocolate,
   melted and left to cool

1 Preheat the oven to 170°C/325°F/gas 3. Draw a 23cm/9in circle on a sheet of baking paper, turn it over and use to line a baking tray.
2 In a bowl, whisk the egg whites until stiff peaks form, using an electric hand mixer, then gradually whisk in the sugar until the mixture is thick and shiny and the sugar has dissolved. Add the cornflour, vinegar and grated chocolate, and whisk until just combined. Spoon on to the prepared tray and, using a palette knife, spread over the circle on the baking paper.
3 Bake in the hot oven for 10 minutes, then turn the oven down to 140°C/275°F/gas 1 and continue cooking for 1 hour. Turn the oven off and leave the pavlova in the oven to cool completely.
4 Remove the pavlova from the oven and transfer to a serving plate. Just before serving, top with the chocolate chantilly cream and drizzle with melted chocolate.

058 Pavlova with white chocolate & passionfruit cream

PREPARATION TIME 15 minutes, plus cooling **COOKING TIME** 30 minutes **SERVES** 4–6

3 egg whites
300g/10¹/₂oz/1¹/₃ cups caster sugar
1 tsp cornflour
1 tsp vanilla essence

100g/3¹/₂oz white chocolate,
   melted and left to cool
250ml/9fl oz/1 cup double cream,
   whipped to soft peaks
2–3 passionfruit

1 Preheat the oven to 150°C/300°F/gas 2. Draw a 25cm/10in circle on a sheet of baking paper, turn it over and use to line a baking tray.
2 In a large bowl, whisk the egg whites, sugar, cornflour, vanilla essence and 4 tbsp boiling water, using an electric hand mixer, for around 10 minutes until the mixture is very stiff. Spoon on to the prepared tray and, using a palette knife, spread over the circle on the baking paper.
3 Bake in the warm oven for 30 minutes, then turn the oven off and leave the pavlova in the oven to cool completely.
4 In a large bowl, gently fold the melted chocolate into the cream, using a metal spoon. Remove the pavlova from the oven, transfer to a serving plate and spread the chocolate cream over the top. Remove the pulp from the passionfruit, using a sharp knife, and scatter evenly over the surface of the pavlova before serving.

059 Mini strawberry pavlovas with chocolate drizzle

PREPARATION TIME 20 minutes, plus cooling   **COOKING TIME** 45 minutes

2 egg whites
125g/4¹/₂oz/¹/₂ cup plus 2 tsp
  caster sugar
¹/₂ tsp white vinegar
¹/₂ tsp vanilla essence
¹/₂ tsp cornflour

200ml/7fl oz/³/₄ cup double cream
2 tbsp icing sugar
150g/5¹/₂oz/1 cup strawberries
100g/3¹/₂oz dark chocolate, melted
  and cooled

1   Preheat the oven to 100°C/200°F/gas ¹/₂. Line a large baking tray with
    baking paper.
2   In a bowl, whisk the egg whites until stiff peaks form, using an electric hand
    mixer, then gradually whisk in the sugar until the mixture is thick and shiny
    and the sugar has dissolved. Fold in the vinegar, vanilla essence and cornflour,
    using a metal spoon. Make 4 circles of the mixture on the prepared tray,
    forming a small indent in the middle of each one with the back of the spoon
    to create a cradle for the cream.
3   Bake in the warm oven for 45 minutes, then turn the oven off and leave the
    pavlovas in the oven to cool completely.
4   In a clean bowl, whip the cream to soft peaks with the icing sugar, using clean
    attachments for the electric hand mixer. Remove the pavlovas from the oven,
    transfer them to 4 plates and divide the whipped cream between them. Divide
    the strawberries evenly between the pavlovas, placing them on top of the
    cream, then drizzle over the melted chocolate.

060 Mini mallow meringues with chocolate cream

PREPARATION TIME 15 minutes, plus cooling   **COOKING TIME** 55–60 minutes
MAKES 12–16 meringues

2 egg whites
125g/4¹/₂oz/¹/₂ cup plus 2 tsp
  caster sugar
¹/₂ tsp white vinegar
¹/₂ tsp vanilla essence

¹/₂ tsp cornflour
1 recipe quantity Chocolate Chantilly
  Cream (see page 208)
icing sugar, sifted, for dusting

1   Preheat the oven to 100°C/200°F/gas ¹/₂. Line 2 baking trays with baking paper.
2   In a bowl, whisk the egg whites until stiff peaks form, using an electric hand
    mixer, then gradually whisk in the sugar until the mixture is thick and shiny and
    the sugar has dissolved. Add the vinegar, vanilla essence and cornflour, and
    whisk for a few seconds until just combined. Place heaped teaspoonfuls of the
    mixture on the prepared baking trays.
3   Bake in the warm oven for 25 minutes. Turn the oven down to 70°C/170°F/gas ¹/₄,
    and leave the meringues in the oven for an extra 30–35 minutes. Remove the
    meringues from the oven and leave on the baking trays to cool completely, then
    place a spoonful of chocolate chantilly cream on top of each one and dust with
    icing sugar.

061 Chocolate meringues with blackberries

PREPARATION TIME 15 minutes, plus cooling   **COOKING TIME** 40 minutes
MAKES 8–10 meringues

3 egg whites
150g/5¹/₂oz/²/₃ cup caster sugar
50g/1³/₄oz dark chocolate, grated,
  plus 50g/1³/₄oz melted and left
  to cool

1 recipe quantity Chocolate Chantilly
  Cream (see page 208)
185g/6¹/₂oz/1¹/₂ cups
  blackberries
icing sugar, sifted, for dusting

1   Preheat the oven to 140°C/275°F/gas 1. Line 2 baking trays with baking paper.
2   In a bowl, whisk the egg whites until stiff peaks form, using an electric hand
    mixer, then gradually whisk in the sugar until the mixture is thick and shiny and
    the sugar has dissolved. Gently fold in the grated chocolate and cocoa, using a
    metal spoon. Place 16–20 heaped tablespoonfuls of the meringue mixture on
    the prepared trays.
3   Bake in the warm oven for 40 minutes, then turn the oven off and leave the
    meringues in the oven to cool completely.
4   Remove the meringues from the oven, and sandwich them together in pairs
    with the chocolate chantilly cream. Divide between 4 plates, and drizzle over
    the melted chocolate. Serve with the blackberries, dusted with icing sugar.

062 Chocolate hazelnut meringues

PREPARATION TIME 20 minutes, plus cooling   **COOKING TIME** 30 minutes
MAKES 10 meringues

3 egg whites
200g/7oz/^{3}/$_4$ cup plus 2 tbsp
   caster sugar
1 tsp cornflour
90g/3^1/$_4$oz/^{2}/$_3$ cup toasted hazelnuts,
   chopped

150g/5^1/$_2$oz dark chocolate, melted
   and cooled
1 recipe quantity Chocolate Chantilly
   Cream (see page 208)

1   Preheat the oven to 150°C/300°F/gas 2. Line 2 large baking trays with
baking paper.
2   In a bowl, whisk the egg whites until stiff peaks form, using an electric hand
mixer, then gradually whisk in the sugar until the mixture is thick and shiny and
the sugar has dissolved. Using a metal spoon, fold in the cornflour, half the
hazelnuts and the melted chocolate, to create a swirled effect. Place 20 heaped
tablespoonfuls of the meringue mixture on the prepared trays and top with the
remaining hazelnuts.
3   Bake in the warm oven for 30 minutes, then turn off the oven and leave the
meringues in the oven to cool completely.
4   To serve, sandwich the chocolate hazelnut meringues together in pairs, using
the chocolate chantilly cream.

063 Poached meringues with chocolate sauce

PREPARATION TIME 20 minutes   **COOKING TIME** 8 minutes

4 egg whites
200g/7oz/^{3}/$_4$ cup plus 2 tbsp
   caster sugar
1 tsp vanilla essence

1 recipe quantity Rich Chocolate
   Sauce (see page 204)
3 tbsp flaked almonds, roasted

1   In a bowl, whisk the egg whites until stiff peaks form, using an electric hand
mixer, then gradually whisk in the sugar until the mixture is thick and shiny and
the sugar has dissolved. Whisk in the vanilla essence.
2   Bring a large, wide pan of water to the boil and turn down to a simmer. Use
2 large spoons to shape the meringue into rounded ovals (you will need to
make 8 in all) and poach them 4 at a time in the water for 2 minutes on each
side.
3   Remove the meringues from the water with a slotted spoon and set aside to
drain on absorbent paper. Place 2 meringues on each plate, and pour over the
rich chocolate sauce. Sprinkle with flaked almonds and serve immediately.

064 Chocolate ganache meringues

PREPARATION TIME 20 minutes, plus cooling   **COOKING TIME** 55 minutes
MAKES 4–6 meringues

3 egg whites
175g/6oz/³/₄ cup caster sugar
1 tsp cornflour
1 tsp vinegar

¹/₂ recipe quantity Dark Chocolate
   Ganache (see page 209)
icing sugar, sifted, for dusting

1   Preheat the oven to 180°C/350°F/gas 4. Line a large baking tray with
    baking paper.
2   In a bowl, whisk the egg whites until stiff peaks form, using an electric hand
    mixer, then gradually whisk in the sugar until the mixture is thick and shiny and
    the sugar has dissolved. Fold in the cornflour and vinegar until well combined,
    using a metal spoon,. Spoon 8–12 flattish rounds on to the prepared tray.
3   Bake in the hot oven for 5 minutes, then turn the oven down to 130°C/250°F/
    gas ¹/₂ and continue to cook for 45 minutes. Remove from the oven and transfer
    the meringues to a wire rack to cool completely.
4   Spread a spoonful of the dark chocolate ganache over half of the meringues
    and top with a spoonful of crème fraîche to complete the filling. Sandwich a
    second meringue on top of the filling and dust all the meringues with icing
    sugar just before serving.

065 Irish coffee meringue with chocolate

PREPARATION TIME 30 minutes, plus cooling   **COOKING TIME** 60 minutes
MAKES 1 x 23cm/9in meringue

6 egg whites
300g/10¹/₂oz/1¹/₃ cups caster sugar
1 tbsp instant coffee granules
1 tbsp cocoa powder

375ml/13fl oz/1¹/₂ cups double cream
2 tbsp coffee liqueur
100g/3¹/₂oz dark chocolate, melted
   and cooled

1   Preheat the oven to 100°C/200°F/gas ¹/₂. Line 2 oven trays with baking paper,
    and draw 2 x 23cm/9in circles on the paper in pencil.
2   In a bowl, whisk the egg whites until stiff peaks form, using an electric hand
    mixer, then gradually whisk in the sugar until the mixture is thick and shiny and
    the sugar has dissolved. Whisk in the coffee and cocoa. Spoon on to the prepared
    trays and, using a palette knife, spread over the circles on the baking paper.
3   Bake in the warm oven for 60 minutes until the meringue is crisp but not brown.
    Remove from the oven, and leave the meringues to cool completely on the trays.
4   In a clean bowl, whisk the cream and liqueur together, using an electric hand
    mixer, to form soft peaks. To assemble the meringue, place 1 round on a
    serving tray, spread over half the liqueur cream and drizzle over half the melted
    chocolate. Repeat with the second meringue, remaining cream and chocolate
    for the top layer, then refrigerate the meringue for 2 hours before serving.

066 Chocolate floating islands

PREPARATION TIME 45 minutes, plus chilling   **COOKING TIME** 25–30 minutes
SERVES 4–6

4 eggs, separated
300g/10¹/₂oz/1¹/₃ cups caster sugar
1 tsp vanilla essence
1 litre/35fl oz /4 cups milk
125g/4¹/₂oz dark chocolate,
   broken into pieces

FOR THE TOPPING:
115g/4oz/¹/₂ cup caster sugar
3 tbsp flaked almonds, toasted

1 In a large bowl, beat the egg yolks together with 100g/3¹/₂oz/¹/₃ cup plus 4 tsp
   of the sugar and the vanilla essence, using an electric hand mixer. In a small
   saucepan, heat the milk and chocolate together over a low heat until just
   melted. Remove from the heat and whisk the chocolate milk into the egg
   mixture, using an electric hand mixer.
2 Return the mixture to the saucepan and cook over a low heat, stirring constantly
   with a wooden spoon until the mixture thickens and coats the back of the spoon.
   Do not allow to boil. Immediately remove from the heat and pour into a large,
   shallow serving bowl. Set aside to cool for 10 minutes. Cover the bowl with
   plastic film (to prevent a skin forming) and leave to cool completely. Refrigerate
   for 2 hours or overnight.
3 For the floating islands, in a clean bowl, whisk the egg whites to soft peaks,
   using an electric hand mixer, then gradually whisk in the sugar until the mixture
   is thick and shiny and the sugar has dissolved.
4 Bring a large, wide pan of water to the boil and turn down to a simmer. Use
   2 large spoons to shape the meringue into rounded ovals, the "floating islands",
   and poach them 4 at a time in the water for 2 minutes on each side. (You will
   need to make 8–12 in all, depending on the number of people.) Remove the
   meringues from the water with a slotted spoon and set aside to drain on
   absorbent paper. Place the meringues on top of the custard to create the
   floating islands.
5 For the topping, in a medium-sized saucepan, dissolve the sugar in 2 tbsp water
   over a low heat, then boil vigorously for 10–12 minutes until the mixture
   becomes a dark golden colour. Cool slightly, then pour the caramel over the
   floating islands and sprinkle over the almonds. Refrigerate the assembled
   dessert for a further 20–30 minutes before serving.

067 Chocolate meringue kisses

PREPARATION TIME 15 minutes   **COOKING TIME** 15 minutes   **MAKES** 12 meringues

2 egg whites
100g/3¹/₂oz/¹/₃ cup plus 4 tsp
   caster sugar

¹/₄ tsp vanilla essence
50g/1³/₄oz dark chocolate, grated

1 Preheat the oven to 140°C/275°F/gas 1. Line a large baking tray with
   baking paper.
2 In a bowl, whisk the egg whites until stiff peaks form, using an electric hand
   mixer, then gradually whisk in the sugar until the mixture is thick and shiny
   and the sugar has dissolved. Whisk in the vanilla essence and chocolate just
   until combined. Place heaped teaspoons of the mixture on the prepared tray.
3 Bake in the warm oven for 15 minutes. Turn the oven off and leave the kisses
   in the oven for 1 hour to cool completely before serving.

068 Hot chocolate soufflés

PREPARATION TIME 25 minutes **COOKING TIME** 20–23 minutes

melted butter, for greasing
80g/2³/₄oz/¹/₃ cup caster sugar,
   plus extra for coating
2 tbsp cornflour
250ml/9fl oz/1 cup milk

100g/3¹/₂oz dark chocolate,
   broken into pieces
3 eggs, separated, plus 2 whites
icing sugar, sifted, for dusting

1 Preheat the oven to 190°C/375°F/gas 5. Grease 4 x 200ml/7fl oz/³/₄ cup capacity ovenproof cups with melted butter and coat lightly with sugar.

2 In a small bowl, mix the cornflour to a paste with 2 tbsp of the milk. In a medium-sized saucepan, heat the remaining milk with the chocolate and 3 tbsp plus 1 tsp of the sugar over a low heat. When the chocolate has melted, whisk in the cornflour paste, using a hand whisk. Continue whisking until the mixture boils and thickens, then turn down to a simmer and cook for 1 minute more. Remove from the heat and allow to cool for a few minutes before beating in the egg yolks. Set the mixture aside to cool completely.

3 In a large bowl, whisk all the egg whites to soft peaks, using an electric hand mixer, then add the remaining sugar and continue to whisk until stiff but not dry. Gently fold the whisked whites into the chocolate mixture, using a metal spoon, and divide equally between the prepared cups.

4 Bake in the hot oven for 15–18 minutes, or until the soufflés are well risen. Remove from the oven, dust with icing sugar and serve immediately.

069 Hot mocha & rum soufflés

PREPARATION TIME 25 minutes   **COOKING TIME** 20–23 minutes

melted butter, for greasing
5 tbsp plus 1 tsp caster sugar,
   plus extra for coating
2 tbsp cornflour
250ml/9fl oz/1 cup milk

100g/3½oz dark chocolate,
   broken into pieces
2 tsp instant coffee granules
1 tbsp dark rum
3 eggs, separated, plus 2 whites
icing sugar, sifted, for dusting

1 Preheat the oven to 190°C/375°F/gas 5. Grease 4 x 200ml/7fl oz/¾-cup capacity ramekins with melted butter and coat lightly with sugar.
2 In a small bowl, mix the cornflour to a paste with 2 tbsp of the milk. In a medium-sized saucepan, heat the remaining milk with 3 tbsp plus 1 tsp of the sugar and the chocolate, coffee and rum. When the chocolate has melted, whisk in the cornflour paste, using a hand whisk. Continue whisking until the mixture boils and thickens, then turn down to a simmer and cook for 1 minute more. Remove from the heat and allow to cool for a few minutes before beating in the egg yolks. Set the mixture aside to cool completely.
3 In a large bowl, whisk all the egg whites to soft peaks, using an electric hand mixer, then add the remaining sugar and continue to whisk until stiff but not dry. Gently fold the whisked whites into the chocolate mixture, using a metal spoon, and divide equally between the prepared ramekins.
4 Bake in the hot oven for 15–18 minutes, or until the soufflés are well risen. Remove from the oven, dust with icing sugar and serve immediately.

070 White chocolate soufflé pots

PREPARATION TIME 30 minutes   **COOKING TIME** 35–40 minutes

melted butter, for greasing
100g/3½oz/⅓ cup plus 4 tsp
   caster sugar, plus extra
   for coating
100g/3½oz butter, softened

150g/5½oz white chocolate,
   broken into pieces
2 eggs, separated
75g/2¾oz/¼ cup plain flour
icing sugar, sifted, for dusting

1 Preheat the oven to 180°C/350°F/gas 4. Grease 4 x 200ml/7fl oz/¾-cup capacity ramekins with melted butter and coat lightly with sugar.
2 In a small saucepan, heat the butter and chocolate together until just melted, remove from the heat, and set aside to cool.
3 In a large bowl, beat the egg yolks and remaining sugar together until light and creamy, using an electric hand mixer, and stir in the cooled chocolate mixture and flour. In a clean bowl, whisk the egg whites until they form stiff peaks, using clean attachments for the electric hand mixer, then gently fold into the chocolate mixture, using a metal spoon. Divide the mixture evenly between the prepared ramekin dishes.
4 Bake in a bain marie (see page 10) in the hot oven for 30–35 minutes, or until slightly puffed and just firm. Remove from the oven and serve the soufflé pots warm, dusted with icing sugar.

071 Chestnut & chocolate soufflés

PREPARATION TIME 35 minutes **COOKING TIME** 20–23 minutes

melted butter, for greasing
80g/2³/₄oz/¹/₃ cup caster sugar,
  plus extra for coating
2 tbsp cornflour
250ml/9fl oz/1 cup milk

100g/3¹/₂oz dark chocolate,
  broken into pieces
100g/3¹/₂oz/¹/₄ cup tinned
  sweetened chestnut purée
3 eggs, separated, plus 2 whites
icing sugar, sifted, for dusting

1 Preheat the oven to 190°C/375°F/gas 5. Grease 4 x 200ml/7fl oz/³/₄-cup capacity ramekins with melted butter and coat lightly with sugar.

2 In a small bowl, mix the cornflour to a paste with 2 tbsp of the milk. In a small saucepan, heat the remaining milk with the chocolate and 3 tbsp plus 1 tsp of the sugar over a low heat. When the chocolate has melted, whisk in the cornflour paste, using a hand whisk. Continue whisking until the mixture boils and thickens, then turn down to a very low heat and cook for 1 minute more. Remove the pan from the heat and allow the mixture to cool for a few minutes before beating in the egg yolks and chestnut purée.

3 In a large bowl, whisk all the egg whites to soft peaks, using an electric hand mixer, then add the remaining sugar, and continue to whisk until stiff but not dry. Gently fold the whisked whites into the chocolate mixture, using a metal spoon, and divide equally between the prepared ramekins.

4 Bake in the hot oven for 15–18 minutes, or until the soufflés are well risen. Remove from the oven, dust with icing sugar and serve immediately.

072 Chilled dark mocha soufflés

PREPARATION TIME 30 minutes, plus chilling **COOKING TIME** 5 minutes

300ml/10¹/₂fl oz/1¹/₄ cups milk
75g/2³/₄oz dark chocolate,
  broken into pieces
2 tsp instant coffee granules
3 egg yolks
4 tbsp caster sugar

3 sheets leaf gelatine
350ml/12fl oz/scant 1¹/₂ cups double
  cream, whipped to soft peaks
chocolate-coated coffee beans,
  to decorate (optional)
cocoa powder, sifted, for dusting

1 Prepare 4 x 150ml/5fl oz/²/₃-cup capacity soufflé dishes by wrapping a 5cm/2in wide strip of foil around the outside of each dish, and tying it in place with string. The foil should stand 2cm/³/₄in above the rim of the dish.

2 In a small saucepan, heat the milk, chocolate and coffee together over a low heat until just melted, then remove the pan from the heat and stir with a wooden spoon until smooth. In a large bowl, beat the yolks and sugar together, using an electric hand mixer, then whisk in the warm chocolate milk. Return the mixture to the pan, return to the heat and continue cooking, stirring constantly with a wooden spoon, until the mixture thickens into a custard and coats the back of the spoon. Do not allow to boil.

3 Meanwhile, in a bowl, soak the gelatine sheets in cold water for 5–10 minutes until soft, then remove them, wring out any excess water and stir into the warm custard until they dissolve. Pour the mixture into a clean bowl and leave to cool. Gently fold three-quarters of the cream into the cooled mixture, using a metal spoon, then divide evenly between the prepared dishes. Refrigerate for 2 hours or overnight.

4 To serve, remove the foil collars and decorate the soufflés with the remaining cream, chocolate-coated coffee beans, if using, and a sprinkling of cocoa.

073 Chilled chocolate & raspberry soufflés

PREPARATION TIME 30 minutes, plus chilling   **COOKING TIME** 5 minutes

250ml/9fl oz/1 cup milk
75g/2¾oz dark chocolate,
  broken into pieces
3 egg yolks
4 tbsp caster sugar

3 sheets leaf gelatine
125ml/4fl oz/½ cup puréed
  raspberries
200ml/7fl oz/¾ cup double cream,
  whipped to soft peaks

1   Prepare 4 x 150ml/5fl oz/⅔-cup capacity soufflé dishes by wrapping a 5cm/2in wide strip of foil around the outside of each dish, tying it in place with string. The foil should stand 2cm/¾in above the rim of the dish.

2   In a small saucepan, heat the milk and chocolate together over a low heat until just melted, then remove the pan from the heat and stir with a wooden spoon until smooth. In a large bowl, whisk the yolks and sugar together, using an electric hand mixer, then whisk in the warm chocolate milk. Return the pan to the heat and continue cooking, stirring constantly with a wooden spoon, until the mixture thickens and coats the back of the spoon. Do not allow to boil.

3   Meanwhile, in a bowl, soak the gelatine sheets in cold water for 5–10 minutes until soft, then remove them, wring out any excess water and stir into the warm custard until they dissolve. Pour the mixture into a clean bowl and leave to cool.

4   Gently fold the raspberry purée and cream into the cooled custard, using a metal spoon, then divide equally between the prepared dishes. Refrigerate for 2 hours or overnight. Remove the foil collars before serving.

074 Chilled white chocolate & passionfruit soufflés

PREPARATION TIME 30 minutes, plus chilling   **COOKING TIME** 5 minutes

300ml/10½fl oz/1¼ cups milk
100g/3½oz white chocolate,
  broken into pieces
1 tsp vanilla essence
3 egg yolks

3 tbsp caster sugar
3 sheets leaf gelatine
425ml/15fl oz/1¾ cups double
  cream, whipped to soft peaks
3 passionfruit

1   Prepare 4 x 150ml/5fl oz/⅔-cup capacity soufflé dishes by wrapping a 5cm/2in wide strip of foil around the outside of each dish, tying it in place with string. The foil should stand 2cm/¾in above the rim of the dish.

2   In a medium-sized saucepan, heat the milk, chocolate and vanilla together over a low heat until just melted. Remove the pan from the heat and stir the mixture with a wooden spoon until smooth. In a large bowl, beat the yolks and sugar together, using an electric hand mixer, and whisk in the warm milk. Return the mixture to the pan, return to the heat and continue cooking, stirring constantly with a wooden spoon, until the mixture thickens and coats the back of the spoon. Do not allow to boil.

3   Meanwhile, in a bowl, soak the gelatine sheets in cold water for 5–10 minutes until soft, then remove them, wring out any excess water and stir into the warm custard until they dissolve. Pour the mixture into a clean bowl and set aside to cool. Gently fold two-thirds of the whipped cream into the cooled mixture, using a metal spoon.

4   Half-fill each of the prepared dishes with soufflé mix, reserving half of the mix for later. Remove the pulp from the passionfruit, using a sharp knife, and place a spoonful in each half-filled dish, reserving some for decoration. Spoon over the remaining soufflé mixture. Refrigerate for 2 hours or overnight.

5   To serve, remove the foil collars and decorate the soufflés with the remaining whipped cream and the reserved passionfruit pulp.

075 Chocolate fondue

PREPARATION TIME 10 minutes   **COOKING TIME** 5 minutes

300g/10½oz dark chocolate,
  broken into pieces
200ml/7fl oz/¾ cup double cream
1 tsp vanilla essence

assorted fruits, cut into pieces, for
  dipping, e.g. apples, pears,
  peaches, bananas

1   In a small saucepan, heat the chocolate and cream together over a low heat
until melted. Remove the pan from the heat and stir the mixture with a wooden
spoon until smooth. Stir in the vanilla essence.
2   Pour the warm fondue into a serving bowl (a purpose-made fondue bowl with
a small candlewarmer underneath would be ideal) or small dish, and surround
it with your choice of fresh fruit pieces.

076 Chocolate & coconut cream fondue

PREPARATION TIME 10 minutes **COOKING TIME** 5 minutes

300g/10½oz dark chocolate,
  broken into pieces
200ml/7fl oz/¾ cup coconut cream
1 tbsp white or dark rum

1 tsp vanilla essence
1 pineapple, cored, peeled and cut
  into bite-sized cubes, for dipping

1   In a small saucepan, heat the chocolate and coconut cream together over a low
heat until the chocolate has just melted. Remove the pan from the heat and stir
the mixture with a wooden spoon until smooth. Add the rum and vanilla essence.
2   Pour the fondue into a fondue bowl (see recipe 075) or small dish and serve with
pineapple pieces for dipping.

077 Marbled chocolate fondue

PREPARATION TIME 10 minutes   **COOKING TIME** 5 minutes

250g/9oz dark chocolate,
  broken into pieces
200ml/7fl oz/¾ cup double cream

1 tsp vanilla essence
50g/1¾oz white chocolate, grated
strawberries, for dipping

1   In a small saucepan, heat the chocolate and cream together over a low heat
until the chocolate has just melted. Remove the pan from the heat and stir the
mixture with a wooden spoon until smooth. Stir in the vanilla essence.
2   Pour the chocolate mixture into a fondue bowl (see recipe 075) or small dish
and sprinkle over the grated white chocolate. As the white chocolate starts to
melt, gently run a knife through the mixture to create a marbled effect. Serve
the fondue immediately, with strawberries for dipping.

078 Chocolate liqueur fondue

PREPARATION TIME 10 minutes   **COOKING TIME** 5 minutes

300g/10½oz dark chocolate,
  broken into pieces
200ml/7fl oz/¾ cup double cream
1 tsp instant coffee granules

1 tbsp coffee or hazelnut liqueur
1 tsp vanilla essence
sponge-finger biscuits, for dipping

1. In a medium-sized saucepan, heat the chocolate, cream and coffee together over a low heat until the chocolate has just melted. Remove the pan from the heat and stir the mixture with a wooden spoon until smooth. Stir in the liqueur and the vanilla essence.
2. Pour the fondue into a fondue bowl (see recipe 075) or small dish and serve immediately with the sponge-finger biscuits for dipping.

079 Italian chocolate custard cake

PREPARATION TIME 20 minutes, plus chilling **COOKING TIME** 15–18 minutes
MAKES 1 x 23cm/9in cake

50g/1³/₄oz butter, melted and left to
  cool, plus extra for greasing
4 eggs, separated
125g/4¹/₂oz/¹/₂ cup plus 2 tsp
  caster sugar

125g/4¹/₂oz/1 cup plain flour
1 recipe quantity Chocolate Pastry
  Cream (see page 12)
1 recipe quantity Chocolate Rum
  Frosting (see page 212)

1 Preheat the oven to 190°C/375°F/gas 5. Grease 2 x 23cm/9in sandwich tins with
   butter, and line the bases with baking paper.
2 In a large bowl, beat the yolks and sugar together with an electric hand mixer
   until thick and creamy. In a clean bowl, whisk the egg whites, using clean
   attachments for the electric hand mixer, and fold into the mixture with the flour
   and melted butter until just combined. Divide the mixture evenly between the
   prepared tins.
3 Bake in the hot oven for 15–18 minutes, or until the cakes are risen and golden
   brown. Remove from the oven and leave the cakes in the tins to cool for
   10 minutes, before turning out to cool completely on a wire rack.
4 Sandwich the cakes together with the chocolate pastry cream. Using a palette
   knife, spread the chocolate rum frosting over the top and sides of the cake.
   Refrigerate for 1 hour before serving.

080 Chocolate mousse cake

PREPARATION TIME 30 minutes **COOKING TIME** 25–30 minutes **MAKES** 1 x 20cm/8in cake

100g/3¹/₂oz butter, chopped,
  plus extra for greasing
150g/5¹/₂oz dark chocolate,
  broken into pieces
5 eggs, separated
125g/4¹/₂oz/¹/₂ cup plus 2 tsp
  caster sugar

150ml/5fl oz/²/₃ cup double cream,
  whipped to soft peaks
2 tbsp icing sugar
1 tbsp orange liqueur (optional)
chocolate curls, for decorating

1 Preheat the oven to 170°C/325°F/gas 3. Grease a 20cm/8in spring-form
   cake tin with butter, and line the base with baking paper.
2 In a small saucepan, heat the chocolate and butter together over a low heat
   until just melted, and stir with a wooden spoon until smooth. Set aside to cool
   for 10 minutes. In a large bowl, beat the egg yolks and caster sugar together
   until thick and creamy, using an electric hand mixer, then stir in the melted
   chocolate mixture to form the cake mixture. Remove 4 tbsp from this mixture to
   make the mousse and keep to one side in a small bowl. In a clean bowl, whisk
   the egg whites until stiff but not dry, using clean attachments for the electric
   hand mixer, then fold them into the cake mixture. Pour into the prepared tin.
3 Bake in the hot oven for 20–25 minutes, or until the cake is firm around the
   edges but still soft in the middle. Remove from the oven and leave in the tin to
   cool completely (the middle will fall, but this will later be filled by the mousse).
4 To make the mousse, fold the cream, icing sugar and liqueur (if using) into the
   reserved cake mixture, using a metal spoon, until just combined. Spoon the
   mousse into the middle of the chocolate cake, then decorate with chocolate
   curls before serving.

081 Chocolate celebration tarts

PREPARATION TIME 25 minutes, plus chilling   **COOKING TIME** 15–17 minutes   **MAKES** 18 tarts

1 recipe quantity Chocolate
  Shortcrust Pastry, uncooked
  (see page 13)
200ml/7fl oz/³/₄ cup double cream
200g/7oz dark chocolate,
  broken into pieces

8 tsp Marsala wine or Kahlua
1 sheet edible gold leaf
  (optional)
icing sugar, sifted, for dusting

1   Preheat the oven to 200°C/400°F/gas 6.
2   Roll the shortcrust pastry dough out to 5mm/¹/₄in thick on a lightly floured
    surface. Using an appropriately sized round pastry cutter, cut out 18 circles to
    fit the holes of 2 x 12-hole jam tart tins and place them in the holes. Prick the
    pastry bases with a fork, then refrigerate for 30 minutes.
3   Bake in the hot oven for 10–12 minutes, or until firm. Remove from the oven,
    and leave the baked pastry cases in the tins to cool for 5 minutes, then remove
    from the tins.
4   For the filling, heat the cream in a small saucepan over a low heat until
    almost simmering, and then remove from the heat. Add the chocolate, and
    stir until smooth, then add the liqueur and set aside to cool. Spoon the cooled
    mixture into the prepared pastry cases, top with a small piece of gold leaf,
    if using, and dust with icing sugar.

082 Chocolate meringue tart

PREPARATION TIME 30 minutes   **COOKING TIME** 50–55 minutes   **MAKES** 1 x 23cm/9in tart

1 x 23cm/9in Chocolate Shortcrust
  Pastry case, baked (see page 13)
250ml/9fl oz/1 cup condensed milk
1 tsp vanilla essence
2 tbsp cocoa powder, sifted

2 tbsp plain flour
3 eggs, separated
50g/1³/₄oz butter, chopped
150g/5¹/₂oz/²/₃ cup caster sugar

1   Preheat the oven to 180°C/350°F/gas 4. Place the baked pastry case on a
    baking tray.
2   In a medium-sized saucepan, heat the condensed milk and vanilla essence over
    a low heat for 3 minutes, stirring constantly with a wooden spoon. Add the cocoa
    and flour, stirring well until combined, then remove the pan from the heat and
    stir in the egg yolks and butter. Pour the mixture into the prepared pastry case,
    being careful not to overfill.
3   Bake in the hot oven for 35–40 minutes, or until the filling is just set. Remove
    the tart from the oven and set aside in the tin.
4   In a clean bowl, whisk the egg whites to stiff peaks, using an electric hand mixer,
    then gradually whisk in the sugar until thick and glossy. Spread the meringue
    over the chocolate filling and return the tart to the hot oven for 8–10 minutes,
    or until the meringue is golden brown. Remove from the oven and serve warm.

083 Chocolate raspberry ganache torte

PREPARATION TIME 40 minutes, plus setting   **COOKING TIME** 25–30 minutes
MAKES 1 x 23cm/9in torte

butter, for greasing
3 eggs, separated, plus 3 yolks
100g/3½oz/⅓ cup plus
   4 tsp caster sugar
4 tbsp plain flour

4 tbsp cocoa powder
½ tsp baking powder
2 x recipe quantity Dark Chocolate
   Ganache (see page 209)
3 tbsp raspberry jam

1   Preheat the oven to 190°C/375°F/gas 5. Grease 2 x 23cm/9in sandwich tins
   with butter, and line the bases with baking paper.
2   In a large bowl, beat all the egg yolks and the sugar together until thick and
   creamy, using an electric mixer. In a separate bowl, sift the flour, cocoa and
   baking powder together, and fold into the egg mixture. In a third bowl, whisk
   the egg whites until stiff but not dry, using clean attachments for the electric
   hand mixer, and fold into the cake mixture. Divide the mixture evenly between
   the prepared tins.
3   Bake in the hot oven for 25–30 minutes, or until the cakes have risen and are
   dark brown. Remove from the oven, and leave the cakes in the tins to cool for
   10 minutes. Remove from the tins and transfer to a wire rack to cool completely.
4   Using a palette knife, sandwich the cakes together with a thick layer of dark
   chocolate ganache and then a layer of raspberry jam. Spread the remaining
   ganache over the top and sides of the torte. Leave the iced cake to set for
   1 hour at room temperature before serving.

084 Mocha truffle tart

PREPARATION TIME 40 minutes, plus chilling   **COOKING TIME** 5 minutes
MAKES 1 x 23cm/9in tart

250g/9oz dark chocolate,
   broken into pieces
150g/5½oz butter, chopped
2 tbsp instant coffee granules
4 egg yolks
100g/3½oz/⅓ cup plus 4 tsp
   caster sugar

1 x 23cm/9in Chocolate Shortcrust
   Pastry case, baked (see page 13)
150ml/5fl oz/⅓ cup double cream,
   whipped to soft peaks
cocoa powder, sifted, for dusting

1   In a small saucepan, melt the chocolate, butter and coffee together over a low
   heat until just melted. Remove the pan from the heat and stir until smooth, then
   pour into a clean bowl and set aside to cool.
2   In a large bowl, beat the egg yolks and sugar together until thick and creamy,
   using an electric hand mixer. Stir in half the chocolate mixture, using a wooden
   spoon, and pour into the baked pastry case. Fold the cream into the remaining
   chocolate mixture, using a metal spoon, and pour into the pastry case, over the
   first layer. Refrigerate for 1 hour. Dust cocoa over the top of the tart before serving.

085 White chocolate & lime tart

PREPARATION TIME 15 minutes, plus chilling **COOKING TIME** 5 minutes
MAKES 1 x 23cm/9in tart

200ml/7fl oz/³/₄ cup double cream
300g/10¹/₂oz white chocolate,
   broken into pieces

zest of 2 limes, plus 1 lime,
   thinly sliced
1 Chocolate Crumb Crust, baked
   (see page 13)

1   In a small saucepan, heat the cream and chocolate together over a low heat until the chocolate has just melted, then remove from the heat and stir until smooth, using a wooden spoon. Stir in the lime zest, then set aside to cool for 10 minutes.

2   Pour the mixture into the baked crumb crust, and refrigerate for 2 hours or until set. Decorate with lime slices before serving.

086 White chocolate mousse cake

PREPARATION TIME 25 minutes   **COOKING TIME** 35–40 minutes   **MAKES** 1 x 23cm/9in cake

25g/1oz butter, chopped,
   plus extra for greasing
200g/7oz white chocolate,
   half broken into pieces and half
   melted and left to cool, plus
   shavings to decorate

300ml/10¹/₂fl oz/1¹/₄ cups
   double cream
4 eggs, separated
3 tbsp plus 1 tsp caster sugar
2¹/₂ tbsp plain flour
125g/4¹/₂oz/1 cup raspberries

1   Preheat the oven to 150°C/300°F/gas 4. Grease a 23cm/9in spring-form cake tin with butter, and line the base with baking paper.

2   In a small saucepan, heat the chocolate pieces, butter and 4 tbsp of the cream together over a low heat until the chocolate just melts. Remove the pan from the heat and stir until smooth, using a wooden spoon, then set aside to cool.

3   In a large bowl, beat the egg yolks and sugar together, using an electric hand mixer, until pale and creamy. Stir in the flour and the chocolate mixture, using a wooden spoon. In a clean bowl, whisk the egg whites until stiff but not dry, using clean attachments for the electric hand mixer. Gently fold the whisked whites into the chocolate cake mixture, using a metal spoon, then pour into the prepared tin.

4   Bake in the hot oven for 30–35 minutes, or until the cake is just firm. Remove from the oven, and leave the cake in the tin to cool completely. When cool, remove the cake from the tin and transfer to a serving plate.

5   In a clean bowl, lightly whip the remaining cream, using clean attachments for the electric hand mixer. (It will thicken when the chocolate is added, so be careful not to make it too stiff.) Gently fold the melted chocolate into it, using a metal spoon, then spoon the chocolate cream into the middle of the cake. Top the cake with raspberries and white chocolate shavings.

087 Chocolate lava cakes

PREPARATION TIME 10 minutes   **COOKING TIME** 15–18 minutes

100g/3½oz butter, chopped,
  plus extra for greasing
150g/5½oz dark chocolate,
  broken into pieces
4 eggs

125g/4½oz/½ cup plus 2 tsp
  caster sugar
150g/5½oz/1 cup plus 2 tbsp
  plain flour

1   Preheat the oven to 180°C/350°F/gas 4. Grease 4 x 200ml/7oz/¾ cup capacity ovenproof ramekins with butter.
2   In a small saucepan, heat the chocolate and butter together over a low heat until just melted. Remove the pan from the heat and stir until smooth, using a wooden spoon, then set aside to cool. In a large bowl, beat the eggs and sugar together until thick and pale, using an electric hand mixer. Stir in the flour, then gently fold in the chocolate mixture, using a metal spoon. Divide the mixture evenly between the ramekins.
3   Bake in the hot oven for 8–10 minutes. Remove from the oven, and leave the lava cakes in the ramekins to cool for a few minutes before turning out on to plates. Serve warm.

088 Sinful chocolate cake

PREPARATION TIME 35 minutes, plus chilling   **COOKING TIME** 5 minutes
SERVES 4–6

1 recipe quantity Chocolate Crumb
  Crust (see page 13)
200ml/7fl oz/¾ cup double cream
1 tsp vanilla essence
200g/7oz dark chocolate,
  broken into pieces

300g/10½oz/2⅓ cups raspberries,
  lightly crushed
2 eggs, separated
cocoa powder, sifted, for dusting

1   Press the prepared chocolate crumb crust into the base of a 23cm/9in square loose-bottomed, fluted flan tin. You may not need all of the crust mixture. Refrigerate the prepared crust for 15 minutes.
2   In a small saucepan, heat the cream, vanilla essence and chocolate together over a low heat until the chocolate has just melted. Remove the pan from the heat and stir with a wooden spoon until smooth. Set aside to cool. Spread the raspberries over the top of the chilled crumb crust.
3   In a clean bowl, whisk the egg whites until stiff, using an electric hand mixer. Stir the egg yolks into the cooled chocolate mixture, using a wooden spoon, then fold in the egg whites, using a metal spoon. Pour the mixture into the crumb crust, over the raspberries.
4   Refrigerate the cake for 2 hours. Remove from the tin and dust with cocoa before serving.

089 Sticky chocolate cake

PREPARATION TIME 25 minutes   **COOKING TIME** 50–55 minutes   **MAKES** 1 x 23cm/9in cake

250g/9oz butter,
  plus extra for greasing
250ml/9fl oz/1 cup double cream
175g/6oz dark chocolate,
  broken into pieces
1 tsp instant coffee granules
250g/9oz/1 cup soft brown sugar
4 eggs, lightly beaten
2 tsp vanilla essence

200g/7oz/1½ cups plus 4 tsp
  self-raising flour
1 tsp ground cinnamon
1 tsp ground nutmeg
125g/4½oz/1 cup raisins
115g/4oz/¾ cup plus 2 tbsp walnuts,
  chopped
1 recipe quantity Rich Chocolate
  Sauce (see page 204)

1   Preheat the oven to 170°F/325°C/gas 3. Grease a 23cm/9in spring-form
    cake tin with butter, and line the base with baking paper.
2   In a small saucepan, heat the cream, chocolate and coffee over a low heat
    until the chocolate has just melted. Remove the pan from the heat, and stir
    the mixture with a wooden spoon until smooth, then leave to cool. In a large
    bowl, beat the butter and sugar together, using an electric hand mixer, until
    light and creamy, then beat in the eggs gradually. Stir in the vanilla essence and
    chocolate mixture, using a wooden spoon. Gently fold in the flour, cinnamon,
    nutmeg, raisins and walnuts, using a metal spoon, then pour the mixture into
    the prepared tin.
3   Bake in the hot oven for 45–50 minutes, or until a skewer inserted into the
    middle comes out with just a few moist crumbs on it. Remove from the oven,
    and leave the cake in the tin to cool for 10 minutes.
4   Remove the cake from the tin and serve warm with the rich chocolate sauce.

090 Lemon roulade with chocolate drizzle

PREPARATION TIME 25 minutes, plus setting   **COOKING TIME** 18–20 minutes
SERVES 4–6

butter, for greasing
175g/6oz/¾ cup caster sugar
6 eggs, separated
225g/8oz dark chocolate,
  melted and left to cool
2 tbsp cocoa powder

4 tbsp lemon curd
juice and rind of 1 lemon,
  finely grated
250ml/9fl oz/1 cup double cream,
  whipped to soft peaks

1   Preheat the oven to 180°C/350°F/gas 4. Grease a 33 x 23cm/13 x 9in Swiss roll tin with butter, and line the base and sides with baking paper.
2   In a large bowl, beat the sugar and egg yolks together, using an electric hand mixer, until thick and creamy. Stir in 175g/6oz of the melted chocolate and the cocoa, using a wooden spoon. In a clean bowl, whisk the egg whites until stiff but not dry, using clean attachments for the electric hand mixer, then gently fold into the chocolate mixture, using a metal spoon. Pour the mixture into the prepared tin and spread evenly, using a palette knife.
3   Bake in the hot oven for 18–20 minutes, or until firm. Remove from the oven and leave to cool completely in the tin. When cool, turn out on to a clean tea towel and remove the lining paper.
4   In a large bowl, mix the lemon curd with the lemon rind and juice, then fold into the cream, using a metal spoon. Spread the lemon cream evenly over the roulade.
5   Using the tea towel to help you, but making sure that it does not get trapped inside the roulade, gradually roll up the roulade Swiss roll style from a short end. Transfer carefully to a serving plate, and drizzle the remaining melted chocolate over the top. Leave to set at room temperature for 30 minutes before serving.

091 White chocolate roulade with raspberries

PREPARATION TIME 30 minutes   **COOKING TIME** 15–18 minutes   **SERVES** 4–6

butter, for greasing
125g/4½oz/½ cup plus 2 tsp
  caster sugar
6 eggs, separated
175g/6oz white chocolate,
  melted and left to cool

2 tbsp plain flour
250ml/9fl oz/1 cup double cream,
  whipped to soft peaks
185g/6½oz/1½ cups raspberries,
  lightly crushed
dark chocolate, grated, to sprinkle

1   Preheat the oven to 180°C/350°F/gas 4. Grease a 33 x 23cm/13 x 9in Swiss roll tin with butter, and line the base and sides with baking paper.
2   In a large bowl, beat the sugar and egg yolks together, using an electric hand mixer, until thick and creamy. Stir in the melted chocolate and flour, using a wooden spoon. In a clean bowl, whisk the egg whites until stiff but not dry, using clean attachments for the electric hand mixer, then gently fold into the chocolate mixture, using a metal spoon. Pour the mixture into the prepared tin and spread evenly, using a palette knife.
3   Bake in the hot oven for 15–18 minutes, or until firm. Remove from the oven and leave to cool completely in the tin. When cool, turn out on to a clean tea towel and remove the lining paper.
4   Spread the cream evenly over the roulade, and scatter over the raspberries. Using the tea towel to help you, but making sure that it does not get trapped inside the roulade, gradually roll up the roulade Swiss roll style from a short end. Transfer carefully to a serving plate. Sprinkle over the grated chocolate before serving.

092 Chocolate roulade with mixed berries & white chocolate cream

PREPARATION TIME 25 minutes   **COOKING TIME** 18–20 minutes   **SERVES** 4–6

butter, for greasing
175g/6oz/³/₄ cup caster sugar
6 eggs, separated
175g/6oz dark chocolate,
    melted and left to cool
2 tbsp cocoa powder

250ml/9fl oz/1 cup double cream,
    whipped to soft peaks
100g/3¹/₂oz white chocolate,
    melted and left to cool
185g/6¹/₂oz/1¹/₂ cups mixed berries
icing sugar, sifted, for dusting

1 Preheat the oven to 180°C/350°F/gas 4. Grease a 33 x 23cm/13 x 9in Swiss roll tin with butter, and line the base and sides with baking paper.
2 In a large bowl, beat the sugar and egg yolks together, using an electric hand mixer, until thick and creamy. Stir in the melted dark chocolate and cocoa, using a wooden spoon. In a clean bowl, whisk the egg whites until stiff but not dry, using clean attachments for the electric hand mixer, then gently fold into the chocolate mixture, using a metal spoon. Pour the mixture into the prepared tin and spread evenly, using a palette knife.
3 Bake in the hot oven for 18–20 minutes, or until firm. Remove from the oven and leave to cool completely in the tin. When cool, turn out on to a clean tea towel and remove the lining paper.
4 In a large bowl, fold the cream and the melted white chocolate together, using a metal spoon, and spread evenly over the roulade. Scatter over the mixed berries, slicing any strawberries.
5 Using the tea towel to help you, but making sure that it does not get trapped inside the roulade, gradually roll up the roulade Swiss roll style from a short end. Transfer carefully to a serving plate, and dust with icing sugar before serving.

093 Mocha roulade with chocolate mascarpone cream

PREPARATION TIME 20 minutes   **COOKING TIME** 18–20 minutes   **SERVES** 4–6

butter, for greasing
175g/6oz/³/₄ cup caster sugar
6 eggs, separated
175g/6oz dark chocolate,
    melted and left to cool
2 tbsp cocoa powder

3 tsp instant coffee granules
1 recipe quantity Chocolate
    Mascarpone Cream (see page 208)
1 tbsp double cream
2 tbsp coffee liqueur
icing sugar, sifted, for dusting

1 Preheat the oven to 180°C/350°F/gas 4. Grease a 33 x 23cm/13 x 9in Swiss roll tin with butter, and line the base and sides with baking paper.
2 In a large bowl, beat the sugar and egg yolks together, using an electric hand mixer, until thick and creamy. Stir in the melted chocolate, cocoa and coffee, using a wooden spoon. In a clean bowl, whisk the egg whites until stiff but not dry, using clean attachments for the electric hand mixer, then gently fold into the chocolate mixture, using a metal spoon. Pour the mixture into the prepared tin and spread evenly, using a palette knife.
3 Bake in the hot oven for 18–20 minutes, or until firm. Remove from the oven and leave to cool completely in the tin. When cool, turn out on to a clean tea towel and remove the lining paper.
4 In a large bowl, mix together the chocolate mascarpone cream, cream and liqueur, then spread evenly over the base.
5 Using the tea towel to help you, but making sure it does not get trapped inside the roulade, gradually roll up the roulade Swiss roll style from a short end. Transfer carefully to a serving plate, and dust with icing sugar before serving.

CHAPTER 2

Baking

There is nothing more wonderful than the smell of freshly baked cakes, cookies or tarts. For me, it brings back precious memories of childhood – coming home after school to a home-made chocolate cake or perhaps a delicious slice or cookie. I passed the tradition down to the next generation, surprising my own children with unexpected treats. And on birthdays, I would always make sure there was a magnificent chocolate cake, decorated with a creamy chocolate icing and dotted with the appropriate number of candles.

Baking can be seen as complicated and time-consuming. However, it really is a very simple skill to master and requires only a light touch and good-quality, fresh ingredients.

I've put a large selection of recipes in this chapter, including cakes, tarts, brownies, slices and biscuits, so that you will find something to suit every occasion. Whether it is Rocky Road Brownies for a family afternoon tea or a Chocolate Angel Food Cake as a centrepiece for a memorable birthday, they're all here – just waiting for you to try them out!

094 Warm chocolate & nut torte

PREPARATION TIME 20 minutes   **COOKING TIME** 40–45 minutes   **MAKES** 1 x 23cm/9in torte

185g/6¹/₂oz butter, softened,
 plus extra for greasing
185g/6¹/₂oz/³/₄ cup plus 1 tbsp
 caster sugar
1 tsp vanilla essence
3 eggs, lightly beaten
185g/6¹/₂oz/1³/₄ cups ground almonds

100g/3¹/₂oz/³/₄ cup walnuts,
 roasted and finely chopped
4 tbsp plain flour
¹/₂ tsp baking powder
4 tbsp Marsala wine
1 recipe quantity Dark Chocolate
 Ganache (see page 209)

1   Preheat the oven to 170°C/325°F/gas 3. Grease a 23cm/9in spring-form cake
    tin with butter, and line the base with baking paper.
2   In a large bowl, beat the butter, sugar and vanilla essence together until light
    and creamy, using an electric hand mixer. Beat in the eggs, one at a time. In a
    clean bowl, mix together the nuts, flour and baking powder, using a wooden
    spoon. Fold into the butter mixture with the Marsala, then pour into the
    prepared tin.
3   Bake in the hot oven for 40–45 minutes, or until the torte is lightly browned and
    firm in the middle. Remove from the oven and leave the torte to cool in the tin
    for 10 minutes. Turn the torte out on to a wire rack, and leave to cool completely.
4   To ice the torte, use a palette knife to spread the dark chocolate ganache
    over the top.

095 Chocolate chestnut cake

PREPARATION TIME 20 minutes   **COOKING TIME** 25–30 minutes   **MAKES** 1 x 23cm/9in cake

butter, for greasing
4 eggs, separated
150g/5¹/₂oz/²/₃ cup caster sugar
1 tsp vanilla essence
250g/9oz tinned, unsweetened
 chestnut purée

75g/2³/₄oz dark chocolate,
 melted and left to cool
1 recipe quantity Shiny Chocolate
 Icing (see page 213)

1   Preheat the oven to 180°C/350°F/gas 4. Grease a 23cm/9in spring-form cake
    tin with butter, and line the base with baking paper.
2   In a large bowl, beat the egg yolks, sugar and vanilla essence until creamy,
    using an electric hand mixer. Add the chestnut purée, mixing well to combine,
    then stir in the melted chocolate. In a clean bowl, using clean attachments for
    the electric hand mixer, whisk the egg whites until stiff but not dry, and fold
    into the chocolate mixture with a metal spoon. Pour into the prepared tin.
3   Bake in the hot oven for 25–30 minutes, or until a skewer inserted into the
    middle of the cake comes out dry. Remove from the oven and leave the cake in
    the tin to cool for 10 minutes, then turn out on to a wire rack to cool completely.
4   To ice the cake, use a palette knife to spread the shiny chocolate icing over the top.

096 Chocolate berry torte

PREPARATION TIME 25 minutes   **COOKING TIME** 35–40 minutes   **MAKES** 1 x 23cm/9in torte

25g/1oz butter, chopped, plus extra for greasing
100g/3½oz dark chocolate, broken into pieces
2 tbsp double cream
4 eggs, separated

110g/3¾oz/⅓ cup plus 2 tbsp caster sugar
2½ tbsp plain flour
2 tbsp cocoa powder
200g/7oz/1 cup blueberries
icing sugar, sifted, for dusting

1 Preheat the oven to 150°C/300°F/gas 2. Grease a 23cm/9in spring-form cake tin with butter, and line the base with baking paper.
2 In a small saucepan, heat the butter, chocolate and cream together over a low heat until the chocolate has just melted. Remove the pan from the heat and set aside to cool.
3 In a large bowl, beat the egg yolks and 5 tbsp of the sugar together until pale and creamy, using an electric hand mixer. Stir in the chocolate mixture, flour and cocoa. In a clean bowl, whisk the egg whites until foamy, using clean attachments for the electric hand mixer, then gradually whisk in the remaining sugar until the mixture is thick and shiny. Gently fold the meringue mixture into the chocolate mixture and pour into the prepared tin. Sprinkle the blueberries over the top.
4 Bake in the warm oven for 30–35 minutes, or until the torte is just firm to the touch. Remove the torte from the oven, leave to cool completely in the tin before turning out, then dust with icing sugar.

097 Chocolate hazelnut torte

PREPARATION TIME 25 minutes   **COOKING TIME** 40–45 minutes   **MAKES** 1 x 23cm/9in torte

175g/6oz butter, chopped, plus extra for greasing
175g/6oz dark chocolate, broken into pieces
3 eggs, separated
175g/6oz/¾ cup caster sugar

100g/3½oz/¾ cup roasted hazelnuts, very finely chopped
2 tbsp plain flour
zest of 1 orange, grated
icing sugar, sifted, for dusting

1 Preheat the oven to 170°C/325°F/gas 3. Grease a 23cm/9in spring-form cake tin with butter, and line the base with baking paper.
2 In a small saucepan, heat the butter and chocolate together over a low heat until just melted. Remove the pan from the heat and stir until smooth, using a wooden spoon, then set aside to cool.
3 In a large bowl, beat the egg yolks and half the sugar until light and creamy, using an electric hand mixer. Mix in the chocolate mixture, hazelnuts, flour and orange zest. In a clean bowl, whisk the egg whites to soft peaks, using clean attachments for the electric hand mixer, then gradually whisk in the remaining sugar until the mixture is thick and shiny. Gently fold the meringue mixture into the chocolate mixture and pour into the prepared tin
4 Bake in the hot oven for 35–40 minutes, or until the torte is just firm in the middle. Remove the torte from the oven, leave to cool completely in the tin before turning out, then dust with icing sugar.

098 Chocolate cake with Marsala

PREPARATION TIME 30 minutes   **COOKING TIME** 25–30 minutes   **MAKES** 1 x 23cm/9in cake

150g/5½oz butter, softened,
   plus extra for greasing
250g/9oz/1 cup plus 4 tsp
   caster sugar
3 eggs, lightly beaten
100g/3½oz dark chocolate,
   melted and left to cool
250g/9oz/2 cups self-raising flour

2 tbsp cocoa powder
185ml/6fl oz/scant ¾ cup milk
8 tbsp Marsala wine
1 recipe quantity Chocolate Marsala
   Cream (see page 207)
1 recipe quantity Dark Chocolate
   Ganache (see page 209)

1   Preheat the oven to 170°C/325°F/gas 3. Grease 2 x 23cm/9in sandwich tins with butter, and line the bases with baking paper.
2   In a large bowl, beat the butter and sugar together until light and creamy, using an electric hand mixer, then beat in the eggs, one at a time, and the melted chocolate. In a clean bowl, sift together the flour and cocoa, then fold into the chocolate mixture with the milk and half of the Marsala until just blended. Pour into the prepared tins.
3   Bake in the hot oven for 25–30 minutes, or until a skewer inserted into the middle of the cakes comes out with just a few moist crumbs on it. Remove from the oven. Pierce the top of the cakes 5 or 6 times with a skewer and brush over the remaining Marsala while they are still warm. Leave the cakes to cool in the tins for 10 minutes, then remove from the tins and transfer to a wire rack to cool completely.
4   To finish the cake, sandwich the 2 halves together with the chocolate Marsala cream, then transfer the cake to a serving plate and spread over the dark chocolate ganache with a palette knife.

099 Mississippi mud cake

PREPARATION TIME 35 minutes   **COOKING TIME** 60–65 minutes   **MAKES** 1 x 23cm/9in cake

200g/7oz butter, chopped,
   plus extra for greasing
100g/3½oz dark chocolate,
   broken into pieces
300g/10½oz/1⅓ cups caster sugar
2 tbsp whisky

150g/5½oz/1 cup plus 2 tbsp
   plain flour
1 tbsp self-raising flour
2 tbsp cocoa powder
2 eggs, lightly beaten
1 recipe quantity Chocolate Fudge
   Frosting (see page 212)

1   Preheat the oven to 170°C/325°F/gas 3. Grease a 23cm/9in spring-form cake tin with butter, and line the base with baking paper.
2   In a small saucepan, melt the butter, chocolate, sugar, whisky and 150ml/5fl oz/ ⅔ cup water together over a low heat until the chocolate has just melted. Pour into a clean bowl and stir with a wooden spoon until smooth, then set aside to cool for 10 minutes. In a clean bowl, mix the flours and cocoa together, then fold into the chocolate mixture with the eggs. Pour into the prepared tin.
3   Bake in the hot oven for 55–60 minutes, or until a skewer inserted into the middle of the cake comes out slightly moist. Remove from the oven and leave in the tin to cool for 15 minutes, then turn out on to a wire rack to cool completely.
4   To ice the cake, use a palette knife to spread over the chocolate fudge frosting.

100 Chocolate banana bread

PREPARATION TIME 20 minutes   **COOKING TIME** 50–55 minutes
MAKES 1 x 24 x 12cm/9 x 4¹/₂in loaf

125g/4¹/₂oz butter, softened, plus
   extra for greasing and to serve
125g/4¹/₂oz/²/₃ cup soft brown sugar
2 eggs, lightly beaten
150g/5¹/₂oz dark chocolate,
   melted and left to cool

3 ripe bananas, mashed
1 tsp vanilla essence
200g/7oz/1²/₃ cups plus
   1 tbsp self-raising flour

1 Preheat the oven to 180°C/350°F/gas 4. Grease a 24 x 12cm/9 x 4¹/₂in loaf tin
   with butter, and line the base with baking paper.
2 In a large bowl, beat the butter and sugar together until light and fluffy, using
   an electric hand mixer. Add the eggs, beating well, then stir in the melted
   chocolate, bananas, vanilla essence and flour until just combined, using
   a wooden spoon. Spoon into the prepared tin.
3 Bake in the hot oven for 50–55 minutes, or until a skewer inserted into the
   middle of the cake comes out with just a few crumbs clinging to it. Remove
   from the oven and leave the cake in the tin to cool for 10 minutes, then turn
   out on to a wire rack to cool completely. Serve with butter for spreading.

101 Banana & chocolate loaf cake with liqueur

PREPARATION TIME 20 minutes   **COOKING TIME** 45–50 minutes
MAKES 1 x 24 x 12cm/9 x 4½in loaf cake

75g/2¾oz butter, softened,
  plus extra for greasing
100g/3½oz/⅓ cup plus 4 tsp
  caster sugar
1 egg, lightly beaten
1 tsp vanilla essence
2 bananas, peeled and mashed

150g/5½oz/1 cup plus 2 tbsp
  self-raising flour
2 tbsp cocoa powder
1 tsp cinnamon
2 tbsp Irish cream liqueur
2 tbsp milk

1   Preheat the oven to 180°C/350°F/gas 4. Grease a 24 x 12cm/9 x 4½in loaf tin
with butter, and line the base with baking paper.
2   In a large bowl, beat the butter and sugar together until light and fluffy, using
an electric hand mixer, and then beat in the egg. Add the vanilla essence and
bananas, and mix well with a wooden spoon to combine. Fold in the flour, cocoa,
cinnamon, liqueur and milk and pour into the prepared tin.
3   Bake in the hot oven for 45–50 minutes, or until a skewer inserted into the middle
of the cake comes out clean. Remove from the oven and leave the cake in the tin
to cool for 10 minutes, then turn out on to a wire rack to cool completely.

102 Chocolate banana swirl cake

PREPARATION TIME 30 minutes   **COOKING TIME** 30–35 minutes   **MAKES** 1 x 23cm/9in cake

175g/6oz butter, softened,
  plus extra for greasing
250g/9oz/1 cup plus 4 tsp
  caster sugar
3 eggs, lightly beaten

250g/9oz/2 cups self-raising flour
1 tbsp cocoa powder
2 tbsp milk
2 ripe bananas, mashed
icing sugar, sifted, for dusting

1   Preheat the oven to 180°C/350°F/gas 4. Grease a 23cm/9in spring-form
cake tin with butter, and line the base with paper.
2   In a large bowl, whisk the butter and sugar together until pale and creamy,
using an electric hand mixer, then add the eggs a little at a time until well
combined. Fold in the flour, using a metal spoon. Divide the mixture in half. Mix
the cocoa with the milk to make a paste, and stir into one half, using a wooden
spoon. Stir the banana into the remaining cake mixture. Spoon tablespoonfuls
of the mixtures into the prepared tin so that both flavours are evenly distributed.
Carefully drag a skewer through the mixture to create a swirl effect.
3   Bake in the hot oven for 30–35 minutes, or until the cake is just firm. Remove
from the oven and leave the cake in the tin to cool for 10 minutes, then turn out
on to a wire rack to cool completely and dust with icing sugar.

103 Chocolate bundt cake

PREPARATION TIME 20 minutes   **COOKING TIME** 55–60 minutes   **MAKES** 1 x 25cm/10in cake

200g/7oz butter, softened,
   plus extra for greasing
400g/14oz/1¹/₂ cups plus 4 tbsp
   caster sugar
3 eggs, lightly beaten
300g/10¹/₂oz/2 cups self-raising flour
2 tbsp cocoa powder

150ml/5fl oz/²/₃ cup milk
1 tsp vanilla essence
125g/4¹/₂oz dark or milk
   chocolate chips
1 recipe quantity Shiny Chocolate
   Icing (see page 213)

1   Preheat the oven to 170°C/325°F/gas 3. Grease a 25cm/10in bundt tin
    with butter.
2   In a large bowl, beat the butter and sugar together until light and creamy,
    using an electric hand mixer, then gradually whisk in the eggs. Fold in the flour,
    cocoa, milk, vanilla essence and chocolate chips until just combined, using
    a metal spoon. Spoon into the prepared tin.
3   Bake in the hot oven for 55–60 minutes, or until a skewer inserted into the
    middle of the cake comes out clean. Remove from the oven, and leave the cake
    in the tin to cool for 10 minutes. Turn the cake out on to a wire rack and, while
    still warm, drizzle over the shiny chocolate icing.

104 All-in-one chocolate & sour cream cake

PREPARATION TIME 15 minutes   **COOKING TIME** 40–45 minutes   **MAKES** 1 x 23cm/9in cake

butter, for greasing
250g/9oz/2 cups self-raising flour
1 tsp baking powder
3 tbsp cocoa powder
200g/7oz/³/₄ cup plus 2 tbsp
   caster sugar
100g/3¹/₂oz/¹/₂ cup plus 2 tsp
   soft brown sugar

100g/3¹/₂oz dark chocolate chips
250ml/9fl oz/1 cup sour cream
3 tbsp vegetable oil
2 eggs
100ml/3¹/₂fl oz/¹/₃ cup milk
1 tsp vanilla essence
1 recipe quantity Creamy Chocolate
   Icing (see page 212)

1   Preheat the oven to 180°C/350°F/gas 4. Grease a 23cm/9in spring-form cake tin
    with butter, and line the base with baking paper.
2   Place all of the ingredients, apart from the icing, in a large bowl, and beat with
    an electric hand mixer on low speed for 2 minutes until just combined. Pour into
    the prepared tin.
3   Bake in the hot oven for 40–45 minutes, or until a skewer inserted in the middle
    of the cake comes out with just a few crumbs on it. Remove from the oven and
    leave the cake in the tin to cool for 15 minutes, then turn out on to a wire rack
    to cool completely.
4   To ice the cake, use a palette knife to spread over the creamy chocolate icing.

105 Simple chocolate & raspberry jam cake

PREPARATION TIME 20 minutes   **COOKING TIME** 50–55 minutes   **MAKES** 1 x 23cm/9in cake

175g/6oz butter, chopped,
  plus extra for greasing
2 tbsp raspberry jam
250g/9oz/1 cup plus 4 tsp
  caster sugar
3 eggs, lightly beaten

250g/9oz/2 cups self-raising flour
150g/5½oz/1 cup plus 2 tbsp
  drinking chocolate
100ml/3½fl oz/⅓ cup milk
1 recipe quantity Creamy Chocolate
  Icing (see page 212)

1   Preheat the oven to 180°C/350°F/gas 4. Grease a 23cm/9in spring-form cake tin
    with butter, and line the base with baking paper.
2   In a small saucepan, melt the butter and raspberry jam together over a low
    heat, then remove from the heat and set aside to cool slightly. In a large bowl,
    beat the sugar and eggs together until thick and pale, using an electric hand
    mixer. In a clean bowl, mix together the flour and drinking chocolate, using a
    wooden spoon. Fold into the egg mixture with the melted butter and jam, and
    the milk. Pour into the prepared tin.
3   Bake in the hot oven for 45–50 minutes until the cake is browned and just firm
    to the touch. Remove from the oven and leave the cake in the tin to cool for
    10 minutes, then turn out on to a wire rack to cool completely.
4   To ice the cake, use a palette knife to spread over the creamy chocolate icing.

106 Flourless chocolate & citrus cake

PREPARATION TIME 25 minutes   **COOKING TIME** 45–50 minutes   **MAKES** 1 x 23cm/9in cake

175g/6oz butter, melted and left to
  cool, plus extra for greasing
6 eggs, separated
200g/7oz/¾ cup plus 2 tbsp
  caster sugar
zest of 1 orange, finely grated
zest of 1 lemon, finely grated

125ml/4fl oz/½ cup
  orange juice
125g/4½oz/1¼ cups
  ground almonds
2 tbsp cocoa powder
250g/9oz dark chocolate,
  melted and left to cool
icing sugar, sifted, for dusting

1   Preheat the oven to 180°C/350°F/gas 4. Grease a deep 23cm/9in spring-form
    round cake tin with butter, and line the base with baking paper.
2   In a large bowl, beat the egg yolks, sugar, orange and lemon zest together until
    thick and pale, using an electric hand mixer. Stir in the melted butter and the
    orange juice. In a clean bowl, combine the ground almonds and cocoa, then fold
    into the egg mixture. In a clean bowl, whisk the egg whites to soft peaks, using
    clean attachments for the electric hand mixer, then pour in the melted
    chocolate and stir together. Fold into the cake mixture until just combined,
    using a metal spoon, then pour into the prepared tin.
3   Bake in the hot oven for 45–50 minutes, or until the cake is firm around the
    edges but still slightly soft in the middle. Remove from the oven and leave
    the cake in the tin to cool completely, then remove the cake from the tin and
    dust with icing sugar.

107 Pear, pistachio & chocolate loaf cake

PREPARATION TIME 30 minutes **COOKING TIME** 55–60 minutes
MAKES 1 x 24 x 12cm/9 x 4¹/₂in loaf cake

150g/5¹/₂oz butter, softened,
  plus extra for greasing
150g/5¹/₂oz/²/₃ cup caster sugar
3 eggs, lightly beaten
1 tsp vanilla essence

200g/7oz dark chocolate,
  finely chopped
1 pear, peeled, cored and diced
60g/2¹/₄oz/¹/₃ cup pistachio nuts
150g/5¹/₂oz/1 cup plus 2 tbsp
  self-raising flour

1   Preheat the oven to 180°C/350°F/gas 4. Grease a 24 x 12cm/9 x 4¹/₂in loaf tin
    with butter.
2   In a large bowl, beat the butter and sugar together until light and fluffy, using
    an electric hand mixer. Add the eggs one at a time, whisking well in between,
    then add the vanilla essence. Fold in the chocolate, pear, pistachio nuts and
    flour until just combined, using a wooden spoon. Pour into the prepared tin.
3   Bake in the hot oven for 55–60 minutes, or until a skewer inserted into the middle
    of the cake comes out clean. Remove from the oven and leave the cake in the tin
    to cool for 10 minutes, then turn out on to a wire rack to cool completely.

108 Devil's food cake

PREPARATION TIME 25 minutes   **COOKING TIME** 20–25 minutes   **MAKES** 1 x 23cm/9in cake

175g/6oz butter, softened,
 plus extra for greasing
125g/4½oz/1 cup cocoa powder
375g/13oz/1½ cups plus 2 tbsp
 caster sugar
1 tsp vanilla essence

1 tbsp chocolate liqueur
4 eggs, lightly beaten
280g/10oz/2¼ cups self-raising flour
1 recipe quantity Creamy Chocolate
 Icing (see page 212)

1   Preheat the oven to 180°C/350°F/gas 4. Grease 2 x 23cm/9in sandwich tins
    with butter, and line the bases with baking paper.
2   Place the cocoa in a small bowl, and blend with 175ml/6fl oz/scant ¾ cup
    boiling water to form a paste. Set aside to cool. In a large bowl, beat the butter,
    sugar and vanilla essence until light and creamy, using an electric hand mixer.
    Gradually add the liqueur and eggs. Stir in some of the flour with a wooden
    spoon, then add the cocoa mixture and finally the remaining flour until just
    combined. Divide the mixture evenly between the prepared tins.
3   Bake in the hot oven for 20–25 minutes, or until a skewer inserted in the middle
    of the cakes comes out clean. Remove from the oven and leave the cakes in the
    tins to cool for 10 minutes, then turn out on to a wire rack to cool completely.
4   To finish the cake, sandwich both halves together with some of the creamy
    chocolate icing, and use a palette knife to spread the remainder over the top.

109 Bourbon chocolate cake

PREPARATION TIME 20 minutes   **COOKING TIME** 35–40 minutes   **MAKES** 1 x 23cm/9in cake

125g/4½oz butter, softened,
 plus extra for greasing
250g/9oz dark chocolate,
 broken into pieces
4 eggs, separated
100g/3½oz/½ cup plus 2 tsp
 soft brown sugar

2 tbsp plain flour
3 tbsp bourbon whiskey
1 tsp vanilla essence
icing sugar, sifted, for dusting
pouring cream, for serving (optional)

1   Preheat the oven to 180°C/350°F/gas 4. Grease a 23cm/9in round spring-form
    cake tin with butter, and line the base with baking paper.
2   In a small saucepan, melt the butter and chocolate together over a low heat,
    then remove from the heat and set aside to cool slightly. In a large bowl, beat
    the egg yolks with the brown sugar until pale and thick, using an electric hand
    mixer. Add the chocolate mixture and stir with a wooden spoon until just
    combined. Fold in the flour, whiskey and vanilla essence, using a metal spoon.
    In a clean bowl, whisk the egg whites to soft peaks, using clean attachments for
    the electric hand mixer. Fold gently into the chocolate mixture, using a metal
    spoon, then pour into the prepared tin.
3   Bake in the hot oven for 30–35 minutes, or until the cake is just set in the middle.
    Remove from the oven and leave in the tin to cool for 10–15 minutes, then remove
    the cake from the tin. Dust with icing sugar and serve with cream, if wanted.

110   Easy fudge cake

PREPARATION TIME 15 minutes   **COOKING TIME** 25–30 minutes   **MAKES** 1 x 23cm/9in cake

75g/2³/₄oz butter, melted,
    plus extra for greasing
200g/7oz/1 cup plus 1 tbsp
    soft brown sugar
2 eggs, lightly beaten

1 tsp vanilla essence
140g/5oz/1¹/₄ cups self-raising flour
2 tbsp cocoa powder
1 recipe quantity Creamy Chocolate
    Icing (see page 212)

1   Preheat the oven to 180°C/350°F/gas 4. Grease a 23cm/9in spring-form cake tin with butter, and line the base with baking paper.
2   In a large bowl, beat the butter and sugar together, using an electric hand mixer, then add the eggs and vanilla essence, beating until well combined. In another bowl, combine the flour and cocoa, then add to the sugar mixture with 125ml/4fl oz/¹/₂ cup hot water, stirring with a wooden spoon just until everything is moist. Pour into the prepared tin.
3   Bake in the hot oven for 25–30 minutes, or until a skewer inserted into the middle of the cake comes out clean. Remove from the oven and leave the cake in the tin to cool for 10 minutes, then turn out on to a wire rack to cool completely.
4   To ice the cake, use a palette knife to spread over the creamy chocolate icing.

111   Sour cream chocolate cake

PREPARATION TIME 25 minutes   **COOKING TIME** 20–25 minutes   **MAKES** 1 x 23cm/9in cake

125g/4¹/₂oz butter, softened,
    plus extra for greasing
200g/7oz/³/₄ cup plus 2 tbsp
    caster sugar
1 tsp vanilla essence
3 eggs, lightly beaten

175g/6oz/1¹/₃ cups plus 1 tbsp
    self-raising flour
3 tbsp cocoa powder
150ml/5fl oz/²/₃ cup sour cream
1 recipe quantity Shiny Chocolate
    Icing (see page 213)

1   Preheat the oven to 170°C/325°F/gas 3. Grease a deep 23cm/9in spring-form round cake tin with butter, and line the base with baking paper.
2   In a large bowl, whisk the butter, sugar and vanilla essence together until light and pale, using an electric hand mixer, then gradually whisk in the eggs. In a clean bowl, combine the flour and cocoa, using a wooden spoon, then fold into the butter mixture with the sour cream. Spoon into the prepared tin.
3   Bake in the hot oven for 20–25 minutes, or until firm and a skewer inserted in the middle of the cake comes out just dry. Remove from the oven and leave the cake in the tin to cool for 10 minutes, then turn out on to a wire rack to cool completely.
4   To ice the cake, use a palette knife to spread over the shiny chocolate icing.

112 Chocolate ricotta cake

PREPARATION TIME 20 minutes **COOKING TIME** 30–35 minutes **MAKES** 1 x 23cm/9in cake

150g/5¹/₂oz butter, softened,
  plus extra for greasing
100g/3¹/₂oz/¹/₃ cup plus 4 tsp
  caster sugar
150g/5¹/₂oz dark chocolate,
  melted and left to cool

3 eggs, separated
250g/9oz ricotta cheese
100g/3¹/₂oz/1 cup ground almonds
2 tbsp plain flour
icing sugar, sifted, for dusting

1 Preheat the oven to 170°C/325°F/gas 4. Grease a 23cm/9in spring-form tin with butter, and line the base with baking paper.

2 In a large bowl, beat the butter and sugar together until light and fluffy, using an electric hand mixer. Add the melted chocolate, egg yolks and ricotta, stirring with a wooden spoon until just combined, then stir in the ground almonds and flour. In a clean bowl, whisk the egg whites to soft peaks, using clean attachments for the electric hand mixer, then fold into the chocolate mixture. Pour into the prepared tin.

3 Bake in the hot oven for 30–35 minutes until the cake is just firm around the edges but still wobbly in the middle. Remove from the oven and leave in the tin to cool for 10–15 minutes, then remove the cake from the tin and transfer to a serving plate. Dust with icing sugar and serve warm.

113 Chocolate beer cake

PREPARATION TIME 30 minutes **COOKING TIME** 20–25 minutes **MAKES** 1 x 20cm/8in cake

125g/4¹/₂oz butter, softened,
  plus extra for greasing
250g/9oz/1¹/₃ cups soft brown sugar
2 eggs, lightly beaten
175g/6oz/1¹/₃ cups plus 1 tbsp
  self-raising flour
2 tbsp cocoa powder

200ml/7fl oz/²/₃ cup beer
1 recipe quantity Chocolate Chantilly
  Cream (see page 208)
1 recipe quantity Chocolate Fudge
  Frosting (see page 212)
50g/1³/₄oz/¹/₂ cup walnuts, roasted,
  finely chopped

1 Preheat the oven to 180°C/350°F/gas 4. Grease 2 x 20cm/8in sandwich tins with butter.

2 In a large bowl, beat the butter and sugar together until light and creamy, using an electric hand mixer, then beat in the eggs, one at a time. In another bowl, combine the flour and cocoa, using a wooden spoon, then fold into the butter mixture with the beer, using a metal spoon. Divide the mixture equally between the tins.

3 Bake in the hot oven for 20–25 minutes, or until the cakes just start to pull away from the sides of the tins and a skewer inserted into the middle of the cakes comes out clean. Remove from the oven and leave the cakes in the tins to cool for 10 minutes, then turn out on to a wire rack to cool completely.

4 To finish the cake, sandwich the halves together with the chocolate chantilly cream, then, using a palette knife, spread the chocolate fudge frosting over the top and sides. Transfer to a serving plate and sprinkle with the chopped walnuts.

114 Chocolate angel food cake

PREPARATION TIME 15 minutes   **COOKING TIME** 45–50 minutes
MAKES 1 x 21 x 10cm/8½ x 4in cake

6 eggs, separated
250ml/9fl oz/1 cup vegetable oil
150g/5½oz/1¼ cups
   drinking chocolate

280g/10oz/2¼ cups self-raising flour
400g/14oz/1½ cups plus 4 tbsp
   caster sugar
icing sugar, sifted, for dusting

1   Preheat the oven to 150°C/300°F/gas 2. Place an ungreased, loose-bottomed angel food cake tin on a baking tray. (If you do not have an angel food cake tin, use a ring tin of the same diameter, but make only half of the recipe.)
2   Place the egg yolks, oil, drinking chocolate, flour, sugar and 250ml/9fl oz/1 cup water in a large bowl, and mix on low speed with an electric hand mixer until just combined. Then beat at the highest setting for 10 minutes. In a clean bowl, whisk the egg whites until stiff, using clean attachments for the electric hand mixer, then fold gently into the chocolate mixture using a metal spoon. Pour into the prepared tin.
3   Bake in the warm oven for 45–50 minutes, or until the cake is firm when touched. Remove from the oven and turn the cake tin upside down on to a wire rack, then leave the cake in the tin until it has cooled completely.
4   When cold, loosen the cake from the tin with a sharp knife, turn out on to a serving plate and dust with icing sugar.

115 Chocolate pear upside-down cake

PREPARATION TIME 20 minutes   **COOKING TIME** 30–35 minutes   **MAKES** 1 x 23cm/9in cake

200g/7oz butter, softened,
plus extra for greasing
200g/7oz dark chocolate,
broken into pieces
150g/5½oz/⅔ cup caster sugar
3 eggs, lightly beaten

1 tsp vanilla essence
100g/3½oz/¾ cup plus 1 tbsp
self-raising flour
3 tbsp soft brown sugar
3 pears, ripe but firm, peeled,
cored and sliced into quarters

1   Preheat the oven to 180°C/350°F/gas 4. Grease a 23cm/9in spring-form
cake tin with butter, and line the base with baking paper.
2   In a small saucepan, combine the butter, chocolate and sugar over a low heat
until just melted, stirring with a wooden spoon. Remove from the heat and set
aside to cool completely. Stir in the eggs, vanilla essence and flour until just
combined. Sprinkle the brown sugar over the base of the tin, arrange the pear
quarters over the top in a spiral shape, and pour over the chocolate batter.
3   Bake in the hot oven for 25–30 minutes, or until a skewer inserted in the middle
of the cake comes out with just a few moist crumbs on it. Remove from the oven
and leave the cake in the tin to cool for 15 minutes, then turn out on to a wire
rack to cool completely, pear side up.

116 Chocolate raisin cake

PREPARATION TIME 30 minutes   **COOKING TIME** 35–40 minutes   **MAKES** 1 x 23 cm/9in cake

150g/5½oz butter, melted,
plus extra for greasing
100g/3½oz/½ cup raisins
2 tbsp Marsala wine
300g/10½oz dark chocolate,
melted and left to cool

100g/3½oz/⅓ cup plus 4 tsp
caster sugar
3 tbsp self-raising flour
2 tbsp cocoa powder, sifted
4 eggs, separated

1   Preheat the oven to 180°C/350°F/gas 4. Grease a 23cm/9in spring-form cake tin
with butter, and line the base with baking paper.
2   Place the raisins in a bowl, and cover with the wine. Microwave on high for
1 minute, then set aside to cool. Place the melted chocolate in a large bowl
and stir in the butter, sugar, flour, cocoa and egg yolks just until combined.
In a clean bowl, whisk the egg whites until stiff but not dry, using an electric
hand mixer, then fold into the chocolate mixture with the raisins, using a metal
spoon. Pour into the prepared tin.
3   Bake in the hot oven for 35–40 minutes, or until a skewer inserted into the
middle of the cake comes out dry. Remove from the oven and leave the cake in
the tin to cool for 15 minutes, then turn out on to a wire rack to cool completely.

117 Chocolate polenta cake

PREPARATION TIME 20 minutes **COOKING TIME** 30–35 minutes **MAKES** 1 x 23cm/9in cake

125g/4½oz butter, softened,
  plus extra for greasing
250g/9oz dark chocolate,
  broken into pieces
5 eggs, separated

150g/5½oz/⅔ cup caster sugar
4 tbsp dark rum
125g/4½oz/¾ cup plus 1 tbsp
  fine polenta
icing sugar, sifted, for dusting

1   Preheat the oven to 180°C/350°F/gas 4. Grease a 23cm/9in spring-form
    cake tin with butter, and line the base with baking paper.
2   In a small saucepan, combine the butter and chocolate over a low heat until the
    chocolate is just melted. Remove from the heat and set aside to cool. In a large
    bowl, beat the egg yolks and sugar together until pale and light, using an
    electric hand mixer. Stir in the chocolate mixture using a wooden spoon. In a
    clean bowl, whisk the egg whites until stiff, using clean attachments for the
    electric hand mixer, then fold into the chocolate base with the rum and polenta.
    Pour into the prepared tin.
3   Bake in the hot oven for 25–30 minutes, or until the cake is just set but still
    slightly wobbly in the middle. Remove from the oven and leave the cake in the
    tin to cool for 15 minutes, then turn out on to a wire rack to cool completely.
    Dust with icing sugar.

118 Chocolate courgette loaf cake

PREPARATION TIME 30 minutes **COOKING TIME** 50–55 minutes
MAKES 1 x 24 x 12cm/9 x 4½in loaf cake

110g/3¾oz butter, softened,
  plus extra for greasing
200g/7oz/¾ cup plus 2 tbsp
  caster sugar
1 tsp orange zest, finely grated
2 eggs, lightly beaten
175g/6oz/1⅓ cups plus 1 tbsp
  self-raising flour

1 tbsp cocoa powder
1 tsp cinnamon
75ml/2½fl oz/⅓ cup milk
125g/4½oz grated courgette
50g/1¾oz/½ cup roasted pecan
  nuts, chopped
1 recipe quantity Chocolate Sour
  Cream Frosting (see page 210)

1   Preheat the oven to 180°C/350°F/gas 4. Grease a 24 x 12cm/9½ x 4½ in loaf tin
    with butter, and line the base with baking paper.
2   In a large bowl, beat together the butter, sugar and orange zest until light and
    creamy, using an electric hand mixer. Gradually beat in the eggs until well
    combined. In a clean bowl, mix together the flour, cocoa and cinnamon with
    a wooden spoon, and fold into the cake mixture with the milk, using a metal
    spoon. Stir in the grated courgette and pecan nuts until just combined. Spoon
    the mixture into the prepared tin.
3   Bake in the hot oven for 50–55 minutes, or until a skewer inserted in the middle
    of the cake comes out just moist. Remove from the oven and leave the cake in
    the tin to cool for 10 minutes, then turn out on to a wire rack to cool completely
    before transferring to a serving plate.
4   To ice the cake, use a palette knife to spread over the chocolate sour
    cream frosting.

119 White chocolate Sauternes cake

PREPARATION TIME 20 minutes   **COOKING TIME** 30–35 minutes   **MAKES** 1 x 23cm/9in cake

175g/6oz butter, softened,
   plus extra for greasing
225g/8oz/1 cup caster sugar
3 eggs, lightly beaten
125g/4½oz/1 cup plain flour
100g/3½oz/¾ cup plus 1 tbsp
   self-raising flour

125ml/4fl oz/½ cup milk
100ml/3½fl oz/⅓ cup Sauternes
200g/7oz white chocolate,
   melted and left to cool
1 recipe quantity White Chocolate
   Frosting (see page 210)

1   Preheat the oven to 180°C/350°F/gas 4. Grease a 23cm/9in spring-form
    cake tin with butter, and line the base with baking paper.
2   In a large bowl, beat the butter and sugar together until light and creamy,
    using an electric hand mixer, then gradually beat in the eggs until smooth.
    In a clean bowl, combine the flours using a wooden spoon, then fold into the
    butter mixture with the milk and half of the Sauternes, using a metal spoon.
    Stir in the melted chocolate, and pour the mixture into the prepared tin.
3   Bake in the hot oven for 30–35 minutes, or until a skewer inserted into the
    middle of the cake comes out clean. Remove from the oven and leave the cake
    in the tin to cool for 10 minutes, then turn out on to a wire rack to cool completely.
    Pierce a few holes in the top of the cake with a skewer, then drizzle over the
    remaining Sauternes. Leave the cake to cool completely.
4   To ice the cake, use a palette knife to spread over the white chocolate frosting.

120 White chocolate cake

PREPARATION TIME 25 minutes **COOKING TIME** 35–40 minutes **MAKES** 1 x 23cm/9in cake

125g/4¹/₂oz butter, softened,
   plus extra for greasing
200g/7oz/³/₄ cup plus 2 tbsp
   caster sugar
1 tsp vanilla essence
3 eggs, lightly beaten
150g/5¹/₂oz white chocolate,
   melted and left to cool

175g/6oz/1¹/₃ cups plus 1 tbsp
   self-raising flour
125ml/4fl oz/¹/₂ cup double cream
1 recipe quantity White Chocolate
   Ganache (see page 210)
raspberries, for serving (optional)

1   Preheat the oven to 170°C/325°F/gas 3. Grease a 23cm/9in spring-form cake tin
    with butter, and line the base with baking paper.
2   In a large bowl, beat the butter, sugar and vanilla essence together until light
    and fluffy, using an electric hand mixer, then gradually beat in the eggs. Stir
    in the melted chocolate, using a wooden spoon, then fold in the flour with the
    cream until just combined, using a metal spoon. Pour into the prepared tin.
3   Bake in the hot oven for 35–40 minutes, or until a skewer inserted in the middle
    of the cake comes out with just a few crumbs sticking to it. Remove from the
    oven and leave the cake in the tin to cool for 10 minutes, then turn out on to
    a wire rack to cool completely.
4   To ice the cake, use a palette knife to spread over the white chocolate ganache.
    Serve with raspberries, if using.

121 Lemon & chocolate drizzle loaf cake

PREPARATION TIME 15 minutes **COOKING TIME** 35–40 minutes
MAKES 1 x 24 x 12cm/9 x 4¹/₂in loaf cake

175g/6oz butter, softened,
   plus extra for greasing
175g/6oz/³/₄ cup caster sugar,
   plus 2 tbsp for sprinkling
2 eggs, lightly beaten
175g/6oz/1¹/₃ cups plus 1 tbsp
   self-raising flour

zest of 1 lemon, grated
1 tbsp milk
100g/3¹/₂oz dark chocolate,
   melted and left to cool
juice of 1 lemon

1   Preheat the oven to 180°C/350°F/gas 4. Grease a 24 x 12cm/9 x 4¹/₂in loaf tin,
    and line the base with baking paper.
2   In a large bowl, beat the butter and sugar together until light and creamy, using
    an electric hand mixer, then beat in the eggs, a little at a time. Fold in the flour,
    lemon zest, milk and melted chocolate, using a metal spoon, and pour into the
    prepared tin.
3   Bake in the hot oven for 35–40 minutes, or until the cake is just firm in the middle.
    Remove from the oven and leave the cake in the tin to cool for 5 minutes. Using
    a skewer, pierce the top of the cake in 5 or 6 places, then brush over the lemon
    juice until it is absorbed. Sprinkle over the extra sugar. Leave the cake in the tin
    for a further 5 minutes, then turn out on to a wire rack to cool completely.

122 Chocolate & almond marble cake

PREPARATION TIME 20 minutes   **COOKING TIME** 18–20 minutes   **MAKES** 1 x 23cm/9in cake

170g/6oz butter, softened,
  plus extra for greasing
170g/6oz/³/₄ cup caster sugar
1 egg, lightly beaten
1 tsp vanilla essence
100g/3¹/₂oz/1 cup ground almonds

100g/3¹/₂oz/³/₄ cup plus 1 tbsp
  self-raising flour
60ml/2fl oz/¹/₄ cup milk
150g/5¹/₂oz milk chocolate,
  melted and left to cool
1 recipe quantity Dark Chocolate
  Ganache (see page 209)

1   Preheat the oven to 180°C/350°F/gas 4. Grease an 23cm/9in square cake tin
    with butter, and line the base with baking paper.
2   In a large bowl, beat the butter and sugar together until light and fluffy, using
    an electric hand mixer. Gradually beat in the egg and vanilla essence until well
    combined. In a clean bowl, mix together the almonds and flour, using a wooden
    spoon, then gently fold into the butter mixture with the milk, using a metal
    spoon. Place half of the cake mixture into the prepared tin. Fold the melted
    chocolate into the remaining mixture and pour into the tin. Gently draw a fork
    through the mix to create a swirled effect.
3   Bake in the hot oven for 18–20 minutes, or until the cake is just firm. Remove
    from the oven and leave the cake in the tin to cool for 10 minutes, then turn out
    on to a wire rack to cool completely.
4   To ice the cake, use a palette knife to spread over the chocolate ganache.

123 Chocolate & orange loaf cake

PREPARATION TIME 30 minutes   **COOKING TIME** 55–60 minutes
MAKES 1 x 24 x 12cm/9 x 4¹/₂in loaf cake

150g/5¹/₂oz butter, softened,
  plus extra for greasing
200g/7oz/³/₄ cup plus 2 tbsp
  caster sugar
1 tsp vanilla essence
2 eggs, lightly beaten
300g/10¹/₂oz/2¹/₃ cups
  self-raising flour

125ml/4fl oz/¹/₂ cup milk
100g/3¹/₂oz dark chocolate,
  melted and left to cool
2 tbsp orange juice
zest of 1 orange, finely grated
icing sugar, sifted, for dusting

1   Preheat the oven to 180°C/350°F/gas 4. Grease a 24 x 12cm/9 x 4¹/₂in loaf tin
    with butter, and line the base with baking paper.
2   In a large bowl, beat the butter and sugar together until light and fluffy, using
    an electric hand mixer, then add the vanilla essence and eggs a little at a time,
    beating well between additions. Fold in the flour and milk until just combined,
    using a metal spoon. Stir in the melted chocolate, orange juice and zest and
    pour into the prepared tin.
3   Bake in the hot oven for 55–60 minutes, or until a skewer inserted in the middle
    of the cake comes out dry. Remove from the oven and leave the cake in the tin
    to cool for 10 minutes, then turn out on to a wire rack to cool completely. Dust
    with icing sugar.

124 Nutty chocolate, rum & fig cake

PREPARATION TIME 30 minutes   **COOKING TIME** 35–40 minutes   **MAKES** 1 x 23cm/9in cake

200g/7oz butter, softened,
plus extra for greasing
200g/7oz/³/₄ cup plus 2 tbsp
caster sugar
3 eggs, lightly beaten
200g/7oz dark chocolate,
melted and left to cool
100g/3¹/₂oz/1 cup ground almonds

75g/2³/₄oz/¹/₂ cup plus 1 tbsp
self-raising flour
125g/4¹/₂oz dried soft figs, stalks
removed and roughly chopped
2 tbsp dark rum
1 recipe quantity Chocolate Rum
Frosting (see page 212)

1   Preheat the oven to 180°C/350°F/gas 4. Grease a 23cm/9in spring-form cake
tin with butter, and line the base with baking paper.
2   In a large bowl, beat the butter and sugar together until light and fluffy, using
an electric hand mixer, then add the eggs one at a time. Stir in the melted
chocolate, almonds, flour, figs and rum, using a wooden spoon, then spoon
the mixture into the prepared tin.
3   Bake in the hot oven for 35–40 minutes, or until a skewer inserted into the
middle of the cake comes out clean. Remove from the oven and leave the cake
in the tin to cool for 10 minutes, then turn out on to a wire rack to cool completely.
4   To ice the cake, use a palette knife to spread over the chocolate rum frosting.

125 Orange loaf cake with chocolate chips

PREPARATION TIME 20 minutes   **COOKING TIME** 40–45 minutes
MAKES 1 x 24 x 12cm/9 x 4¹/₂in loaf cake

175g/6oz butter, softened,
plus extra for greasing
175g/6oz/³/₄ cup caster sugar
2 eggs, lightly beaten
175g/6oz/1¹/₃ cups plus 1 tbsp
self-raising flour

100g/3¹/₂oz dark or milk
chocolate chips
zest of 1 orange, grated, plus juice
1 tbsp milk
1 recipe quantity Chocolate
Buttercream (see page 208)

1   Preheat the oven to 180°C/350°F/gas 4. Grease a 24 x 12cm/9 x 4¹/₂in loaf tin
with butter, and line the base with baking paper.
2   In a large bowl, beat the butter and sugar together until light and fluffy, using
an electric hand mixer, then gradually beat in the eggs. Fold in the flour,
chocolate chips, orange zest and milk until just combined, and pour into the
prepared tin.
3   Bake in the hot oven for 40–45 minutes, or until a skewer inserted into the
centre comes out with just a few moist crumbs on it. Remove from the oven.
4   Pierce the top of the cake in 3 or 4 places with the skewer and brush over the
orange juice. Cool for 10 minutes, then turn out on to a wire rack and top with
chocolate buttercream.

126 Chocolate brownie cake

PREPARATION TIME 25 minutes   **COOKING TIME** 40–45 minutes   **MAKES** 1 x 23cm/9in cake

175g/6oz butter, softened,
  plus extra for greasing
175g/6oz dark chocolate,
  broken into pieces
3 eggs, separated
175g/6oz/³/₄ cup caster sugar

100g/3¹/₂oz/1 cup walnuts, chopped
100g/3¹/₂oz dark or milk
  chocolate chips
2 tbsp plain flour
icing sugar, sifted, for dusting

1 Preheat the oven to 170°C/325°F/gas 3. Grease a 23cm/9in spring-form cake
   tin with butter, and line the base with baking paper.
2 In a small saucepan, heat the butter and chocolate together over a low heat
   until just melted. Remove the pan from the heat and stir until smooth, using
   a wooden spoon. Set aside to cool. In a large bowl, beat the egg yolks and half
   the sugar together until light and creamy, using an electric hand mixer. Using
   a wooden spoon, mix in the chocolate mixture, then stir in the walnuts,
   chocolate chips and flour.
3 In a clean bowl, whisk the egg whites to soft peaks, using clean attachments for
   the electric hand mixer, then continue whisking, gradually adding the remaining
   sugar, until thick and shiny. Gently fold the whisked whites into the chocolate
   mixture, then pour into the prepared tin.
4 Bake in the hot oven for 35–40 minutes, or until the cake is just firm in the
   middle. Leave the cake in the tin to cool completely before turning out, then
   dust with icing sugar.

127 Peanut butter chocolate cake

PREPARATION TIME 20 minutes   **COOKING TIME** 30–35 minutes   **MAKES** 1 x 23cm/9in cake

125g/4¹/₂oz butter, chopped,
  plus extra for greasing
1 tsp vanilla essence
275g/9³/₄oz/1 cup plus 3 tbsp
  caster sugar
3 eggs, separated
125g/4¹/₂oz dark chocolate,
  melted and left to cool

2 tbsp smooth peanut butter
140g/5oz/1 cup plus 1 tbsp
  self-raising flour
100g/3¹/₂oz/³/₄ cup plus 1 tbsp
  plain flour
250ml/9fl oz/1 cup milk
1 recipe quantity Chocolate Fudge
  Frosting (see page 212)

1 Preheat the oven to 170°C/325°F/gas 3. Grease a deep 23cm/9in square cake
   tin with butter, and line the base with baking paper.
2 In a large bowl, beat the butter, vanilla essence and sugar together until light
   and creamy, using an electric hand mixer. Whisk in the egg yolks, then stir in
   the melted chocolate and peanut butter. In a clean bowl, combine the flours
   and fold into the chocolate mixture with the milk, using a metal spoon. In a
   clean bowl, whisk the egg whites to stiff peaks, using clean attachments for
   the electric hand mixer, then gently fold into the cake mixture. Pour into the
   prepared tin.
3 Bake in the hot oven for 30–35 minutes, or until the cake is dark brown and
   firm. Remove from the oven and leave the cake in the tin to cool for 15 minutes,
   then turn out on to a wire rack to cool completely.
4 Using a large knife, split the cake in half and sandwich the two halves back
   together with half of the chocolate fudge frosting. To ice the cake, use a palette
   knife to spread the remaining frosting over the top.

128   Chocolate cream roll with strawberries

PREPARATION TIME 35 minutes   **COOKING TIME** 10–12 minutes   **MAKES** 1 x cream roll

butter, for greasing
4 eggs, separated
200g/7oz/³/₄ cup plus 2 tbsp
  caster sugar, plus 2 tbsp for
  sprinkling
75g/2³/₄oz dark or milk
  chocolate, grated

75g/2³/₄oz/¹/₂ cup plus 1 tbsp
  self-raising flour
1 recipe quantity Chocolate Chantilly
  Cream (see page 208)
150g/5¹/₂ oz/1 cup strawberries,
  hulled and sliced

1   Preheat the oven to 180°C/350°F/gas 4. Grease a 33 x 23cm/13 x 9in Swiss roll tin with butter, and line the base and sides with baking paper.

2   In a large bowl, beat the egg yolks and half the sugar together until thick and creamy, using an electric hand mixer. Stir in 2 tbsp water, the grated chocolate and flour, using a wooden spoon. In a clean bowl, whisk the egg whites to soft peaks, using clean attachments for the electric hand mixer, then continue whisking, gradually adding the remaining sugar, until thick and shiny. Fold into the chocolate mixture until just combined, using a metal spoon. Pour the mixture into the prepared tin and spread evenly, using a palette knife.

3   Bake in the hot oven for 10–12 minutes, or until just firm. Remove from the oven and turn out on to a large sheet of baking paper that has been sprinkled with sugar. Remove the lining paper, then, using the baking paper to help you, roll up from a short side, enclosing the paper in the cake. Leave to cool completely.

4   When cool, unroll the cake carefully, spread with the chocolate chantilly cream and scatter over the strawberries. Re-roll, transfer to a serving plate and refrigerate until ready to serve.

129 Chocolate Lamingtons

PREPARATION TIME 40 minutes   COOKING TIME 15–20 minutes   MAKES 16 Lamingtons

25g/1oz butter, melted,
  plus extra for greasing
4 eggs
100g/3½oz/⅓ cup plus 4 tsp
  caster sugar
100g/3½oz/¾ cup plus 1 tbsp
  self-raising flour
1 tbsp cornflour

FOR THE COATING:
500g/1lb 2oz/4 cups icing sugar,
  sifted
3 tbsp cocoa powder, sifted
25g/1oz butter, melted
125ml/4fl oz/½ cup milk
175g/6oz/2 cups desiccated coconut

1   Preheat the oven to 180°C/350°F/gas 4. Grease a shallow 23cm/9in square cake tin with butter, and line the base with baking paper.
2   In a large bowl, beat the eggs and sugar together, using an electric hand mixer, until thick and pale (around 5–10 minutes). In a clean bowl, combine the flour and cornflour and fold into the egg mixture with the melted butter until just mixed, using a metal spoon. Pour into the prepared tin.
3   Bake in the hot oven for 15–20 minutes until the cake is firm and lightly golden. Remove from the oven and leave the cake in the tin to cool for 10 minutes, then turn out on to a wire rack to cool completely. With a sharp knife, cut the cooled cake into 16 squares, removing the crusts.
4   For the coating, combine the icing sugar and cocoa in a large bowl. Using a wooden spoon, stir in the melted butter, milk, and as much of 125ml/4fl oz/½ cup hot water as is needed to make the mixture the consistency of thick cream. Dip each piece of cake into the coating until it is well covered, then toss the coated cake in the coconut until completely covered. Leave to set on a wire rack.

130 Double chocolate Lamingtons

PREPARATION TIME 40 minutes   COOKING TIME 15–20 minutes   MAKES 16 Lamingtons

25g/1oz butter, melted,
  plus extra for greasing
4 eggs
100g/3½oz/⅓ cup plus 4 tsp
  caster sugar
100g/3½oz/¾ cup plus 1 tbsp
  self-raising flour
1 tbsp cornflour
2 tbsp cocoa powder

FOR THE COATING:
500g/1lb 2oz/4 cups icing sugar,
  sifted
3 tbsp cocoa powder, sifted
25g/1oz butter, melted
125ml/4fl oz/½ cup milk
175g/6oz/2 cups desiccated coconut

1   Preheat the oven to 180°C/350°F/gas 4. Grease a shallow 23cm/9in square cake tin with butter, and line the base with baking paper.
2   In a large bowl, beat the eggs and sugar together, using an electric hand mixer, until thick and pale (around 5–10 minutes). In a clean bowl, combine the flour, cornflour and cocoa and fold into the egg mixture with the melted butter until just mixed, using a metal spoon. Pour into the prepared tin.
3   Bake in the hot oven for 15–20 minutes until the cake is firm and lightly golden. Remove from the oven and leave the cake in the tin to cool for 10 minutes, then turn out on to a wire rack to cool completely. Using a sharp knife, cut the cooled cake into 16 squares, removing the crusts.
4   For the coating, combine the icing sugar and cocoa in a large bowl. Using a wooden spoon, stir in the melted butter, milk, and as much of 125ml/4fl oz/½ cup hot water as is needed to make the mixture the consistency of thick cream. Dip each piece of cake into the coating until it is well covered, then toss the coated cake in the coconut until completely covered. Leave to set on a wire rack.

131 White chocolate Lamingtons

PREPARATION TIME 40 minutes   **COOKING TIME** 15–20 minutes   **MAKES** 16 Lamingtons

25g/1oz butter, melted,
  plus extra for greasing
4 eggs
100g/3½oz/⅓ cup plus 4 tsp
  caster sugar
100g/3½oz/¾ cup plus 1 tbsp
  self-raising flour
1 tbsp cornflour

FOR THE COATING:
500g/1lb 2oz/4 cups icing sugar,
  sifted
25g/1oz butter, melted
125ml/4fl oz/½ cup milk
125g/4½oz white chocolate,
  melted and left to cool
1 tbsp coconut liqueur
175g/6oz/2 cups desiccated coconut,
  toasted

1 Preheat the oven to 180°C/350°F/gas 4. Grease a 23cm/9in square tin with butter, and line the base with baking paper.
2 In a large bowl, beat the eggs and sugar together, using an electric hand mixer, until thick and pale (around 5–10 minutes). In a clean bowl, combine the flour and cornflour and fold into the egg mixture with the melted butter until just mixed, using a metal spoon. Pour into the prepared tin.
3 Bake in the hot oven for 15–20 minutes until the cake is firm and lightly golden. Remove from the oven and leave the cake in the tin to cool for 10 minutes, then turn out on to a wire rack to cool completely. With a sharp knife, cut the cooled cake into 16 squares, removing the crusts.
4 For the coating, place the icing sugar in a large bowl, and add the melted butter and milk. Using a wooden spoon, stir in the white chocolate and liqueur. Dip each piece of cake into the coating until it is well covered, then toss the coated cake in the coconut until completely covered. Leave to set on a wire rack.

132 Apple chocolate cake

PREPARATION TIME 20 minutes   **COOKING TIME** 30–35 minutes   **MAKES** 1 x 23cm/9in cake

175g/6oz butter, softened,
  plus extra for greasing
200g/7oz/¾ cup plus 2 tbsp
  caster sugar
3 eggs, lightly beaten
2 tbsp cocoa powder

¼ tsp bicarbonate of soda
2 large apples, peeled and chopped
250g/9oz/2 cups self-raising flour
1 recipe quantity Chocolate Cream
  Cheese Frosting (see page 211)

1 Preheat the oven to 170°C/325°F/gas 3. Grease a shallow 23cm/9in square cake tin with butter, and line the base with baking paper.
2 Place the butter, sugar, eggs, cocoa, bicarbonate of soda, apples, flour and 85ml/3fl oz/scant ⅓ cup water in the bowl of a processor, and pulse until just smooth. Pour into the prepared tin.
3 Bake in the hot oven for 30–35 minutes, or until the cake is dark brown and firm in the middle. Remove from the oven and leave the cake in the tin to cool for 15 minutes, then turn out on to a wire rack to cool completely.
4 To ice the cake, use a palette knife to spread over the chocolate cream cheese frosting.

133 Chocolate ginger cake

PREPARATION TIME 25 minutes   **COOKING TIME** 35–40 minutes   **MAKES** 1 x 23cm/9in cake

150g/5½oz butter, softened,
  plus extra for greasing
150g/5½oz/¾ cup plus
  1 tbsp soft brown sugar
2 eggs, lightly beaten
2 tbsp chopped stem ginger
1 tbsp clear honey

100g/3½oz dark chocolate,
  melted and left to cool
150g/5½oz/1 cup plus 2 tbsp
  self-raising flour
2 tsp ground ginger
1 tbsp dark rum
1 recipe quantity Chocolate Rum
  Frosting (see page 212)

1   Preheat the oven to 180°C/350°F/gas 4. Grease a 23cm/9in square cake tin with butter, and line the base with baking paper.
2   In a large bowl, beat the butter and sugar together until light and fluffy, using an electric hand mixer, then add the eggs and beat until smooth. Stir in the chopped ginger, honey and melted chocolate until just combined, using a wooden spoon. Sift the flour and ground ginger together and fold into the cake mixture with the rum, using a metal spoon. Spoon into the prepared tin.
3   Bake in the hot oven for 35–40 minutes, or until the cake is just firm in the middle. Remove from the oven and leave the cake in the tin to cool for 10 minutes, then turn out on to a wire rack to cool completely.
4   To ice the cake, use a palette knife to spread over the chocolate rum frosting.

134 White chocolate, ginger & apricot loaf cake

PREPARATION TIME 30 minutes   **COOKING TIME** 50–55 minutes
MAKES 1 x 24 x 12cm/9 x 4½in loaf cake

125g/4½oz butter, softened,
  plus extra for greasing
125g/4½oz/½ cup plus 2 tsp
  caster sugar
3 eggs, lightly beaten
175g/6oz white chocolate,
  melted and left to cool

200g/7oz/1⅓ cups plus
  1 tbsp self-raising flour
2 tbsp chopped preserved ginger
100g/3½oz soft dried apricots,
  chopped

1   Preheat the oven to 180°C/350°F/gas 4. Grease a 24 x 12cm/9 x 4½in loaf tin with butter, and line the base with baking paper.
2   In a large bowl, beat the butter and sugar together until light and fluffy, using an electric hand mixer. Gradually beat in the eggs. Using a wooden spoon, stir in the melted chocolate, then fold in the flour, ginger and apricots with a metal spoon until just combined. Spoon into the prepared tin.
3   Bake in the hot oven for 50–55 minutes, or until the loaf is just firm to the touch. Remove from the oven and leave the cake in the tin to cool for 10 minutes, then turn out on to a wire rack to cool completely.

135   Chocolate cup cakes

PREPARATION TIME 20 minutes   **COOKING TIME** 12–15 minutes   **MAKES** 12 cup cakes

125g/4^1/$_2$oz butter, softened
125g/4^1/$_2$oz/^{1}/$_2$ cup plus 2 tsp
  caster sugar
2 eggs, lightly beaten
125g/4^1/$_2$oz/1 cup self-raising flour

3 tbsp cocoa powder
2 tbsp milk
^{1}/$_2$ tsp vanilla essence
1 recipe quantity Creamy Chocolate
  Icing (see page 212)

1   Preheat the oven to 180°C/350°F/gas 4. Place 12 paper cake cases into the
   holes of a 12-hole muffin tin.
2   In a large bowl, beat the butter and sugar until light and creamy, using an
   electric hand mixer, then gradually whisk in the eggs until well blended. In
   a clean bowl, sift the flour and cocoa together, then fold into the butter mixture,
   using a metal spoon, along with the milk and vanilla essence. Divide the
   mixture evenly between the cake cases.
3   Bake in the hot oven for 12–15 minutes, or until the cakes are firm to the touch.
   Remove from the oven and transfer to wire racks to cool completely.
4   To ice the cakes, use a palette knife to spread over the creamy chocolate icing.

136 Dark & white chocolate cup cakes

PREPARATION TIME 20 minutes   **COOKING TIME** 12–15 minutes   **MAKES** 12 cup cakes

125g/4¹/₂oz butter, softened
100g/3¹/₂oz/¹/₃ cup plus 4 tsp
  caster sugar
2 eggs, lightly beaten
125g/4¹/₂oz/1 cup self-raising flour
3 tbsp cocoa powder

100g/3oz white chocolate chips
2 tbsp milk
¹/₂ tsp vanilla essence
1 recipe quantity Creamy Chocolate
  Icing (see page 212)

1   Preheat the oven to 180°C/350°F/gas 4. Place 12 paper cake cases into the
    holes of a 12-hole muffin tin.
2   In a large bowl, beat the butter and sugar together until light and creamy, using
    an electric hand mixer, then gradually whisk in the eggs. In a clean bowl, sift
    the flour and cocoa together, then fold into the butter mixture with the white
    chocolate chips, milk and vanilla essence, using a metal spoon. Divide the
    mixture evenly between the cake cases.
3   Bake in the hot oven for 12–15 minutes, or until the cakes are firm to the touch.
    Remove from the oven and transfer to wire racks to cool completely.
4   To ice the cakes, use a palette knife to spread over the creamy chocolate icing.

137 Chocolate surprise cup cakes

PREPARATION TIME 15 minutes   **COOKING TIME** 12–15 minutes   **MAKES** 12 cup cakes

125g/4¹/₂oz butter, softened
125g/4¹/₂oz/¹/₂ cup plus 2 tsp
  caster sugar
2 eggs, lightly beaten
125g/4¹/₂oz/1 cup self-raising flour

3 tbsp cocoa powder
4 tbsp milk
¹/₂ tsp vanilla essence
24 small dark chocolate buttons
icing sugar, sifted, for dusting

1   Preheat the oven to 180°C/350°F/gas 4. Place 12 paper cake cases into
    the holes of a 12-hole muffin tin.
2   In a large bowl, beat the butter and sugar until light and creamy, using an
    electric hand mixer, then gradually whisk in the eggs until well blended. In a
    clean bowl, sift the flour and cocoa together, then fold into the butter mixture,
    using a metal spoon, along with the milk and vanilla essence.
3   Place a small spoonful of the mixture into the bottom of each paper case. Place
    2 chocolate buttons on top of each spoonful, then divide the remaining mixture
    evenly between the cake cases, to cover the chocolate buttons.
4   Bake in the hot oven for 12–15 minutes, or until the cakes are firm to the touch.
    Remove from the oven and transfer to wire racks to cool a little. Dust with icing
    sugar and serve warm.

138   White chocolate cup cakes

PREPARATION TIME 20 minutes   **COOKING TIME** 17–20 minutes   **MAKES** 16 cup cakes

125g/4¹/₂oz white chocolate,
  broken into pieces
100g/3¹/₂oz butter, chopped
125ml/4fl oz/¹/₂ cup milk
100g/3¹/₂oz/¹/₃ cup plus 4 tsp
  caster sugar

1 tsp vanilla essence
1 egg, lightly beaten
125g/4¹/₂oz/1 cup self-raising flour
1 recipe quantity White Chocolate
  Ganache (see page 210)

1   Preheat the oven to 180°C/350°F/gas 4. Place16 paper cake cases into the holes of 2 x 12-hole muffin tins.
2   In a medium-sized saucepan, melt the chocolate, butter, milk and sugar together over a low heat, stirring occasionally. When smooth, remove from the heat and set aside to cool for 15 minutes. In a bowl, whisk the vanilla essence and egg together, and add to the chocolate mixture. Place the flour in a large bowl and whisk in the chocolate and egg mixture until well combined. Pour the mixture into a jug and divide it evenly between the cake cases.
3   Bake in the hot oven for 12–15 minutes, or until the cakes are firm to the touch. Remove from the oven and transfer to wire racks to cool completely.
4   To ice the cakes, use a palette knife to spread over the white chocolate ganache.

139   White chocolate, lime & coconut cup cakes

PREPARATION TIME 20 minutes   **COOKING TIME** 18–20 minutes   **MAKES** 12 cup cakes

150g/5¹/₂oz/1 cup plus 2 tbsp
  self-raising flour
3 tbsp plus 1 tsp caster sugar
50g/1³/₄oz butter, melted
1 egg, lightly beaten
100ml/3¹/₂fl oz/¹/₃ cup milk
1 tsp vanilla essence

juice and zest of 1 lime
100g/3¹/₂oz white chocolate,
  broken into pieces
45g/1¹/₂oz/¹/₂ cup desiccated coconut
1 recipe quantity White Chocolate
  Frosting (see page 210)

1   Preheat the oven to 180°C/350°F/gas 4. Place 12 paper cake cases into the holes of a 12-hole muffin tin.
2   In a large bowl, combine the flour and sugar, and make a well in the middle. Mix together the butter, egg, milk, vanilla essence, lime juice and zest, using a wooden spoon, and stir into the flour mixture until just combined. Stir in the white chocolate and coconut, then use a dessertspoon to divide the mixture evenly between the cake cases.
3   Bake in the hot oven for 18–20 minutes, or until the cakes are firm to the touch. Remove from the oven and transfer to wire racks to cool completely.
4   To ice the cakes, use a palette knife to spread over the white chocolate frosting.

140 Butterfly cakes with chocolate cream

PREPARATION TIME 20 minutes **COOKING TIME** 15–20 minutes **MAKES** 12 cakes

125g/4¹/₂oz butter, softened
125g/4¹/₂oz/¹/₂ cup plus 2 tsp
 caster sugar
2 eggs, lightly beaten
1 tsp vanilla essence
200g/7oz/1¹/₂ cups plus 4 tsp
 self-raising flour

2 tbsp cocoa powder
3 tbsp milk
1 recipe quantity Chocolate Chantilly
 Cream (see page 208)
icing sugar, sifted, for dusting

1 Preheat the oven to 180°C/350°F/gas 4. Place 12 paper cake cases into a
 12-hole shallow muffin tin.
2 In a large bowl, beat the butter and sugar together until light and fluffy, using
 an electric hand mixer, then gradually beat in the eggs and vanilla essence until
 combined. In a clean bowl, sift the flour and cocoa together, and fold into the
 mixture with the milk, using a metal spoon. Divide the mixture evenly between
 the cake cases.
3 Bake in the hot oven for 15–20 minutes, or until the cakes are firm to the touch.
 Remove from the oven and lift the cakes out to cool on a wire rack.
4 Using a sharp knife, make a small circular incision in the top of each cake and
 remove the small circle of cake, then cut the circle in half, to form two semi-
 circular pieces. Place a spoonful of the chocolate cream in the middle of each
 cake, then replace the two pieces of cake on the top at an angle to form 'wings'
 and dust with icing sugar.

141 Apple & chocolate upside-down cakes

PREPARATION TIME 25 minutes **COOKING TIME** 15–20 minutes **MAKES** 12 cakes

100g/3¹/₂oz butter, softened,
 plus extra for greasing
2 apples, peeled, cored and diced
3 tbsp plus 1 tsp caster sugar
4 tbsp icing sugar, plus extra, sifted,
 for dusting

2 eggs, lightly beaten
150g/5¹/₂oz/1 cup plus 2 tbsp
 self-raising flour
2 tbsp cocoa powder
3 tbsp milk

1 Preheat the oven to 180°C/350°F/gas 4. Grease a 12-hole muffin tin with butter,
 and distribute the diced apple evenly over the base of each hole.
2 In a large bowl, beat the butter and sugars together, using an electric hand
 mixer, then add the eggs one at a time until well combined. In a clean bowl,
 sift the flour and cocoa together, then fold into the cake mixture with the milk,
 using a metal spoon. Divide the mixture evenly between the muffin holes.
3 Bake in the hot oven for 15–20 minutes, or until the cakes are just firm in the
 middle. Remove from the oven and leave the cakes in the tin to cool for
 10 minutes, then turn out on to a wire rack, apple side up, and leave to cool
 completely. Dust with icing sugar.

142 Chocolate madeleines

PREPARATION TIME 15 minutes   **COOKING TIME** 15–17 minutes   **MAKES** 12–14 madeleines

100g/3¹/₂oz butter, chopped,
  plus extra for greasing
75g/2³/₄oz dark chocolate,
  broken into pieces
75g/2³/₄oz/¹/₂ cup plus 1 tbsp
  plain flour

¹/₂ tsp baking powder
pinch salt
2 eggs
100g/3¹/₂oz/¹/₃ cup plus
  4 tsp caster sugar
icing sugar, sifted, for dusting

1   Preheat the oven to 180°C/350°F/gas 4. Grease a 12-hole madeleine tin
    with butter.
2   In a small saucepan, heat the butter and chocolate together over a low heat
    until just melted, then set aside to cool. Sift the flour and baking powder into
    a bowl, and add the salt. In a large bowl, beat the eggs and sugar together until
    the mixture is light in colour, using an electric hand mixer, then whisk in the
    chocolate mixture. Using a metal spoon, gently fold in the flour mix, then divide
    the mixture between the holes in the prepared tin, taking care not to overfill.
3   Bake in the hot oven for 10–12 minutes until the cakes are firm to the touch. Remove
    from the oven and leave the madeleines in the tin to cool for 10 minutes, then
    turn out on to a wire rack to cool completely and dust with icing sugar.

143 White chocolate, coconut & blueberry friands

PREPARATION TIME 15 minutes   **COOKING TIME** 17–20 minutes   **MAKES** 24 friands

100g/3¹/₂oz butter, softened,
  plus extra for greasing
100g/3¹/₂oz white chocolate,
  broken into pieces
90q/3¹/₄oz/1 cup desiccated coconut
225g/8oz/1³/₄ cups icing sugar

70g/2¹/₂oz/¹/₂ cup plus 1 tbsp
  plain flour
6 egg whites
1 tsp vanilla essence
24 blueberries

1   Heat the oven to 180°C/350°F/gas 4. Grease 24 friand moulds or 2 x 12-hole mini-muffin tins with butter.

2   In a small saucepan, combine the butter and chocolate, and melt together over a low heat. Remove from the heat and set aside to cool slightly. Mix together the coconut, sugar and flour, using a wooden spoon, then stir in the egg whites, vanilla essence and chocolate mixture until well combined. Divide the mixture between the holes in the prepared tin, taking care not to overfill, and place a blueberry on top of each friand.

3   Bake in the hot oven for 12–15 minutes until the friands are lightly browned. Remove from the oven and leave the friands in the tins to cool for 5 minutes, then turn out on to a wire rack to cool completely.

144 Chocolate-almond friands with raspberries

PREPARATION TIME 15 minutes   **COOKING TIME** 12–15 minutes   **MAKES** 24 friands

100g/3¹/₂oz butter, melted,
  plus extra for greasing
90g/3oz/³/₄ plus 1 tbsp cup
  ground almonds.
225g/8oz/1³/₄ cups icing sugar
70g/2¹/₂oz/¹/₂ cup plus
  1 tbsp plain flour

2 tbsp cocoa powder
6 egg whites
1 tsp vanilla essence
24 raspberries

1   Heat the oven to 180°C/350°F/gas 4. Grease 24 friand moulds or 2 x 12-hole mini-muffin tins with butter.

2   In a large bowl, mix the butter, ground almonds, sugar, flour, cocoa, egg whites and vanilla essence together until combined, using a wooden spoon. Divide the mixture between the moulds or holes in the prepared tin, taking care not to overfill, and place a raspberry on top of each friand.

3   Bake in the hot oven for 12–15 minutes until the friands are lightly browned. Remove from the oven and leave the friands in the tins to cool for 5 minutes, then turn out on to a wire rack to cool completely.

145 Cream liqueur brownies

PREPARATION TIME 20 minutes   **COOKING TIME** 20–25 minutes   **MAKES** 12 brownies

100g/3½oz butter, chopped,
  plus extra for greasing
100g/3½oz dark chocolate,
  broken into pieces
2 eggs, lightly beaten
200g/7oz/¾ cup plus 2 tbsp
  caster sugar
3 tbsp Irish cream liqueur

100g/3½oz/¾ cup plus
  1 tbsp plain flour

FOR THE ICING:
400g/14oz/3 cups icing sugar
2 tbsp cocoa powder
2 tbsp Irish cream liqueur

1   Preheat the oven to 180°C/350°F/gas 4. Grease a shallow 23cm/9in square tin
    with butter and line the base with baking paper, leaving some hanging over the
    edges to make removing the brownies easier.
2   In a small saucepan, heat the butter and chocolate together over a low heat
    until just melted, then remove from the heat. In a large bowl, beat the eggs and
    sugar together until light and creamy, using an electric hand mixer. Stir in the
    chocolate mixture, liqueur and flour until just combined, using a wooden spoon.
    Pour into the prepared tin.
3   Bake in the hot oven for 15–20 minutes, or until the brownie is firm around the
    edges and still slightly soft in the middle. Remove from the oven and leave in
    the tin to cool.
4   For the icing, sift the icing sugar and cocoa into a bowl and make a well in
    the middle. Add the liqueur, then, using a wooden spoon, mix in just enough
    boiling water to make a spreading consistency. Ice the brownies while still
    warm, using a palette knife. Leave to set, then cut into 12 squares.

146 Chocolate cream cheese brownies

PREPARATION TIME 20 minutes   **COOKING TIME** 20–25 minutes   **MAKES** 12 brownies

350g/12oz butter, chopped,
  plus extra for greasing
350g/12oz dark chocolate,
  broken into pieces
300g/10½oz/1⅓ cups caster sugar
3 eggs, lightly beaten

1 tsp vanilla essence
200g/7oz/1½ cups plus 4 tsp
  plain flour
pinch salt
300g/10½oz cream cheese,
  cut into thin slices and chilled

1   Preheat the oven to 180°C/350°F/gas 4. Grease a shallow 23cm/9in square tin
    with butter and line the base with baking paper, leaving some hanging over the
    edges to make removing the brownies easier.
2   In a medium-sized saucepan, melt the butter and chocolate together over a low
    heat, stirring constantly, until the chocolate has just melted. Remove from the
    heat. Add the sugar and mix well, using a wooden spoon, then set aside to cool
    to room temperature. Gradually mix the beaten eggs into the chocolate mixture
    with the vanilla essence, using a wooden spoon, then fold in the flour and salt.
    Pour half the mixture into the prepared tin and top with the chilled cream
    cheese slices. Pour over the remaining brownie mixture.
3   Bake in the hot oven for 15–20 minutes, or until the brownie is firm around the
    edges and still slightly soft in the middle. Remove from the oven and leave in
    the tin to cool completely, then cut into 12 squares.

147 Chocolate fudge brownies

PREPARATION TIME 15 minutes   **COOKING TIME** 20–25 minutes   **MAKES** 12 brownies

200g/7oz butter, chopped,
  plus extra for greasing
200g/7oz dark chocolate,
  broken into pieces
250g/9oz/1 cup plus 4 tsp
  caster sugar

3 eggs, lightly beaten
1 tsp vanilla essence
125g/4½oz/1 cup plain flour
pinch salt

1   Preheat the oven to 180°C/350°F/gas 4. Grease a shallow 23cm/9in square tin
    with butter and line the base with baking paper, leaving some hanging over the
    edges to make removing the brownies easier.
2   In a medium-sized saucepan, melt the butter and chocolate over a low heat
    until the chocolate has just melted, stirring constantly with a wooden spoon,
    then remove the pan from the heat. Add the sugar, and mix well, then leave to
    cool to room temperature. In a large bowl, gradually mix the eggs into the
    chocolate mixture, with the vanilla essence, then fold in the flour and salt, using
    a metal spoon. Pour the mixture into the prepared tin.
3   Bake in the hot oven for 15–20 minutes, or until the brownie is firm around the
    edges and still slightly soft in the middle. Remove from the oven and leave
    in the tin to cool completely, then cut into 12 squares.

148 Cashew & chocolate-chip brownies

PREPARATION TIME 20 minutes   **COOKING TIME** 20–25 minutes   **MAKES** 12 brownies

175g/6oz butter, chopped,
  plus extra for greasing
2 tbsp cocoa powder
250g/9oz/1 cup plus 4 tsp
  caster sugar
pinch salt
2 eggs, lightly beaten
1 tsp vanilla essence

150g/5½oz/1 cup plus 2 tbsp
  plain flour
125g/4½oz dark or milk
  chocolate chips
100g/3½oz/⅔ cup unsalted
  cashew nuts, roasted and
  roughly chopped

1   Preheat the oven to 180°C/350°F/gas 4. Grease a shallow 23cm/9in square tin
    with butter and line the base with baking paper, leaving some hanging over the
    edges to make removing the brownies easier.
2   In a small saucepan, heat the butter with the cocoa and sugar over a low heat
    until just melted, then remove from the heat and set aside to cool. When cool,
    add the salt, eggs, vanilla essence, flour and chocolate chips, and stir with a
    wooden spoon until just combined. Pour into the prepared tin and scatter the
    cashew nuts over the top.
3   Bake in the hot oven for 15–20 minutes, or until the brownie is firm around the
    edges and still slightly soft in the middle. Remove from the oven and leave
    in the tin to cool completely, then cut into 12 squares.

149 Dark & white chocolate brownies

PREPARATION TIME 25 minutes   **COOKING TIME** 20–25 minutes   **MAKES** 12 brownies

175g/6oz butter, chopped,
  plus extra for greasing
2 tbsp cocoa powder
300g/10$\frac{1}{2}$oz/1$\frac{1}{3}$ cups caster sugar
2 eggs, lightly beaten
1 tsp vanilla essence

150g/5$\frac{1}{2}$oz/1 cup plus 2 tbsp
  plain flour
60g/2$\frac{1}{4}$oz white chocolate chips
60g/2$\frac{1}{4}$oz dark chocolate chips
60g/2$\frac{1}{4}$oz/$\frac{2}{3}$ cup walnuts,
  roughly chopped

1   Preheat the oven to 180°C/350°F/gas 4. Grease a shallow 23cm/9in square tin
    with butter and line the base with baking paper, leaving some hanging over the
    edges to make removing the brownies easier.
2   In a large saucepan, heat the butter with the cocoa and sugar over a low heat
    until just melted, remove from the heat and set aside to cool. When cool, add
    the remaining ingredients, and stir with a wooden spoon until just combined.
    Pour into the prepared tin.
3   Bake in the hot oven for 15–20 minutes, or until the brownie is firm around the
    edges and still slightly soft in the middle. Remove from the oven and leave in
    the tin to cool completely, then cut into 12 squares.

150 Cakey chocolate brownies

PREPARATION TIME 20 minutes   **COOKING TIME** 12–15 minutes   **MAKES** 12 brownies

60g/2¼oz butter, softened,
  plus extra for greasing
150g/5½oz/⅔ cup caster sugar
2 eggs, lightly beaten
1 tsp vanilla essence
4 tbsp milk
125g/4½oz dark chocolate,
  melted and left to cool

75g/2¾oz/½ cup plus 1 tbsp
  self-raising flour
icing sugar, sifted, for dusting
  (optional)

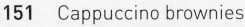

1   Preheat the oven to 180°C/350°F/gas 4. Grease a shallow 23cm/9in square tin
    with butter and line the base with baking paper, leaving some hanging over the
    edges to make removing the brownies easier.
2   In a large bowl, whisk the butter and sugar together, using an electric hand
    mixer, then add the eggs, whisking well until combined. Stir in the vanilla
    essence, milk, melted chocolate and flour, using a wooden spoon, then pour
    into the prepared tin.
3   Bake in the hot oven for 12–15 minutes, or until the brownie is firm around the
    edges and still slightly soft in the middle. Remove from the oven and leave in
    the tin to cool completely, then cut into 12 squares. Dust with icing sugar, if liked.

151 Cappuccino brownies

PREPARATION TIME 20 minutes   **COOKING TIME** 20–25 minutes   **MAKES** 12 brownies

175g/6oz butter, chopped,
  plus extra for greasing
2 tbsp cocoa powder
2 tsp instant coffee granules
250g/9oz/1 cup plus 4 tsp
  caster sugar
2 eggs, lightly beaten

1 tsp vanilla essence
150g/5½oz/1 cup plus 2 tbsp
  plain flour
1 recipe quantity White Chocolate
  Frosting (see page 210)
1 tbsp cocoa powder, sifted

1   Preheat the oven to 180°C/350°F/gas 4. Grease a shallow 23cm/9in square tin
    with butter and line the base with baking paper, leaving some hanging over the
    edges to make removing the brownies easier.
2   In a small saucepan, heat the butter with the cocoa, coffee and sugar over a low
    heat until just melted, remove from the heat and set aside to cool. When cool,
    add the eggs, vanilla essence and flour, and stir with a wooden spoon until just
    combined. Pour into the prepared tin.
3   Bake in the hot oven for 15–20 minutes, or until the brownie is firm around the
    edges and still slightly soft in the middle. Remove from the oven and leave in
    the tin to cool completely.
4   To ice the brownie, use a palette knife to spread the white chocolate frosting
    over the top. Sprinkle with the cocoa, then cut into 12 squares.

152 Rocky road brownies

PREPARATION TIME 20 minutes, plus setting   **COOKING TIME** 20–25 minutes
MAKES 12 brownies

175g/6oz butter, chopped,
  plus extra for greasing
2 tbsp cocoa powder
250g/9oz/1 cup plus
  4 tsp caster sugar
2 eggs, lightly beaten
1 tsp vanilla essence
150g/5¹/₂oz/1 cup plus 2 tbsp
  plain flour

100g/3¹/₂oz dark or milk
  chocolate chips

FOR THE TOPPING:
200g/7oz white and pink
  marshmallows, chopped
1 recipe quantity Shiny Chocolate
  Icing (see page 213)

1   Preheat the oven to 180°C/350°F/gas 4. Grease a shallow 23cm/9in square tin with butter and line the base with baking paper, leaving some hanging over the edges to make removing the brownies easier.
2   In a small saucepan, heat the butter with the cocoa and sugar over a low heat until just melted, then remove from the heat and set aside to cool. When cool, add the eggs, vanilla essence, flour and chocolate chips, and stir with a wooden spoon until just combined. Pour the mixture into the prepared tin.
3   Bake in the hot oven for 15–20 minutes, or until the edges of the brownie are firm and the middle is still moist. Remove from the oven and leave the brownie in the tin to cool completely.
4   Stir the marshmallows into the shiny chocolate icing until they are well coated, then spread the mixture evenly over the top of the brownie. Leave the icing to set for 30 minutes, then cut the brownie into 12 squares.

153 Brown sugar brownies

PREPARATION TIME 25 minutes   **COOKING TIME** 25–30 minutes   **MAKES** 24 brownies

125g/4¹/₂oz butter, softened,
  plus extra for greasing
300g/10¹/₂oz/1¹/₂ cups plus 2 tbsp
  soft brown sugar
2 eggs, lightly beaten
200g/7oz/1¹/₂ cups plus 4 tsp
  plain flour
1 tsp vanilla essence

125g/4¹/₂oz/1¹/₄ cups
  pecan nuts, chopped

FOR THE TOPPING:
175g/6oz dark chocolate,
  melted and left to cool
180ml/6fl oz/³/₄ cup sour cream

1   Preheat the oven to 180°C/350°F/gas 4. Grease a shallow 23cm/9in square tin with butter and line the base with baking paper, leaving some hanging over the edges to make removing the brownies easier.
2   In a large bowl, beat the butter and sugar together until light, using an electric hand mixer, then beat in the eggs. Fold in the flour, vanilla essence and pecan nuts, using a metal spoon, and pour into the prepared tin.
3   Bake in the hot oven for 25–30 minutes, or until the brownie is firm around the edges and still slightly soft in the middle. Remove the brownie from the oven and leave to cool in the tin for 10 minutes while making the topping.
4   Mix the melted chocolate and sour cream together in a small bowl, then spread over the brownie. Leave the brownie in the tin to cool completely, then cut into 24 small squares.

154   Blondies

PREPARATION TIME 20 minutes   **COOKING TIME** 25–30 minutes   **MAKES** 12 blondies

100g/3¹/₂oz butter, chopped,
 plus extra for greasing
125g/4¹/₂oz white chocolate,
 broken into pieces
200g/7oz/³/₄ cup plus 2 tbsp
 caster sugar
3 eggs, lightly beaten

1 tsp vanilla essence
100g/3¹/₂oz/³/₄ cup hazelnuts,
 skinned and chopped
100g/3¹/₂oz white chocolate chips
175g/6oz/1¹/₃ cups plus 1 tbsp
 plain flour

1   Preheat the oven to 180°C/350°F/gas 4. Grease a shallow 23cm/9in square tin
    with butter, and line the base with baking paper.
2   In a small saucepan, heat the butter and chocolate together over a low heat
    until the chocolate has just melted, then remove from the heat and stir gently
    until smooth. In a large bowl, combine the sugar and eggs, then stir in the
    chocolate mixture, vanilla essence, hazelnuts, chocolate chips and flour, using
    a wooden spoon. Pour into the prepared tin.
3   Bake in the hot oven for 20–25 minutes, or until the cake is firm around the
    edges but still moist in the middle. Remove from the oven, and leave the cake in
    the tin to cool completely. Remove the cake from the tin and cut into 12 squares.

155 Chewy chocolate biscuits

PREPARATION TIME 15 minutes   **COOKING TIME** 12–15 minutes   **MAKES** 18 biscuits

butter, for greasing
4 egg whites
350g/12oz/2³/₄ cups icing sugar
3 tbsp cocoa powder

2 tbsp plain flour
125g/4¹/₂oz/1 cup walnuts,
  finely chopped

1   Preheat the oven to 180°C/350°F/gas 4. Grease 2 large baking trays with butter.
2   In a large bowl, whisk the egg whites to soft peaks, using an electric hand
    mixer, then whisk in the icing sugar, cocoa and flour until well combined. Add
    1 tbsp water, and continue to whisk until the mixture becomes very thick and
    shiny. Gently fold in the walnuts, using a metal spoon. Place 18 tablespoonfuls
    of the mixture on the prepared trays, leaving approximately 10cm/4in between
    them to allow for spreading.
3   Bake in the hot oven for 12–15 minutes, or until the tops are firm but not dry
    (they will look cracked). (You may need to cook them in batches.) Remove the
    biscuits from the oven and leave to cool on the trays for 10 minutes before
    transferring to a wire rack to cool completely.

156 Double chocolate biscuits

PREPARATION TIME 15 minutes   **COOKING TIME** 10–12 minutes   **MAKES** 24 biscuits

125g/4¹/₂oz butter, softened,
  plus extra for greasing
1 tsp vanilla essence
75g/2³/₄oz/¹/₃ cup plus 1 tbsp
  soft brown sugar
5 tbsp caster sugar
1 egg, lightly beaten

185g/6¹/₂oz/1¹/₃ cups plus 2 tbsp
  plain flour
1 tbsp cocoa powder
100g/3¹/₂oz dark or milk
  chocolate chips
100g/3¹/₂oz white chocolate chips

1   Preheat the oven to 180°C/350°F/gas 4. Grease 2 large baking trays with butter.
2   In a large bowl, beat together the butter, vanilla essence and both sugars until
    light and creamy, using an electric hand mixer. Add the egg until well combined.
    Fold in the flour, cocoa and both kinds of chocolate chips, using a metal spoon.
    Place 24 tablespoonfuls of the mixture on the prepared trays, leaving
    approximately 10cm/4in between them to allow for spreading.
3   Bake in the hot oven for 10–12 minutes, or until the biscuits are dark brown.
    (You may need to cook them in batches.) Remove the biscuits from the oven and
    leave to cool on the trays for 10 minutes before transferring to a wire rack to
    cool completely.

157   Chocolate macaroons

PREPARATION TIME 20 minutes   **COOKING TIME** 10–15 minutes   **MAKES** 24 macaroons

butter, for greasing
3 egg whites
200g/7oz/³/₄ cup plus 2 tbsp
   caster sugar

1¹/₂ tbsp plain flour
2 tbsp cocoa powder
150g/5¹/₂oz/1¹/₂ cups
   ground almonds

1   Preheat the oven to 180°C/350°F/gas 2. Line 2 large baking trays with
     baking paper.
2   In a clean bowl, whisk the egg whites to soft peaks, using an electric hand
     mixer. Gradually add the sugar, and continue to whisk until stiff and the sugar
     has dissolved (around 5 minutes). In a clean bowl, combine the flour, cocoa and
     ground almonds, using a wooden spoon, then gently fold into the egg whites
     until just combined. Place 24 tablespoonfuls of the mixture on the prepared
     tray, leaving approximately 5cm/2in between them to allow for spreading.
3   Bake in the warm oven for 10–15 minutes, or until the macaroons are dry on the
     outside but still moist in the middle. (You may need to cook them in batches.)
     Remove the macaroons from the oven and leave on the trays to cool completely.

158   Chocolate melting moments

PREPARATION TIME 20 minutes   **COOKING TIME** 8–10 minutes   **MAKES** 20 biscuits

125g/4¹/₂oz butter, softened,
   plus extra for greasing
4 tbsp icing sugar, plus extra,
   sifted, for dusting

125g/4¹/₂oz/1 cup plain flour
3 tbsp cocoa powder

1   Preheat the oven to 180°C/350°F/gas 4. Grease 2 large baking trays with butter.
2   In a large bowl, mix the butter and sugar together, using a wooden spoon,
     until light and fluffy. In a clean bowl, combine the flour and cocoa, then stir into
     the butter mixture until just combined (the mixture will be soft). Place a little
     flour on your hands, and roll the mixture into 20 balls. Place 10 balls of dough
     on each baking tray, leaving approximately 5cm/2in between them to allow for
     spreading, and press the top of each biscuit down with a lightly floured fork.
3   Bake in the hot oven for 8–10 minutes, or until the biscuits are firm. (You may
     need to cook them in batches.) Remove the melting moments from the oven
     and leave to cool on the trays for 5 minutes before transferring to a wire rack
     to cool completely. Dust with the extra sugar.

159 Chocolate cherry macaroons

PREPARATION TIME 10 minutes, plus chilling   **COOKING TIME** 18–20 minutes
MAKES 20 macaroons

butter, for greasing
150g/5¹/₂oz/1²/₃ cups desiccated
  coconut
200ml/7fl oz/³/₄ cup coconut cream
2 tbsp cocoa powder

100g/3¹/₂oz/³/₄ cup plus 1 tbsp
  icing sugar
2 large egg whites
100g/3¹/₂oz/¹/₂ cup glacé cherries,
  finely chopped

1   Preheat the oven to 170°C/325°F/gas 3. Line 2 large baking trays with
    baking paper.
2   In a large bowl, mix all of the ingredients until well combined, using a wooden
    spoon. Refrigerate the mixture for 30 minutes. Place 20 heaped teaspoonfuls
    of the mixture on the prepared baking tray, leaving approximately 5cm/2in
    between them to allow for spreading.
3   Bake in the hot oven for 18–20 minutes, or until the macaroons look just firm.
    (You may need to cook them in batches.) Remove the macaroons from the oven
    and leave to cool on the trays for 5 minutes before transferring to a wire rack
    to cool completely.

160 Chocolate Anzac biscuits

PREPARATION TIME 20 minutes   **COOKING TIME** 20–23 minutes   **MAKES** 20 biscuits

75g/2³/₄oz butter, chopped,
  plus extra for greasing
2 tbsp clear honey
¹/₂ tsp bicarbonate of soda
50g/1¹/₄ oz/¹/₂ cup rolled oats

75g/2³/₄oz/¹/₂ cup plus 1tbsp
  plain flour
100g/3¹/₂oz/¹/₃ cup plus 4 tsp
  caster sugar
3 tbsp desiccated coconut
50g/2oz milk or dark chocolate chips

1 Preheat the oven to 170°C/325°F/gas 3. Grease 2 large baking trays with butter.
2 In a small saucepan, heat the butter and honey over a low heat until just
   melted, then add the bicarbonate of soda. The mixture should fizz up for
   a moment or two, and then settle down. Remove from the heat and set aside
   to cool. In a large bowl, combine the remaining ingredients, using a wooden
   spoon, then pour over the cooled mixture and mix together. Place 20 large
   teaspoonfuls of the mixture on the prepared tray, leaving approximately
   10cm/4in between them to allow for spreading.
3 Bake in the hot oven for 15–18 minutes (the biscuits will still look soft). (You may
   need to cook them in batches.) Remove the biscuits from the oven and leave to
   cool on the tray for 5 minutes, then transfer to a wire rack to cool completely.

161 Dark chocolate & coffee biscuits

PREPARATION TIME 20 minutes   **COOKING TIME** 15–20 minutes   **MAKES** 20 biscuits

150g/5¹/₂oz butter, softened,
  plus extra for greasing
175g/6oz/1¹/₃ cups plus 1 tbsp
  plain flour
2 tbsp cocoa
50g/1³/₄oz dark chocolate,
  broken into very small pieces

¹/₄ tsp instant coffee granules
125g/4¹/₂oz/¹/₂ cup plus 2 tsp
  caster sugar
2 tbsp milk
1 tsp vanilla essence
icing sugar, for dusting

1 Preheat the oven to 180°C/350°F/gas 4. Grease 2 large baking trays with butter.
2 Place the flour, cocoa, chocolate, coffee and sugar in the bowl of a food processor,
   and process until combined. Add the butter, milk and vanilla essence, and pulse
   briefly until the mixture forms a dough. Roll 20 large teaspoonfuls of the dough
   into balls roughly the size of a walnut, and place on the prepared trays, leaving
   approximately 5cm/2in between them to allow for spreading.
3 Bake in the hot oven for 15–20 minutes, or until the biscuits spread slightly and
   become firm, but still soft in the middle. (You may need to cook them in batches.)
   Remove the biscuits from the oven and leave to cool on the trays for 5 minutes
   before transferring to a wire rack to cool completely. Dust with icing sugar.

162 Chocolate & hazelnut biscuits

PREPARATION TIME 20 minutes   **COOKING TIME** 10–12 minutes   **MAKES** 24 biscuits

125g/4¹/₂oz butter, softened,
  plus extra for greasing
100g/3¹/₂oz/¹/₃ cup plus 4 tsp
  caster sugar

125g/4¹/₂oz/1 cup plain flour
1 tbsp cocoa powder
3 tbsp roasted
  ground hazelnuts

1 Preheat the oven to 180°C/350°F/gas 4. Grease 2 large baking trays with butter.
2 In a large bowl, beat the butter and sugar together until light and creamy, using an electric hand mixer. In a clean bowl, mix together the flour, cocoa and ground hazelnuts, using a metal spoon, and fold into the butter mixture until well blended. Roll 24 large teaspoonfuls of the mixture into balls between lightly floured hands, and place on the prepared baking trays, leaving approximately 5cm/2in between them to allow for spreading. Press down on each ball to flatten them slightly.
3 Bake in the hot oven for 10–12 minutes, or until the biscuits are firm. (You may need to cook them in batches.) Remove the biscuits from the oven and leave to cool on the trays for 10 minutes, then transfer to a wire rack to cool completely.

163 Chocolate & peanut butter biscuits

PREPARATION TIME 20 minutes, plus chilling   **COOKING TIME** 10–12 minutes
MAKES 18 biscuits

125g/4¹/₂oz butter, softened,
  plus extra for greasing
125g/4¹/₂oz/¹/₂ cup plus 2 tsp
  caster sugar
125g/4¹/₂oz/¹/₂ cup
  crunchy peanut butter

2 tbsp golden syrup
1 tbsp milk
175g/6oz/1¹/₃ cups plus 1 tbsp
  plain flour
2 tbsp cocoa powder
¹/₂ tsp bicarbonate of soda

1 Preheat the oven to 180°C/350°F/gas 4. Grease 2 large baking trays with butter.
2 In a large bowl, beat together the butter and sugar until light and creamy, using an electric hand mixer, then mix in the remaining ingredients with a wooden spoon. Mix together until well blended and the ingredients form a dough. Shape the dough into a log measuring approximately 30 x 4cm/12 x 1½in, and wrap in plastic film. Refrigerate the dough for 1 hour, or until firm but not solid.
3 Cut the dough into 18 x 5mm/¹/₄in slices, and place the slices on the prepared trays, leaving approximately 5cm/2in between them to allow for spreading.
4 Bake in the hot oven for 10–12 minutes, or until the biscuits are firm. (You may need to cook them in batches.) Remove the biscuits from the oven and leave to cool on the trays for 10 minutes, then transfer to a wire rack to cool completely.

164   Chocolate soufflé biscuits

PREPARATION TIME 20 minutes   **COOKING TIME** 10–12 minutes   **MAKES** 20 biscuits

1 egg white
pinch cream of tartar
1 tsp vanilla essence
2 tbsp caster sugar

50g/1³/₄oz/¹/₃ cup plus 2 tbsp
   walnuts, finely chopped
100g/3¹/₂oz dark chocolate,
   melted and left to cool

1 Preheat the oven to 180°C/350°F/gas 4. Line 2 large baking trays with
baking paper.
2 In a large bowl, whisk the egg white and cream of tartar to soft peaks, using an
electric hand mixer, then add the vanilla essence. Gradually whisk in the sugar
until the egg whites are stiff, but not dry. Fold in the walnuts and melted
chocolate until just combined, using a metal spoon. Place 20 teaspoonfuls of
the mixture on to the prepared trays, leaving approximately 10cm/4in between
them to allow for spreading.
3 Bake in the hot oven for 10–12 minutes until the biscuits are shiny and cracked
on the surface, but still moist in the middle. (You may need to cook them in
batches.) Remove from the oven and transfer to wire racks to cool completely.

165   Orange chocolate-chip biscuits

PREPARATION TIME 20 minutes   **COOKING TIME** 10–12 minutes   **MAKES** 24 biscuits

125g/4¹/₂oz butter, softened,
   plus extra for greasing
1 tsp vanilla essence
75g/2³/₄oz/¹/₃ cup plus 1 tbsp
   soft brown sugar
5 tbsp caster sugar
1 egg, lightly beaten

185g/6¹/₂oz/1¹/₃ cups plus 2 tbsp
   plain flour
1 tsp cardamom
1 tsp cinnamon
zest of 1 orange, grated
200g/7oz orange-flavoured
   chocolate, broken into pieces

1 Preheat the oven to 180°C/350°F/gas 4. Grease 2 large baking trays with butter.
2 In a large bowl, beat together the butter, vanilla essence and both sugars until
light and creamy, using an electric hand mixer. Add the egg until well combined,
then stir in the remaining ingredients. Place 24 tablespoonfuls of the mixture on
the prepared baking trays, leaving approximately 5cm/2in between them to
allow for spreading.
3 Bake in the hot oven for 10–12 minutes, or until the biscuits are dark brown.
(You may need to cook them in batches.) Remove the bisuits from the oven and
transfer to wire racks to cool completely.

166 Chocolate & pistachio biscotti

PREPARATION TIME 35 minutes   **COOKING TIME** 50–65 minutes
MAKES approximately 20 biscotti

125g/4¹/₂oz/¹/₂ cup plus 2 tsp
  caster sugar
1 egg
125g/4¹/₂oz/1 cup plain flour

2 tbsp cocoa powder
¹/₂ tsp baking powder
50g/1³/₄oz/³/₄ cup pistachio nuts,
  roughly chopped

1   Preheat the oven to 170°C/325°F/gas 3. Line a large baking tray with baking paper.
2   In a large bowl, beat the sugar and egg together until pale and thick, using an
    electric hand mixer. In a separate bowl, combine the remaining ingredients,
    using a metal spoon, and fold into the egg mixture to form a dough. Remove the
    dough from the bowl and gently knead it on a lightly floured surface for about
    30 seconds. Form a log about 18 x 5cm/7 x 2in in size, and place on the
    prepared baking tray.
3   Bake in the hot oven for 20–25 minutes, or until the dough is firm to the touch.
    Remove from the oven, turning the temperature down to 140°C/275°F/gas 1,
    and leave to cool completely. When the dough is cold, cut it into approximately
    20 slices around 5mm/¹/₄in thick, using a serrated knife.
4   Place the biscotti slices on a fresh baking tray, and bake them in the warm oven
    for 30–40 minutes, turning once, until they are very dry. Remove the biscotti from
    the oven and leave to cool completely.

167 Chocolate-chip biscotti

PREPARATION TIME 35 minutes   **COOKING TIME** 50–65 minutes
MAKES approximately 20 biscotti

125g/4½oz/½ cup plus 2 tsp
   caster sugar
1 egg

125g/4½oz/1 cup plain flour
½ tsp baking powder
100g/3½oz dark chocolate chips

1 Preheat the oven to 170°C/325°F/gas 3. Line a baking tray with baking paper.
2 In a large bowl, beat the sugar and egg together until pale and thick, using an
   electric hand mixer. In a separate bowl, combine the remaining ingredients,
   using a metal spoon, and fold into the egg mixture to form a dough. Remove the
   dough from the bowl, and gently knead it on a lightly floured surface for about
   30 seconds. Form a dough log about 25 x 5cm/10 x 2in in size, and place on the
   prepared baking tray.
3 Bake in the hot oven for 20–25 minutes, or until the dough is firm to the touch.
   Remove from the oven, turning the temperature down to 140°C/275°F/gas 1,
   and leave to cool completely. When the dough is cold, cut it into approximately
   20 slices around 5mm/¼in thick, using a serrated knife.
4 Place the biscotti slices on a fresh baking tray, and bake them in the warm oven
   for 30–40 minutes, turning once, until they are very dry. Remove the biscotti from
   the oven and leave to cool completely.

168 Double chocolate biscotti with hazelnuts

PREPARATION TIME 35 minutes   **COOKING TIME** 50–65 minutes
MAKES approximately 20 biscotti

125g/4½oz/½ cup plus 2 tsp
   caster sugar
1 egg
125g/4½oz/1 cup plain flour
2 tbsp cocoa powder
½ tsp baking powder

50g/1¾oz dark chocolate,
   broken into rough pieces
50g/1¾oz white chocolate,
   broken into rough pieces
100g/3½oz/¾ cup roasted
   hazelnuts, skinned and
   roughly chopped

1 Preheat the oven to 170°C/325°F/gas 3. Line a large baking tray with baking paper.
2 In a large bowl, beat the sugar and egg together until pale and thick, using an
   electric hand mixer. In a separate bowl, combine the remaining ingredients,
   using a metal spoon, and fold into the egg mixture to form a dough. Remove
   the dough from the bowl and gently knead it on a lightly floured surface for
   about 30 seconds. Form a dough log about 25 x 5cm/10 x 2in in size, and place
   on the prepared baking tray.
3 Bake in the hot oven for 20–25 minutes, or until the dough is firm to the touch.
   Remove from the oven, turning the temperature down to 140°C/275°F/gas 1,
   and leave to cool completely. When the dough is cold, cut into approximately
   20 slices around 5mm/¼in thick, using a serrated knife.
4 Place the biscotti slices on a fresh baking tray, and bake them in the warm oven
   for 30–40 minutes, turning once, until they are very dry. Remove the biscotti from
   the oven and leave to cool completely.

169 Crispy chocolate chip cookies

PREPARATION TIME 15 minutes **COOKING TIME** 10–12 minutes **MAKES** 24 cookies

125g/4¹/₂oz butter, softened,
  plus extra for greasing
1 tsp vanilla essence
75g/2³/₄oz/¹/₃ cup plus 1 tbsp
  soft brown sugar
5 tbsp caster sugar
1 egg, lightly beaten

185g/6¹/₂oz/1¹/₃ cups plus 2 tbsp
  plain flour
200g/7oz dark or milk
  chocolate chips

1   Preheat the oven to 180°C/350°F/gas 4. Grease 2 large baking trays with butter.
2   In a large bowl, beat the butter, vanilla essence and both sugars together until light and creamy, using an electric hand mixer, then beat in the egg. Stir in the flour and chocolate chips, using a wooden spoon. Place 24 tablespoonfuls of the mixture on the prepared trays, leaving approximately 10cm/4in between them to allow for spreading.
3   Bake in the hot oven for 10–12 minutes, or until the cookies are golden brown. (You may need to cook them in batches.) Remove the cookies from the oven and transfer to wire racks to cool completely.

170 Chocolate-chip pecan cookies

PREPARATION TIME 20 minutes **COOKING TIME** 10–12 minutes **MAKES** 30 cookies

140g/5oz butter, softened,
  plus extra for greasing
3 tbsp caster sugar
60g/2¹/₄oz/¹/₃ cup soft brown sugar
1 egg, lightly beaten
125g/4¹/₂oz/1 cup plain flour

¹/₂ tsp bicarbonate of soda
150g/5¹/₂oz/scant 1 cup
  dark or milk chocolate chips
100g/3¹/₂oz/1 cup pecan nuts,
  finely chopped

1   Preheat the oven to 180°C/350°F/gas 4. Grease 2 large baking trays with butter.
2   In a large bowl, beat the butter and both sugars together until light and creamy, using an electric hand mixer, then beat in the egg. In a separate bowl, mix the remaining ingredients together using a wooden spoon, then stir into the butter mixture until well combined (do this in 2 batches). Roll 30 large teaspoonfuls of the mixture between floured hands to form balls. Place on the prepared trays, leaving approximately 5cm/2in between them to allow for spreading. Press down lightly to flatten the balls into rounds.
3   Bake in the hot oven for 10–12 minutes until the cookies are lightly browned. (You may need to cook them in batches.) Remove the cookies from the oven and leave on the baking sheets to cool for 10 minutes, then transfer the cookies to wire racks to cool completely.

171 Truffle dough cookies

PREPARATION TIME 15 minutes, plus chilling **COOKING TIME** 10–12 minutes
MAKES 20 cookies

100g/3½oz/⅓ cup plus 4 tsp
  caster sugar
75g/2¾oz/½ cup plus 1 tbsp
  self-raising flour
3 tbsp cocoa powder
pinch salt

25g/1oz butter, chopped
1 egg, lightly beaten
1 tsp vanilla essence
icing sugar, sifted, for rolling
  and dusting

1 Line a large baking tray with baking paper.
2 Place the sugar, flour, cocoa, salt and butter in the bowl of a food processor, and pulse for 30 seconds. Add the egg and vanilla essence, and pulse for 15 seconds more, or until the mixture forms a dough. Remove the dough from the processor and refrigerate for 30 minutes. Preheat the oven to 180°C/350°F/gas 4.
3 Roll the dough into 20 balls about the size of a walnut, then roll these balls in icing sugar and place on the prepared tray, leaving approximately 10cm/4in between them to allow for spreading.
4 Bake in the hot oven for 10–12 minutes until the cookies are just set. (You may need to cook them in batches.) Remove the cookies from the oven and transfer to a wire rack to cool completely. Dust with icing sugar.

172   White & dark truffle dough cookies

PREPARATION TIME 20 minutes, plus chilling   **COOKING TIME** 10–12 minutes
MAKES 20 cookies

5 tbsp caster sugar	25g/1oz butter, chopped
75g/2³/₄oz/¹/₂ cup plus 1 tbsp self-raising flour	1 egg, lightly beaten
3 tbsp cocoa powder	1 tsp vanilla essence
pinch salt	100g/3¹/₂oz white chocolate chips
	icing sugar, sifted, for rolling

1   Line a large baking tray with baking paper.
2   Place the sugar, flour, cocoa, salt and butter in the bowl of a food processor, and pulse for 30 seconds. Add the egg and vanilla essence, and pulse for 15 seconds more, or until the mixture forms a dough. Remove the dough from the processor, place in a bowl and fold in the chocolate chips, then refrigerate for 30 minutes. Preheat the oven to 180°C/350°F/gas 4.
3   Roll the dough into 20 balls about the size of a walnut, then roll these balls in icing sugar and place on the prepared tray, leaving approximately 10cm/4in between them to allow for spreading.
4   Bake in the hot oven for 10–12 minutes until the cookies are just set. (You may need to cook them in batches.) Remove the cookies from the oven and transfer to a wire rack to cool completely.

173   Chocolate pine nut cookies

PREPARATION TIME 20 minutes   **COOKING TIME** 15–18 minutes   **MAKES** 20 cookies

125g/4¹/₂oz butter, softened, plus extra for greasing	1 tbsp cocoa powder
75g/2³/₄oz/¹/₂ cup plus 1 tbsp icing sugar	125g/4¹/₂oz/1 cup plain flour
1 tsp vanilla essence	75g/2³/₄oz/¹/₂ cup pine nuts, finely chopped, plus 50g/1³/₄oz/¹/₃ cup for decorating

1   Preheat the oven to 170°C/325°F/gas 3. Grease 2 large baking trays with butter.
2   In a large bowl, beat the butter, sugar and vanilla essence together until light and creamy, using an electric hand mixer. Fold in the cocoa, flour and pine nuts until the mixture forms a soft dough, using a metal spoon.
3   Roll the dough into 20 balls about the size of a walnut and place on the prepared baking trays, leaving approximately 10cm/4in between them to allow for spreading. Press a few pine nuts on top of each cookie.
4   Bake in the hot oven for 15–18 minutes, or until the cookies just begin to look dry. (You may need to cook them in batches.) Remove the cookies from the oven and leave to cool on the trays for 5 minutes, before transferring to a wire rack to cool completely.

174 Chocolate brownie cookies

PREPARATION TIME 15 minutes **COOKING TIME** 11–13 minutes **MAKES** 12 cookies

25g/1oz butter, chopped
175g/6oz dark chocolate,
  broken into pieces
1 egg, lightly beaten
100g/3½oz/⅓ cup plus 4 tsp
  caster sugar

1 tsp vanilla essence
40g/1¼oz/⅓ cup
  self-raising flour
60g/2¼oz/⅔ cup pecan nuts,
  chopped and toasted

1 Preheat the oven to 180°C/350°F/gas 4. Grease 2 large baking trays with butter.
2 In a small saucepan, melt the butter and chocolate together over a low heat, and stir with a wooden spoon until smooth. Remove the pan from the heat and set aside to cool. In a large bowl, beat the egg and sugar together until thick and creamy, using an electric hand mixer. Stir in the chocolate mixture, vanilla essence, flour and nuts, using a wooden spoon. Place tablespoonfuls of the mixture on the prepared trays, leaving approximately 10cm/4in between them to allow for spreading.
3 Bake in the hot oven for 6–8 minutes, or until the cookies are puffed and cracked, but still moist. Remove the cookies from the oven and transfer the to a wire rack to cool completely.

175 Spiced chocolate cookies

PREPARATION TIME 20 minutes **COOKING TIME** 12–15 minutes **MAKES** 24 cookies

125g/4½oz butter, softened,
  plus extra for greasing
100g/3½oz/⅓ cup plus 4 tsp
  caster sugar
100g/3½oz/½ cup plus
  2 tsp soft brown sugar
1 tsp vanilla essence

1 egg, lightly beaten
100g/3½oz/1 cup rolled oats
125g/4½oz/1 cup self-raising flour
2 tbsp cocoa powder
50g/1¾oz/½ cup ground almonds
1 tsp cinnamon
1 tsp allspice

1 Preheat the oven to 180°C/350°F/gas 4. Grease 2 large baking trays with butter.
2 In a large bowl, beat the butter and both sugars together until light and creamy, using an electric hand mixer, then beat in the vanilla essence and egg. Stir in the remaining ingredients until just combined. Place tablespoonfuls of the mixture on the prepared trays, leaving approximately 5cm/2in between them to allow for spreading.
3 Bake in the hot oven for 12–15 minutes, or until the cookies are golden brown. (You may need to cook them in batches.) Remove the cookies from the oven and transfer to wire racks to cool completely.

176 Hazelnut thumbprints

PREPARATION TIME 20 minutes   **COOKING TIME** 10–12 minutes   **MAKES** 24 biscuits

125g/4^1/$_2$oz butter, softened,
plus extra for greasing
125g/4^1/$_2$oz/^{1}/$_2$ cup plus 2 tsp
caster sugar
1 egg, lightly beaten
75g/2^3/$_4$oz/^{1}/$_2$ cup plus 1 tbsp
plain flour

75g/2^3/$_4$oz/^{1}/$_2$ cup plus 1 tbsp
self-raising flour
2 tbsp cocoa powder
150g/5^1/$_2$oz chocolate
hazelnut spread
icing sugar, sifted, for dusting

1 Preheat the oven to 180°C/350°F/gas 4. Grease 2 large baking trays with butter.
2 In a large bowl, beat the butter and sugar together until pale and creamy, using an electric hand mixer, then add the egg, beating well to combine. In a separate bowl, mix together both flours and the cocoa, using a wooden spoon, and stir into the butter mixture to form a dough.
3 Roll into 24 balls about the size of a walnut, and place on the prepared trays, leaving approximately 5cm/2in between them to allow for spreading. Push the middle of each ball of dough down with your thumb to create an indent, then place a teaspoonful of the chocolate hazelnut spread into each indented hole.
4 Bake in the hot oven for 10–12 minutes, or until the biscuits are firm. (You may need to cook them in batches.) Remove the thumbprints from the oven and leave to cool on the trays for 10 minutes before transferring to a wire rack to cool completely. Dust with icing sugar.

177 Chocolate shortbread

PREPARATION TIME 15 minutes   **COOKING TIME** 25–30 minutes   **MAKES** 16 shortbreads

250g/9oz butter, chopped
300g/10^1/$_2$oz/2^1/$_3$ cups plain flour

100g/3^1/$_2$oz/^{1}/$_3$ cup plus 4 tsp
caster sugar, plus extra for
sprinkling
1 tbsp cocoa powder

1 Preheat the oven to 150°C/300°F/gas 2. Line a large baking tray with baking paper.
2 Place all the ingredients in the bowl of a food processor, and pulse until the mixture just forms a dough. Divide the dough into 2 equal halves, place them on the prepared tray and press into 2 circles approximately 23cm/9in in diameter. Mark each circle lightly into 8 pieces, using the back of a knife. Prick 6 or 7 times with a fork, and sprinkle with some sugar.
3 Bake in the warm oven for 35–40 minutes, or until the shortbreads are firm. Remove from the oven and leave the shortbreads to cool on the tray for 10 minutes before transferring to a wire rack to cool completely. Cut each shortbread round into 8 pieces along the scored lines.

178   Chocolate-dipped shortbreads

PREPARATION TIME 15 minutes   **COOKING TIME** 10–12 minutes   **MAKES** 18 shortbreads

125g/4¹/₂oz butter, softened
75g/2³/₄oz/¹/₂ cup plus 1 tbsp
  icing sugar

125g/4¹/₂oz/1 cup plain flour
100g/3¹/₂oz dark chocolate,
  melted and left to cool

1   Preheat the oven to 180°C/350°F/gas 4. Line a large baking tray with baking paper.
2   In a large bowl, mix together the butter, sugar and flour until well combined, using a wooden spoon. Roll teaspoonfuls of the mixture into balls and place on the prepared tray, flattening them slightly, leaving approximately 10cm/4in between them to allow for spreading.
3   Bake in the hot oven for 10–12 minutes, or until the shortbreads are lightly browned. Remove from the oven and transfer the shortbreads to a wire rack to cool completely.
4   Dip the cooled shortbreads into the melted chocolate and leave on a clean sheet of baking paper to set.

179   Nutty white chocolate shortbreads

PREPARATION TIME 20 minutes   **COOKING TIME** 35–40 minutes   **MAKES** 16 shortbreads

150g/5¹/₂oz/1 cup plus 2 tbsp
  plain flour
150g/5¹/₂oz/³/₄ cup plus 2 tbsp
  rice flour
100g/3¹/₂oz/¹/₃ cup plus 4 tsp
  caster sugar

225g/8oz chilled butter, chopped
125g/4¹/₂oz white chocolate,
  broken into small pieces
125g/4¹/₂oz/ ³/₄ cup plus 2 tbsp
  hazelnuts, roasted, skins removed,
  finely chopped

1   Preheat the oven to 150°C/300°F/gas 2. Line a large baking tray with baking paper.
2   Place both flours and the sugar in the bowl of a food processor and pulse briefly to combine. Add the butter, chocolate and hazelnuts and pulse several times until all the ingredients are combined and the mixture begins to form a dough.
3   Remove from the food processor and shape the dough to form 2 x 20cm/8in rounds, approximately 5mm/¹/₄in thick, on the prepared tray. Prick each round with a fork, then score each round into 8 pieces using the back of a knife.
4   Bake in the warm oven for 35–40 minutes, or until the shortbreads are firm and lightly browned. Remove from the oven and leave the shortbreads to cool on the tray for 10 minutes before transferring to a wire rack to cool completely. Cut each shortbread round into 8 pieces along the scored lines.

180 Chocolate almond squares

PREPARATION TIME 15 minutes   **COOKING TIME** 20–25 minutes   **MAKES** 16 squares

100g/3½oz butter, softened,
  plus extra for greasing
5 tbsp caster sugar
4 eggs, separated
100g/3½oz dark chocolate, grated

185g/6½oz/1¾ cups ground almonds
4 tbsp plain flour
1 tbsp brandy
1 recipe quantity Shiny Chocolate
  Icing (see page 213)

1   Preheat the oven to 180°C/350°F/gas 4. Grease a shallow 23cm/9in square tin
    with butter, then line the base with baking paper.
2   In a large bowl, mix together the butter, sugar, egg yolks, chocolate, ground
    almonds, flour and brandy, using a wooden spoon. In a clean bowl, whisk the
    egg whites to soft peaks, using an electric hand mixer, then fold into the
    chocolate mixture, using a metal spoon. Pour into the prepared tin.
3   Bake in the hot oven for 20–25 minutes, or until the cake is firm and lightly
    browned. Remove from the oven and leave the cake to cool completely in the tin.
4   To ice, use a palette knife to spread over the shiny chocolate icing, then cut into
    16 squares.

181 Crunchy chocolate-topped squares

PREPARATION TIME 20 minutes   **COOKING TIME** 17–20 minutes   **MAKES** 16 squares

75g/2³⁄₄oz butter, melted,
  plus extra for greasing
100g/3¹⁄₂oz dark chocolate,
  broken into pieces
150g/5¹⁄₂oz/1 cup plus 2 tbsp
  self-raising flour
45g/1¹⁄₄oz/¹⁄₂ cup
  desiccated coconut

4 tbsp cornflakes
85g/3oz/¹⁄₃ cup plus 2 tbsp
  soft brown sugar

FOR THE TOPPING:
100g/3¹⁄₂oz dark chocolate,
  broken into pieces
25g/1oz butter, chopped

1   Preheat the oven to 180°C/350°F/gas 4. Grease a shallow 23cm/9in square cake
    tin with butter, and line the base with baking paper.
2   In a small saucepan, heat the butter and chocolate together over a low heat
    until just melted. Place the flour, coconut, cornflakes, brown sugar and melted
    butter into a large bowl and mix together, using a wooden spoon. Add the
    chocolate mixture, and stir until well combined. Spoon into the prepared tin.
3   Bake in the hot oven for 12–15 minutes, or until the cake is just firm. Remove
    from the oven and leave in the tin to cool completely.
4   For the topping, heat the chocolate and butter together in a small saucepan
    over a low heat until just melted. Set aside to cool for 10 minutes. Spread the
    topping over the slice, and leave to set before cutting into 16 squares.

182 Crunchy chocolate crisp slice

PREPARATION TIME 15 minutes, plus chilling   **COOKING TIME** 5 minutes
MAKES 18 squares

75g/6oz butter, plus
  extra for greasing
600g/21oz/3 cups rice crispies
2 tbsp cocoa powder

100g/3¹⁄₂oz dark chocolate,
  broken into pieces
125g/4¹⁄₂oz marshmallows

1   Grease a shallow 30 x 20cm/12 x 8in tin with butter, and line with baking paper.
2   Mix the rice crispies and cocoa together in a bowl until well combined. In a
    small saucepan, melt the butter and chocolate together over a low heat, then
    remove from the heat and add the marshmallows. Using a wooden spoon, stir
    until melted, then pour over the rice crispies and stir well to combine.
3   Press the mixture into the prepared tin and leave to cool, then refrigerate for
    1 hour before cutting into 18 squares.

183   Chocolate & coconut rough slice

PREPARATION TIME 20 minutes, plus chilling   **COOKING TIME** 12–15 minutes
MAKES 12 squares

125g/4¹/₂oz butter, melted,
  plus extra, for greasing
75g/2³/₄oz/¹/₂ cup plus 1 tbsp
  self-raising flour
75g/2³/₄oz/¹/₂ cup plus 1 tbsp
  plain flour
2 tbsp cocoa powder
5 tbsp caster sugar
45g/1¹/₂oz/¹/₂ cup
  desiccated coconut

FOR THE TOPPING:
100g/3¹/₂oz/³/₄ cup plus 1 tbsp
  icing sugar
2 tbsp cocoa powder
45g/1¹/₂oz/¹/₂ cup
  desiccated coconut
125m/4fl oz/¹/₂ cup condensed milk

1. Preheat the oven to 180°C/350°F/gas 4. Grease a shallow 23cm/9in square cake tin with butter, and line with baking paper.
2. In a large bowl, sift both flours and the cocoa together, then add the sugar and coconut. Add the melted butter, and stir with a wooden spoon until well combined. Press the mixture into the prepared tin.
3. Bake in the hot oven for 12–15 minutes, or until the cake is just firm. Remove from the oven and leave in the tin to cool completely.
4. For the topping, sift the icing sugar and cocoa together into a clean bowl, add the remaining ingredients and stir to combine. Spread the topping evenly over the slice using a palette knife. Refrigerate the iced cake for 30 minutes or until set before cutting into 12 squares.

184   Chocolate & coconut cherry slice

PREPARATION TIME 20 minutes   **COOKING TIME** 15–20 minutes   **MAKES** 16 squares

butter, for greasing
200g/7oz dark chocolate, melted
75g/2³/₄oz/³/₄ cup plus 2 tbsp
  desiccated coconut

5 tbsp caster sugar
210g/7¹/₂oz/1 cup glacé cherries,
  chopped
1 egg white

1. Preheat the oven to 180°C/350°F/gas 4. Grease a shallow 23cm/9in square cake tin with butter. Line with baking paper, leaving a little overhanging the edges.
2. Spread the melted chocolate evenly over the base of the prepared tin, and leave to set. In a large bowl, mix the coconut, sugar, cherries and egg white together, using a wooden spoon, and spread over the chocolate.
3. Bake in the hot oven for 15–20 minutes, or until the slice is just firm. Remove from the oven and leave the slice in the tin to cool completely before removing and cutting into 16 squares.

185 Rocky road slice

PREPARATION TIME 20 minutes   **COOKING TIME** 15–17 minutes   **MAKES** 16 squares

125g/4¹/₂oz butter, chopped,
   plus extra for greasing
2 tbsp cocoa powder
100g/3¹/₂oz/¹/₃ cup plus 4 tsp
   caster sugar
1 egg, lightly beaten
60g/2¹/₄oz/¹/₃ cup walnuts, chopped
250g/9oz digestive biscuits, crushed

FOR THE TOPPING:
150g/5¹/₂oz milk chocolate,
   melted and left to cool
200g/7oz marshmallows, chopped

1   Preheat the oven to 180°C/350°F/gas 4. Grease a shallow 23cm/9in square cake
    tin with butter, and line with baking paper.
2   In a small saucepan, melt the butter over a low heat , then stir in the cocoa and
    sugar, using a wooden spoon. Remove from the heat and set aside to cool.
    Whisk in the egg. In a large bowl, combine the walnuts and crushed biscuits,
    then pour the butter mixture over the biscuit mix. Stir until well combined,
    using a wooden spoon. Press the mixture into the prepared tin.
3   Bake in the hot oven for 10–12 minutes, or until the slice is just firm. Remove
    the slice from the oven.
4   For the topping, mix the melted chocolate and marshmallows together in
    a bowl, and spread over the baked slice. Leave the slice in the tin to cool
    completely, then refrigerate for 30 minutes before cutting into 16 squares.

186 Chocolate-chip & nut slice

PREPARATION TIME 15 minutes   **COOKING TIME** 20–25 minutes   **MAKES** 16 squares

100g/3¹/₂oz butter, melted,
   plus extra for greasing
125g/4¹/₂oz digestive biscuits,
   finely crushed
200g/7oz milk or dark
   chocolate chips

90g/3¹/₄oz/1 cup desiccated coconut
100g/3¹/₂oz/³/₄ cup mixed nuts,
   chopped
397g/14oz can condensed milk

1   Preheat the oven to 180°C/350°F/gas 4. Grease a shallow 23cm/9in square
    cake tin with butter, and line with baking paper.
2   Pour the melted butter into the tray and spread over the paper-lined base
    to coat it evenly. Sprinkle over the crushed biscuits, chocolate chips, coconut
    and nuts, then pour over the condensed milk as evenly as possible.
3   Bake in the hot oven for 20–25 minutes, or until lightly browned. Remove from
    the oven and leave the slice in the tin to cool completely before cutting into
    16 squares and transferring to a serving plate.

187 White chocolate fruit & nut slice

PREPARATION TIME 20 minutes   **COOKING TIME** 35–40 minutes   **MAKES** 16 slices

butter, for greasing
100g/3½oz/1 cup flaked almonds
200g/7oz/2 cups walnuts, chopped
150g/5½oz/1⅔ cups desiccated
   coconut
150g/5½oz/¾ cup dried apricots,
   chopped

150g/5½oz/1 cup plus 2 tbsp raisins
2 tbsp plus 1 tsp rice flour
25g/1oz/¼ cup ground almonds
150g/5½oz/½ cup apricot jam
125ml/4fl oz/½ cup honey
250g/9oz white chocolate,
   melted and left to cool

1 Preheat the oven to 170°C/325°F/gas 3. Grease a shallow 30 x 22cm/12 x 8in tin
with butter, and line with baking paper.
2 In a large bowl, mix the almonds, walnuts, coconut, apricots, raisins, flour
and ground almonds together. In a small saucepan, gently warm the jam and
honey together over a low heat until melted. Pour the jam and honey mixture
into the fruit mixture, stir well to combine, then pour into the prepared tin.
3 Bake in the hot oven for 30–35 minutes, or until the slice is lightly browned.
Remove from the oven, and leave the slice in the baking tray to cool completely
before spreading the melted chocolate over the top. Leave to set before cutting
into 16 slices.

188 Chocolate coconut slice

PREPARATION TIME 20 minutes   **COOKING TIME** 15–20 minutes   **MAKES** 16 slices

125g/4¹/₂oz butter, melted,
   plus extra for greasing
100g/3¹/₂oz/¹/₂ cup plus 2 tsp
   soft brown sugar
90g/3¹/₄oz/1 cup desiccated coconut,
   plus 2 tbsp for sprinkling
1 egg, lightly beaten

75g/2³/₄oz/¹/₂ cup plus 1 tbsp
   plain flour
4 tbsp self-raising flour
1 tbsp cocoa powder
1 recipe quantity Chocolate Fudge
   Frosting (see page 212)

1   Preheat the oven to 180°C/350°F/gas 4. Grease a shallow 30 x 20cm/12 x 8in
    tin with butter, and line with baking paper.
2   In a large bowl, mix together the melted butter, brown sugar, coconut, egg,
    both flours and the cocoa until well combined, using a wooden spoon. Press
    the mixture into the prepared tin.
3   Bake in the hot oven for 15–20 minutes until the slice is firm and golden brown.
    Remove from the oven and leave the slice in the tin to cool completely.
4   To decorate the slice, use a palette knife to spread over the chocolate fudge
    frosting, then sprinkle over the coconut before cutting into 16 slices.

189 Chocolate peppermint slice

PREPARATION TIME 30 minutes, plus chilling   **COOKING TIME** 12–15 minutes
MAKES 24 squares

25g/1oz butter, melted,
   plus extra for greasing
100g/3¹/₂oz/³/₄ cup plus 1 tbsp
   self-raising flour
2 tbsp cocoa powder
¹/₄ tsp bicarbonate of soda
5 tbsp caster sugar
1 egg, lightly beaten

FOR THE FILLING
300g/10¹/₂oz/2¹/₃ cups icing sugar
1 tbsp vegetable oil
2 tbsp milk (approximately)
1 tsp peppermint essence

FOR THE TOPPING
125g/4¹/₂oz dark chocolate,
   broken into pieces
100g/3¹/₂oz butter, chopped

1   Preheat the oven to 180°C/350°F/gas 4. Grease a shallow 23cm/9in square cake
    tin with butter, and line with baking paper.
2   In a large bowl, mix the flour, cocoa, bicarbonate of soda, sugar, butter and
    5 tbsp water together until smooth, using a wooden spoon. Add the egg, and
    mix until well combined. Pour into the prepared tin.
3   Bake in the hot oven for 12–15 minutes, or until the slice is just firm. Remove
    from the oven and leave the slice to cool in the tin.
4   For the filling, sift the icing sugar into a bowl, and mix all of the ingredients plus
    4 tbsp hot water together until smooth, using as much of the milk as is necessary
    for a soft consistency. Spread the filling evenly over the cake base, using a palette
    knife. Refrigerate the slice for 1 hour until firm.
5   For the filling, melt the chocolate and butter together in a small saucepan until
    the chocolate has just melted, and stir until smooth, using a wooden spoon.
    Spread the topping over the filling, then refrigerate the slice for 1 hour. Remove
    the slice from the refrigerator and cut into 24 squares.

190 Mincemeat & chocolate slice

PREPARATION TIME 15 minutes   **COOKING TIME** 20–25 minutes   **MAKES** 16 squares

125g/4½oz butter, melted,
  plus extra for greasing
150g/5½oz/1 cup plus 2 tbsp
  self-raising flour
2 tbsp cocoa powder

100g/3½oz/⅓ cup plus 4 tsp
  caster sugar
400g/14oz/1½ cups mincemeat
1 egg, lightly beaten
1 recipe quantity Shiny Chocolate
  Icing (see page 213)

1 Preheat the oven to 180°C/350°F/gas 4. Grease a shallow 23cm/9in square cake tin with butter, and line with baking paper.
2 Mix together the butter, flour, cocoa, sugar, mincemeat and egg until just combined, using a wooden spoon. Press the mixture into the prepared cake tin.
3 Bake in the hot oven for 20–25 minutes until the slice is firm and lightly browned. Leave the slice in the tin to cool completely.
4 To ice the slice, use a palette knife to spread over the shiny chocolate icing before cutting into 16 squares.

191 Butterscotch & chocolate slice

PREPARATION TIME 15 minutes   **COOKING TIME** 35–40 minutes   **MAKES** 16 squares

250g/9oz butter, softened,
  plus extra for greasing
175g/6oz/¾ cup plus 3 tbsp
  soft brown sugar
2 eggs, lightly beaten
1 tsp vanilla essence

200g/7oz dark or plain chocolate,
  finely chopped
350g/12oz/2¾ cups self-raising flour
125g/4½ oz/1 cup walnuts,
  finely chopped

1 Preheat the oven to 170°C/325°F/gas 3. Grease a shallow 30 x 23cm/13 x 9in tin with butter and line with baking paper.
2 In a large bowl, beat together the butter and brown sugar, using an electric hand mixer, then add the eggs, a little at a time. Add the vanilla essence, then gently fold in the chocolate and flour until just combined, using a metal spoon. Spread the mixture evenly over the base of the prepared tin and scatter the walnuts evenly over the top of the mixture.
3 Bake in the hot oven for 35–40 minutes, or until the middle is just firm and the top is golden brown. Remove from the oven, and leave the cake in the tin to cool completely before cutting into 16 squares.

192 Chocolate flapjacks

PREPARATION TIME 20 minutes   **COOKING TIME** 15–20 minutes   **MAKES** 18 flapjacks

350g/12oz butter, chopped,
  plus extra for greasing
3 tbsp golden syrup
175g/6oz/³⁄₄ cup plus 3 tbsp
  soft brown sugar

100g/3¹⁄₂oz/¹⁄₃ cup plus 4 tsp
  caster sugar
5 tbsp cocoa powder
350g/12oz/3¹⁄₂ cups rolled oats

1   Preheat the oven to 150°C/300°F/gas 2. Grease a shallow 23cm/9in square
    cake tin with butter, and line the base with baking paper.
2   In a small saucepan, melt the butter with the golden syrup, over a low heat.
    Remove from the heat and set aside. In a large bowl, mix together both sugars,
    cocoa and rolled oats, using a wooden spoon, then pour the butter mixture into
    the bowl. Stir until well combined then press the mixture into the prepared tin.
3   Bake in the warm oven for 15–20 minutes, or until just firm in the middle.
    Remove from the oven, and leave in the tin to cool completely before cutting
    into 18 pieces.

193   Chocolate & almond tuiles

PREPARATION TIME 15 minutes   **COOKING TIME** 6–8 minutes   **MAKES** 18 tuiles

75g/2³/₄oz butter, melted
50g/1³/₄oz/¹/₂ cup ground almonds
4 tbsp plain flour
1 tbsp cocoa powder

3 tbsp plus 1 tsp caster sugar
pinch salt
2 egg whites
50g/1³/₄oz/¹/₂ cup flaked almonds

1   Preheat the oven to 170°C/325°F/gas 4. Line a large baking tray with baking paper.
2   Place all of the ingredients except the flaked almonds in a large bowl, and stir until combined, using a wooden spoon. Place tablespoonfuls of the mixture on the prepared tray and spread thinly, using the back of a spoon or a knife. Sprinkle over the flaked almonds.
3   Bake in the hot oven for 6–8 minutes, or until the tuiles are golden brown. Remove from the oven and leave the tuiles to cool on the tray for 5 minutes, then transfer to a wire rack to cool completely.

194   Macadamia & chocolate wafers

PREPARATION TIME 15 minutes   **COOKING TIME** 8–10 minutes   **MAKES** 18 wafers

100g/3¹/₂oz butter, softened,
   plus extra for greasing
175g/6oz/³/₄ cup caster sugar
3 tbsp golden syrup or clear honey
150g/5¹/₂oz/1 cup plus 2 tbsp
   plain flour

1 tbsp cocoa powder
2 egg whites
80g/3oz/¹/₂ cup macadamia nuts,
   chopped
4 tbsp chocolate chips

1   Preheat the oven to 180°C/350°F/gas 4. Line 2 large baking trays with baking paper.
2   Place the butter, sugar, syrup, flour, cocoa and egg whites in the bowl of a food processor, and pulse until smooth. Spoon 9 tablespoonfuls of the mixture on each of the prepared trays. Spread out each one thinly, using the back of the spoon, leaving approximately 10cm/4in between them to allow for spreading. Sprinkle with the chopped nuts and chocolate chips.
3   Bake in the hot oven for 8–10 minutes until the wafers are golden brown. Remove from the oven, and leave the wafers on the trays to cool completely.

195 Chocolate scones

PREPARATION time 20 minutes   COOKING TIME 15–20 minutes   MAKES 6 large scones

75g/2³/₄oz chilled butter, chopped,
   plus extra for greasing
350g/12oz/2³/₄ cups self-raising
   flour, plus extra for dusting
2 tbsp cocoa powder
1 tsp cinnamon

100g/3¹/₂oz/¹/₃ cup plus 4 tsp
   caster sugar
100ml/3¹/₂fl oz/¹/₃ cup milk,
   plus extra for brushing
1 egg, lightly beaten
1 recipe quantity Chocolate Chantilly
   Cream (see page 208)

1   Preheat the oven to 190°C/375°F/gas 5. Grease a large baking tray with butter.
2   Sift the flour and cocoa into a large bowl, then add the cinnamon and sugar. Add
    the butter, and, working lightly, rub it into the flour using your fingertips until
    the mixture resembles breadcrumbs. In a small bowl, beat together the milk
    and egg. Add the milk mixture to the flour mixture until it forms a soft dough,
    using a rounded knife and a cutting motion.
3   Turn the dough out on to a lightly floured board and pat it out until it is around
    2.5cm/1in thick. Cut out 6 circles using a scone cutter, and place on the
    prepared tray. Brush the tops with a little extra milk, using a pastry brush.
4   Bake in the hot oven for 15–20 minutes, or until the scones are golden brown.
    Remove from the oven and transfer to a wire rack to cool completely, then
    transfer to a serving plate and serve with the chocolate chantilly cream.

196 Chocolate chunk scones

PREPARATION TIME 20 minutes   COOKING TIME 15–20 minutes   MAKES 6 large scones

75g/2³/₄oz chilled butter, chopped,
   plus extra for greasing
350g/12oz/2³/₄ cups self-raising
   flour, plus extra for dusting
5 tbsp caster sugar
100g/3¹/₂oz dark or milk chocolate,
   broken into pieces

100ml/3¹/₂fl oz/¹/₃ cup milk,
   plus extra for brushing
1 egg, lightly beaten
1 recipe quantity Chocolate Chantilly
   Cream (see page 208)

1   Preheat the oven to 190°C/375°F/gas 5. Grease a baking tray with butter.
2   Place the flour and sugar in a large bowl, and, working lightly, rub in the butter
    with your fingertips until the mixture resembles breadcrumbs. Stir in the
    chocolate with a wooden spoon. In a small bowl, beat together the milk and
    egg. Add the milk mixture to the flour mixture until it forms a soft dough, using
    a rounded knife and a cutting motion.
3   Turn the dough out on to a lightly floured board and pat it out until it is around
    2.5cm/1in thick. Cut out 6 circles using a scone cutter, and place on the
    prepared tray. Brush the tops with a little extra milk, using a pastry brush.
4   Bake in the hot oven for 15–20 minutes, or until the scones are golden brown.
    Remove from the oven and transfer to a wire rack to cool completely, then
    transfer to a serving plate and serve with the chocolate chantilly cream.

197   Cranberry and white chocolate scones

PREPARATION TIME 20 minutes   **COOKING TIME** 15–20 minutes   **MAKES** 6 large scones

75g/2³/₄oz butter, chilled and
  chopped, plus extra for greasing
  and to serve
250g/9oz/2 cups self-raising flour
3 tbsp plus 1 tsp caster sugar

75g/2³/₄oz white chocolate chips
100g/3¹/₂oz/³/₄ cup plus 1 tbsp
  dried cranberries
6 tbsp milk, plus extra for brushing
1 egg, lightly beaten

1   Preheat the oven to 190°C/375°F/gas 5. Grease a large baking tray with butter.
2   Place the flour and sugar in a large bowl, and, working lightly, rub in the butter
    with your fingertips until the mixture resembles breadcrumbs. Stir in the
    chocolate chips and cranberries, using a wooden spoon. In a small bowl, beat
    together the milk and egg. Add the milk mixture to the flour mixture until it
    forms a soft dough, using a rounded knife and a cutting motion.
3   Turn the dough out on to a lightly floured board and pat it out until it is around
    2.5cm/1in thick. Cut out 6 circles using a scone cutter, and place on the
    prepared tray. Brush the tops with a little extra milk, using a pastry brush.
4   Bake in the hot oven for 15–20 minutes, or until the scones are golden brown.
    Remove from the oven and transfer to a wire rack to cool completely, then
    transfer to a serving plate and serve warm or cold with butter.

198 Chocolate coconut drops

PREPARATION TIME 15 minutes   **COOKING TIME** 10–12 minutes   **MAKES** 20 biscuits

butter, for greasing
75g/2³/₄oz dark chocolate,
  melted and left to cool
90g/3¹/₄oz/1 cup desiccated coconut

125g/4¹/₂oz/¹/₂ cup plus 2 tsp
  caster sugar
1 tbsp cocoa powder
1 egg white
1 tbsp icing sugar, sifted

1 Preheat the oven to 180°C/350°F/gas 4. Grease 2 baking trays with butter.
2 In a large bowl, mix together the melted chocolate, coconut, caster sugar, cocoa and egg white until well combined, using a wooden spoon. Shape large teaspoonfuls of the mixture into balls and place them on the prepared trays, leaving approximately 5cm/2in between them to allow for spreading. Flatten each ball slightly, and sprinkle over the icing sugar.
3 Bake in the hot oven for 10–12 minutes, or until the biscuits are just firm. Remove from the oven and leave the biscuits to cool on the trays for 10 minutes, then transfer to wire racks to cool completely.

199 Chocolate donut mini-muffins

PREPARATION TIME 20 minutes   **COOKING TIME** 15–20 minutes   **MAKES** 24 mini-muffins

85g/3oz butter, softened,
  plus extra for greasing
145g/5¹/₄oz/²/₃ cup caster sugar
1 egg, lightly beaten
185g/6¹/₂oz/1¹/₃ cups plus 2 tbsp
  self-raising flour

2 tbsp cocoa powder
¹/₄ tsp bicarbonate of soda
1 tsp ground nutmeg
125ml/4fl oz/¹/₂ cup milk
1 tsp cinnamon
25g/1oz butter, melted

1 Preheat the oven to 180°C/350°F/gas 4. Grease 2 x 12-hole mini-muffin tins with butter.
2 In a large bowl, beat the butter and 100g/3¹/₂oz/¹/₃ cup plus 4 tsp of the sugar together until pale and creamy, using an electric hand mixer, then whisk in the egg. In a clean bowl, combine the flour, cocoa, bicarbonate of soda and nutmeg, then fold into the butter mixture with the milk. Spoon the mixture evenly into the prepared tin holes.
3 Bake in the hot oven for 15–20 minutes until the mini-muffins are firm and lightly browned. Remove from the oven and leave the mini-muffins in the tins to cool for 5 minutes.
4 In a clean bowl, combine the remaining sugar and the cinnamon. While still warm, brush the top of each mini-muffin with the melted butter, then sprinkle over the cinnamon sugar. Remove the mini-muffins from the tins and transfer to a wire rack to cool completely.

200 Chocolate-chip & coconut muffins

PREPARATION TIME 15 minutes   **COOKING TIME** 15–20 minutes   **MAKES** 12 muffins

100g/3½oz butter, melted,
  plus extra for greasing
375g/13oz/3 cups self-raising flour
175g/6oz/¾ cup caster sugar
45g/1¼oz/½ cup desiccated coconut

125ml/4fl oz/½ cup sour cream
60ml/2fl oz/¼ cup milk
2 eggs, lightly beaten
100g/3½oz dark chocolate chips

1   Preheat the oven to 190°C/375°F/gas 5. Grease a 12-hole muffin tin with butter.
2   In a large bowl, mix all of the ingredients together, using a wooden spoon, until well combined. Spoon the mixture evenly into the prepared tin holes.
3   Bake in the hot oven for 15–20 minutes until the muffins have risen and are golden brown. Remove from the oven and leave in the tin to cool for 5–10 minutes, then remove from the tin and transfer to a wire rack to cool completely.

201 Chocolate cherry muffins

PREPARATION TIME 15 minutes   **COOKING TIME** 18–20 minutes   **MAKES** 12 large muffins

15g/½oz butter, melted,
  plus extra for greasing
150g/5½oz/1 cup plus 2 tbsp
  self-raising flour
75g/2¾oz/½ cup plus 1 tbsp
  plain flour
3 tbsp cocoa powder
250g/9oz/1 cup plus 4 tsp
  caster sugar

1 egg, lightly beaten
250ml/9fl oz/1 cup milk
110g/3¾oz/½ cup glacé cherries,
  roughly chopped
100g/3½oz dark chocolate chips
50g/1¼oz/½ cup desiccated coconut

1   Preheat the oven to 190°C/375°F/gas 5. Grease a 12-hole muffin tin with butter.
2   In a large bowl, mix both flours, the cocoa, sugar, egg, butter and milk until just combined, using a wooden spoon. Stir in the cherries, chocolate chips and coconut and spoon the mixture evenly into the prepared tin holes.
3   Bake in the hot oven for 18–20 minutes until the muffins have risen and are dark brown. Remove from the oven and leave in the tin to cool for 5–10 minutes, then remove from the tin and transfer to a wire rack to cool completely.

202 Banana & white chocolate muffins

PREPARATION TIME 15 minutes   **COOKING TIME** 15–20 minutes   **MAKES** 12 muffins

125g/4¹/₂oz butter, melted,
  plus extra for greasing
375g/13oz/3 cups self-raising flour
175g/6oz/³/₄ cup caster sugar
2 eggs lightly beaten

2 ripe bananas, mashed
125g/4¹/₂oz white chocolate chips
250ml/9fl oz/1 cup milk
icing sugar, sifted, for dusting

1 Preheat the oven to 190°F/375°C/gas 5. Grease a 12-hole muffin tin with butter.
2 In a large bowl, mix together all the ingredients until just combined, using a
   wooden spoon. Divide the mixture evenly between the prepared tin holes.
3 Bake in the hot oven for 15–20 minutes until the muffins have risen and are
   golden brown. Remove from the oven and leave the muffins in the tin to cool
   for 5–10 minutes, then remove from the tin and transfer to a wire rack to cool
   completely. Dust with icing sugar.

203 White chocolate & blueberry muffins

PREPARATION TIME 15 minutes   **COOKING TIME** 15–20 minutes   **MAKES** 12 muffins

125g/4¹/₂oz butter, melted,
  plus extra for greasing
250g/9oz/2 cups
  self-raising flour
100g/3¹/₂oz/¹/₃ cup plus 4 tsp
  caster sugar

125g/4¹/₂oz white chocolate,
  broken into pieces
1 egg, lightly beaten
125ml/4fl oz/¹/₂ cup milk
1 tsp vanilla essence
150g/5¹/₂oz/1 cup blueberries

1 Preheat the oven to 190°C/375°F/gas 5. Grease a 12-hole muffin tin with butter.
2 In a large bowl, mix all the ingredients together until just combined, using a
   wooden spoon. Divide the mixture evenly between the prepared tin holes.
3 Bake in the hot oven for 15–20 minutes until the muffins have risen and are
   golden brown. Remove from the oven and leave the muffins in the tin to cool
   for 5–10 minutes, then remove the muffins from the tin and transfer to a wire
   rack to cool completely.

204 Orange chocolate-chip muffins

PREPARATION TIME 20 minutes   **COOKING TIME** 20–25 minutes   **MAKES** 12 muffins

75g/2³/₄oz butter, melted,
  plus extra for greasing
250g/9oz/2 cups self-raising flour
pinch salt
100g/3¹/₂oz/¹/₃ cup plus 4 tsp
  caster sugar

1 egg, lightly beaten
125ml/4fl oz/¹/₂ cup milk
125ml/4fl oz/¹/₂ cup plain yogurt
zest of 1 orange
100g/3¹/₂oz orange-flavoured
  chocolate, broken into pieces

1 Preheat the oven to 180°C/350°F/gas 4. Grease a 12-hole muffin tin with butter.
2 In a large bowl, combine the flour, salt and sugar, using a wooden spoon. In a
   separate bowl, beat together the egg, milk, yogurt melted butter and orange
   zest until combined, using a hand whisk, then stir into the flour mixture. Fold
   in the chocolate, using a metal spoon. Divide the mixture evenly between the
   prepared tin holes.
3 Bake in the hot oven for 20–25 minutes until the muffins have risen and are
   golden brown. Remove from the oven and leave in the tin to cool for 5–10 minutes,
   then remove from the tin and transfer to a wire rack to cool completely.

205 Double chocolate muffins

PREPARATION TIME 15 minutes **COOKING TIME** 20–25 minutes **MAKES** 12 muffins

125g/4¹/₂oz butter, melted,
   plus extra for greasing
375g/13oz/3 cups
   self-raising flour
3 tbsp cocoa powder

175g/6oz/³/₄ cup caster sugar
2 eggs, lightly beaten
125g/4¹/₂oz dark or milk
   chocolate chips
250ml/9fl oz/1 cup milk

1 Preheat the oven to 190°C/375°F/gas 5. Grease a 12-hole muffin tin with butter.
2 In a large bowl, mix together all the ingredients until just combined, using a
   wooden spoon. Divide the mixture evenly between the prepared tin holes.
3 Bake in the hot oven for 20–25 minutes until the muffins have risen and are
   golden brown. Remove from the oven and leave in the tin to cool for 5–10 minutes,
   then remove from the tin and transfer to a wire rack to cool completely.

206   White chocolate & strawberry muffins

PREPARATION TIME 15 minutes   **COOKING TIME** 18–20 minutes   **MAKES** 12 muffins

125g/4¹/₂oz butter, melted,
   plus extra for greasing
100g/3¹/₂oz/¹/₃ cup plus 4 tsp
   caster sugar
125ml/4fl oz/¹/₂ cup milk
1 egg, lightly beaten

1 tsp vanilla essence
250g/9oz/2 cups self-raising flour
250g/9oz white chocolate chips
160g/5¹/₂oz/¹/₂ cup strawberry jam

1   Preheat the oven to 180°C/350°F/gas 4. Grease a 12-hole muffin tin with butter.
2   In a large bowl, mix together all the ingredients except for the jam until blended. Spoon the mixture evenly between the prepared tin holes, to fill approximately halfway, then top with a spoonful of the strawberry jam. Cover the jam with the remaining muffin mixture.
3   Bake in the hot oven for 18–20 minutes until the muffins have risen and are golden brown. Remove from the oven and leave in the tin to cool for 5–10 minutes, then remove from the tin and transfer to a wire rack to cool completely.

207   Flourless chocolate muffins

PREPARATION TIME 15 minutes   **COOKING TIME** 20–25 minutes   **MAKES** 12 muffins

150g/5¹/₂oz butter,
   plus extra for greasing
200g/7oz dark chocolate,
   broken into pieces
5 eggs, separated

125g/4¹/₂oz/¹/₂ cup plus 2 tsp
   caster sugar
150g/5¹/₂oz/1¹/₂ cups
   ground almonds

1   Preheat the oven to 170°C/325°F/gas 3. Grease a 12-hole muffin tin with butter.
2   In a small saucepan, heat the butter and chocolate together over a low heat until just melted, then remove from the heat and set aside to cool slightly. When cool, add the egg yolks and 5 tbsp of the sugar, and combine well, using a wooden spoon.
3   In a clean bowl, whisk the egg whites to soft peaks, using an electric hand mixer, then gradually add the remaining sugar and continue beating until thick, but not dry. Fold the chocolate mixture and the ground almonds into the whisked egg whites, using a metal spoon. Divide the mixture evenly between the prepared tin holes.
4   Bake in the hot oven for 20–25 minutes until the muffins have risen and are golden brown. Remove from the oven and leave in the tin to cool for 5–10 minutes, then remove from the tin and transfer to a wire rack to cool completely.

208 Chocolate mud pastries

PREPARATION TIME 20 minutes   **COOKING TIME** 20–25 minutes   **MAKES** 12 pastries

375g/13oz packet ready-rolled
   puff pastry
75g/2³⁄₄oz dark chocolate,
   broken into pieces
25g/1oz butter, chopped

5 tbsp caster sugar
1 egg, lightly beaten
1 tsp vanilla essence
1 tbsp plain flour
icing sugar, sifted, for dusting

1 Preheat the oven to 200°C/400°F/gas 6.
2 Cut the pastry into 12 squares of approximately 10cm/4in, which will roughly fit the holes of a 12-hole muffin tin with around 1cm/½in extra. Gently ease each pastry square into a hole without stretching it, and refrigerate while preparing the filling.
3 In a small saucepan, heat the chocolate and butter over a low heat, and stir until just melted. Remove from the heat and set aside to cool for 10 minutes, then stir in the sugar, egg, vanilla essence and flour. Spoon 1–2 tbsp of the chocolate mixture into the middle of each pastry cup, taking care not to overfill.
4 Bake in the hot oven for 15–20 minutes, or until the pastry is golden and the filling has puffed up. Remove from the oven and leave the pastries in the tins for 5 minutes, then transfer to a wire rack to cool completely. Dust the pastries with icing sugar.

209 Chocolate caramel tarts

PREPARATION TIME 35 minutes, plus setting   **COOKING TIME** 15 minutes
MAKES 4 x 10cm/4in tarts

400g/14oz/1³⁄₄ cups plus 2 tbsp
   granulated sugar
125g/4¹⁄₂oz butter, chopped,
   plus extra for greasing
125ml/4fl oz/¹⁄₂ cup double cream

4 x 10cm/4in Chocolate Shortcrust
   Pastry cases, baked (see page 13)
1 recipe quantity Dark Chocolate
   Ganache (see page 209)

1 In a medium-sized saucepan, mix 125ml/4fl oz/¹⁄₂ cup water and the sugar together over a low heat, and stir with a metal spoon from time to time until the sugar has dissolved completely. Turn up the heat, and boil vigorously for 10–12 minutes until the mixture forms a dark caramel, swirling the pan from time to time. Remove from the heat, add the butter and cream (being careful as the mixture will hiss and spit) and stir well until combined, using a wooden spoon. Set the caramel mixture aside to cool for 15 minutes, then divide it equally between the baked pastry cases and leave to set for 15–20 minutes.
2 Top each tart with dark chocolate ganache, spreading it over evenly with a palette knife. Leave the tarts to set at room temperature for 1–2 hours.

210 Mincemeat & chocolate tart

PREPARATION TIME 30 minutes   **COOKING TIME** 15–20 minutes   **MAKES** 1 x 23cm/9in tart

1 x 23cm/9in Chocolate Shortcrust
  Pastry case, baked (see page 13)
1 tbsp brandy
400g/14oz/1½ cups mincemeat
50g/1¾oz dark chocolate,
  melted and left to cool

FOR THE TOPPING:
3 tbsp plain flour
2 tbsp soft brown sugar
50g/1¾oz butter, chopped
½ tsp cinnamon

1 Preheat the oven to 180°C/350°F/gas 4. Place the baked pastry case on
   a baking tray.
2 In a large bowl, combine the brandy and mincemeat, using a wooden spoon,
   and spread evenly over the base of the tart case. Place the topping ingredients
   in the bowl of a food processor, and pulse until smooth. Sprinkle the topping
   mixture evenly over the mincemeat.
3 Bake in the hot oven for 15–20 minutes until the tart is golden brown. Remove
   from the oven, and leave the tart on the baking sheet to cool for 15 minutes.
   Place the melted chocolate in a piping bag with a fine nozzle and drizzle
   randomly over the top of the tart. Serve warm or cold.

211 Chocolate pear tart

PREPARATION TIME 30 minutes   **COOKING TIME** 30–35 minutes   **MAKES** 1 x 23cm/9in tart

1 x 23cm/9in Chocolate Shortcrust
  Pastry case, baked (see page 13)
200g/7oz dark chocolate,
  melted and left to cool
1 egg, lightly beaten

250ml/9fl oz/1 cup double cream
1 tsp vanilla essence
3 large ripe pears, peeled, cored
  and halved

1 Preheat the oven to 180°C/350°F/gas 4. Place the baked pastry case on
   a baking tray.
2 In a large bowl, beat the chocolate, egg, cream and vanilla essence together,
   using an electric hand mixer, to make a chocolate custard. Place the pears
   on the base of the pastry case, and pour the chocolate custard mixture over
   the top, taking care not to overfill.
3 Bake in the hot oven for 30–35 minutes, or until the custard has set. Remove
   from the oven, and leave the tart on the baking sheet to cool for 30 minutes
   before transferring to a serving plate.

212 Chocolate & raspberry tart

PREPARATION TIME 20 minutes   **COOKING TIME** 35–40 minutes   **MAKES** 1 x 23cm/9in tart

1 x 23cm/9in Sweet Shortcrust
   Pastry case, baked (see page 13)
150g/5¹/₂oz dark chocolate,
   broken into pieces
75ml/2¹/₂fl oz/¹/₃ cup double cream
75g/2³/₄oz butter, chopped
2 eggs

3 tbsp plus 1 tsp caster sugar
1 tbsp golden syrup
125g/4¹/₂oz/1 cup raspberries,
   plus extra for serving (optional)
icing sugar, for dusting
1 recipe quantity Chocolate Marsala
   Cream (see page 352)

1   Preheat the oven to 150°C/300°F/gas 2. Place the baked pastry case on
    a baking tray.
2   In a small saucepan, melt the chocolate, cream and butter together over a low
    heat, then remove the pan from the heat and set aside to cool. In a large bowl,
    beat the eggs, sugar and golden syrup together for a few minutes until pale and
    light, using an electric hand mixer. Stir in the chocolate mixture, using a wooden
    spoon. Scatter the raspberries over the base of the tart, and pour the chocolate
    filling on top, taking care not to overfill.
3   Bake in the warm oven for 35–40 minutes, or until the middle of the tart is just
    set. Remove from the oven, and leave on the baking tray to cool completely.
4   Dust the tart with icing sugar just before serving, and serve with extra
    raspberries, if wanted, and some chocolate Marsala cream.

213 Chocolate tart with cardamom

PREPARATION TIME 30 minutes   **COOKING TIME** 20–25 minutes   **MAKES** 1 x 23cm/9in tart

1 x 23cm/9in Sweet Shortcrust
   Pastry case, baked (see page 13)
50g/1³/₄oz butter
250g/9oz dark chocolate,
   broken into pieces

3 eggs, separated
5 tbsp caster sugar
125ml/4fl oz/¹/₂ cup double cream
1 tsp ground cardamom

1 Preheat the oven to 200°C/400°F/gas 6. Place the baked pastry case
   on a baking tray.
2 In a small saucepan, melt the butter and chocolate together over a low heat,
   then remove the pan from the heat and and set aside to cool. In a separate
   bowl, whisk the egg whites to soft peaks, using an electric hand mixer, then
   gradually add the sugar and whisk until stiff. Beat the yolks into the chocolate
   mixture, then fold in the cream, cardamom and whisked egg whites, using a
   metal spoon until just combined. Pour the mixture into the baked pastry case,
   taking care not to overfill.
3 Bake in the hot oven for 20–25 minutes, or until the tart is just firm around the
   edges but the middle is still soft. Remove the tart from the oven and serve warm.

214 Chocolate-crusted lemon tart

PREPARATION TIME 35 minutes   **COOKING TIME** 30–35 minutes   **MAKES** 1 x 23cm/9in tart

1 recipe quantity Chocolate
   Crumb Crust (see page 13)
juice and finely grated zest of
   3 lemons

150g/5¹/₂oz/²/₃ cup caster sugar
150ml/5fl oz/²/₃ cup double cream
4 eggs, lightly beaten
icing sugar, sifted, for dusting

1 Preheat the oven to 150°C/300°F/gas 2. Press the chocolate crumb crust into the
   bottom and sides of a fluted, loose-bottomed 23cm/9in flan tin, 3–4cm/1¹/₂in deep.
2 In a large bowl, beat together the lemon juice and zest and the sugar until the
   sugar has dissolved, using an electric hand mixer. Whisk in the cream and
   eggs, then pour the lemon filling into the prepared crumb crust, taking care not
   to overfill.
3 Bake in the warm oven for 30–35 minutes, or until the tart is just set but the
   middle is still slightly wobbly. Remove from the oven and leave the tart in the tin
   to cool completely, then remove the tart from the tin and dust with icing sugar.

215 Chocolate custard tart

PREPARATION TIME 25 minutes   **COOKING TIME** 35–40 minutes   **MAKES** 1 x 23cm/9in tart

1 x 23cm/9in Sweet Shortcrust
  Pastry case, baked (see page 13)
2 eggs plus 2 egg yolks
3 tbsp plus 1 tsp caster sugar

500ml/17fl oz/2 cups milk
100g/3^1/$_2$oz dark chocolate,
  broken into pieces
1 tsp vanilla essence

1   Preheat the oven to 150°C/300°F/gas 2. Place the baked pastry case on a
   baking tray.
2   In a large bowl, beat together the eggs, egg yolks and sugar, using an electric
   hand mixer. In a small saucepan, heat the milk and chocolate together over a
   low heat until the chocolate has just melted. Whisk the warm chocolate milk
   into the egg mixture and stir in the vanilla essence, then pour the resulting
   custard mixture into the pastry case, taking care not to overfill.
3   Bake in the warm oven for 35–40 minutes, or until the custard is set but still
   wobbly. Remove from the oven and leave on the baking tray to cool completely.

216 White chocolate & berry tarts

PREPARATION TIME 30 minutes   **COOKING TIME** 8–10 minutes   **MAKES** 12 tarts

125g/4^1/$_2$oz butter, melted,
  plus extra for greasing
8 sheets filo pastry
5 tbsp caster sugar
150ml/5fl oz/^{2}/$_3$ cup double cream,
  whipped to soft peaks

125g/4^1/$_2$oz white chocolate,
  melted and left to cool
185g/6^1/$_2$oz/1^1/$_2$ cups mixed
  raspberries and blackberries

1   Preheat the oven to 180°C/350°F/gas 4. Grease a 12-hole muffin tin with butter.
2   Lay a sheet of filo pastry on the work surface and brush with melted butter.
   Sprinkle over some of the sugar. Place a second layer of pastry on top of the
   first layer, lightly butter, then sprinkle with sugar. Repeat until all of the layers
   have been used, finishing with a butter and sugar layer. Cut the pastry stack into
   12 squares and ease a square into each hole of the muffin tin.
3   Bake in the hot oven for 8–10 minutes, or until the pastry is golden brown.
   Remove from the oven and leave the filo cases in the tin to cool.
4   For the filling, gently fold the cream and melted chocolate together in a bowl,
   using a metal spoon. Remove the tart cases from the tin and, just before
   serving, divide the filling mixture evenly between them and spoon over the
   mixed berries.

217 Double chocolate tart

PREPARATION TIME 25 minutes   **COOKING TIME** 25–30 minutes   **MAKES** 1 x 23cm/9in tart

1 x 23cm/9in Sweet Shortcrust
  Pastry case, baked (see page 13)
200g/7oz dark chocolate,
  broken into pieces
175g/6oz milk chocolate,
  broken into pieces

175g/6oz butter, chopped,
4 eggs, lightly beaten
5 tbsp caster sugar
icing sugar, for dusting

1   Preheat the oven to 180°C/350°F/gas 4. Place the baked pastry case on
a baking tray.
2   In a small saucepan, heat both chocolates and the butter over a low heat until
just melted. Remove the pan from the heat and set aside to cool slightly. In a
large bowl, beat the eggs and sugar together until thick and pale, using an
electric hand mixer, then fold in the cooled chocolate mixture, using a metal
spoon. Pour the mixture into the pastry case, taking care not to overfill.
3   Bake in the hot oven for 25–30 minutes, or until the tart is just firm. Remove
from the oven and leave the tart on the baking tray to cool completely, then
dust with icing sugar.

218 Italian-style chocolate tart

PREPARATION TIME 25 minutes   **COOKING TIME** 30–35 minutes
MAKES 1 x 35 x 12cm/14 x 4½in rectangular tart

1 recipe quantity Chocolate
  Shortcrust Pastry (see page 13),
  baked in a 35 x 12cm/14 x 4½in
  rectangular tin, 3–4cm/1½in deep
250ml/9fl oz/1 cup milk
100g/3½oz dark chocolate,
  broken into pieces

1 tsp vanilla essence
4 tbsp caster sugar
2 eggs
1½ tbsp plain flour
1 tbsp Marsala wine
icing sugar, sifted, for dusting

1   Preheat the oven to 170°C/325°F/gas 3. Place the baked pastry case on a
baking tray.
2   In a medium-sized saucepan, heat the milk, chocolate and vanilla essence over
a low heat until the chocolate has just melted. In a large bowl, beat the sugar,
eggs and flour together, using an electric hand mixer, then beat in the warm
chocolate mixture. Return the mixture to the saucepan and heat until the
mixture has thickened, stirring constantly with a wooden spoon. Remove from
the heat, stir in the Marsala wine, then pour the mixture into the pastry case,
taking care not to overfill.
3   Bake in the hot oven for 25–30 minutes, or until the custard is firm around the
edges but still wobbly in the middle. Remove from the oven and leave the tart
on the baking tray to cool completely, then dust with icing sugar.

219 Tangy lemon & chocolate tarts

PREPARATION TIME 35 minutes   **COOKING TIME** 17–20 minutes   **MAKES** 4 x 10cm/4in tarts

4 x 10cm/4in Sweet Shortcrust
   Pastry cases, baked (see page 13)
juice and finely grated zest of
   3 lemons
150g/5½oz/⅔ cup caster sugar

5 eggs, lightly beaten
150g/5½oz butter, chopped
100g/3½oz dark chocolate, melted,
   plus shards to decorate
cocoa powder, sifted, for dusting

1   Preheat the oven to 180°C/350°F/gas 4. Place the baked pastry cases on a
    baking tray.
2   Place the lemon juice and zest, the sugar, eggs and butter in the top of a double
    boiler and heat, stirring constantly with a wooden spoon, for approximately
    15 minutes until the mixture thickens and coats the back of the spoon. Remove
    from the heat and stir in the melted chocolate. Pour the mixture into the baked
    pastry cases, filling them about two-thirds full.
3   Bake in the hot oven for 12–15 minutes, or until the custard is just firm. Remove
    from the oven and leave the tarts on the tray to cool completely. Place a shard
    of chocolate on each tart and dust with cocoa just before serving.

220 Chocolate Bakewell tart

PREPARATION TIME 35 minutes   **COOKING TIME** 30–35 minutes   **MAKES** 1 x 23cm/9in tart

1 x 23cm/9in Chocolate Shortcrust
  Pastry case, baked (see page 13)
160g/5½oz raspberry or
  strawberry jam
75g/2¾oz butter, softened
5 tbsp caster sugar

1 egg, lightly beaten
2 tbsp ground almonds
75g/2¾oz/½ cup plus 1 tbsp
  self-raising flour
2 tbsp cocoa powder
3 tbsp milk

1   Preheat the oven to 190°C/375°F/gas 5. Place the baked pastry case on a
    baking tray and spread the jam over the base.
2   In a large bowl, beat the butter and sugar together until light and creamy, using
    an electric hand mixer, then beat in the egg. Fold in the almonds, flour, cocoa
    and milk, using a metal spoon, and spread the filling mixture over the jam in the
    pastry case, taking care not to overfill.
3   Bake in the hot oven for 15 minutes, then lower the oven temperature to 175°C/
    325°F/gas 3 and bake for a further 15 minutes, or until the top of the tart is firm.
    Remove from the oven and serve warm or cold.

221 Chocolate-glazed peanut butter tart

PREPARATION TIME 20 minutes, plus chilling   **COOKING TIME** 5 minutes
MAKES 1 x 35 x 12cm/14 x 4½in rectangular tart

3 egg yolks
75g/2¾oz/⅓ cup plus 1 tbsp
  soft brown sugar
2 tsp plain flour
300ml/10½fl oz/1¼ cups milk
100g/3½oz smooth peanut butter
1 tsp vanilla essence

1 recipe quantity Sweet Shortcrust
  Pastry (see page 13), baked in a
  35 x 12cm/14 x 4½in rectangular
  tin, 3–4cm/1½in deep
100g/3½oz dark chocolate,
  melted and left to cool

1   In a medium-sized bowl, beat together the egg yolks, brown sugar and flour
    until well combined, using a wooden spoon. In a medium-sized saucepan, heat
    the milk until it just comes to the boil, and then whisk the hot milk into the egg
    yolk mixture, stirring well. Return the mixture to the pan and place over a low
    heat. Bring the mixture to the boil until it boils and thickens, stirring constantly
    with a wooden spoon. Allow to boil gently for 1 minute, then remove from the
    heat. Whisk in the peanut butter and vanilla essence. Set the filling mixture
    aside to cool for 10 minutes.
2   Pour the filling mixture into the baked pastry case on a serving plate. While the
    mixture is still warm, pour the melted dark chocolate over the top. Leave to cool
    completely, then refrigerate the tart for 30 minutes before serving.

222 Chocolate mascarpone tart

PREPARATION TIME 35 minutes, plus chilling   **COOKING TIME** 5 minutes
MAKES 1 x 23cm/9in tart

350g/12oz dark chocolate,
  broken into pieces
250ml/9fl oz/1 cup milk
50g/1³/₄oz butter, chopped
2 tsp vanilla essence
1 Chocolate Crumb Crust, baked
  (see page 13)

250g/9oz mascarpone cheese,
  softened
250ml/9fl oz/1 cup double cream
2 tbsp caster sugar
cocoa powder, sifted, for dusting

1   Place the chocolate, milk, butter and half the vanilla essence in a saucepan, and stir constantly over a low heat until the chocolate has just melted, using a wooden spoon. Remove from the heat and set aside until cool. Do not allow it to set. Pour the chocolate mixture into the baked crumb crust and chill for an hour.

2   In a large bowl, beat the mascarpone, cream, sugar and remaining vanilla essence together until light, using an electric hand mixer. Spoon over the top of the chocolate mixture. Refrigerate the tart for another hour, or until firm. Dust with cocoa just before serving.

223 Chocolate pecan tart

PREPARATION TIME 15 minutes   **COOKING TIME** 40–45 minutes   **MAKES** 1 x 23cm/9in tart

1 x 23cm/9in Chocolate Shortcrust
  Pastry case, baked (see page 13)
200g/7oz/³/₄ cup plus 2 tbsp
  caster sugar
3 tbsp cocoa powder
2 eggs

1 tsp vanilla essence
175ml/5³/₄fl oz/²/₃ cup double cream
50g/1¹/₄oz butter, melted and left
  to cool
75g/2³/₄oz/²/₃ cup plus 1 tsp pecans,
  roughly chopped

1   Preheat the oven to 180°C/350°F/gas 4. Place the baked pastry case on a baking tray.

2   In a large bowl, whisk the sugar, cocoa, eggs, vanilla essence, cream and butter together until smooth, using an electric hand mixer. Sprinkle the pecans into the bottom of the pastry case and pour over the filling mixture, taking care not to overfill.

3   Bake in the hot oven for 40–45 minutes, or until the tart is just firm. Remove from the oven, transfer to a wire rack and leave to cool completely.

CHAPTER 3

Desserts

In this chapter you will find a range of hot and cold desserts that make the perfect ending for any occasion. I have included a versatile collection of crêpe recipes – from the basic Chocolate Crêpes to a more exotic version filled with orange, white chocolate and ricotta. And for custard lovers, the assortment of crème brûlée and crème caramel recipes will really hit the spot. The Chocolate, Panettone & Raisin Puddings and the Fig & Chocolate Bread Pudding provide delicious variations on a traditional comfort-food favourite. There are also a few indulgent puddings – the Chocolate Puddings with Rum Sauce are a real favourite of mine. They are served with a very adult sauce, which can be substituted with cream for younger gourmets!

If you are trying to tone down the chocolate just a little, you will also find some fruity chocolate recipes such as Baked Bananas with Chocolate Rum Sauce or Fruit Kebabs with Chocolate Fruit & Nut Sauce, any of which make a delicious and healthy finale to a meal. Whatever kind of dessert you're looking for, there is a recipe in this chapter just for you.

224 Chocolate Scotch pancakes

PREPARATION TIME 10 minutes   **COOKING TIME** 15 minutes
MAKES approximately 12 mini pancakes

250g/9oz/2 cups self-raising flour
1 tbsp cocoa powder
100g/3½oz/⅓ cup plus 4 tsp
  caster sugar

250ml/9fl oz/1 cup milk
1 egg, lightly beaten
butter, melted, for cooking pancakes
icing sugar, sifted, for dusting

1 Sift the flour and cocoa into a large bowl, mix in the sugar, and make a well in the middle of the mixture. In a small bowl, whisk the milk and egg together with a hand whisk, and pour into the well. Stir to form a smooth batter with a wooden spoon.

2 Heat a non-stick frying pan over a medium heat and brush with melted butter. Pour in the batter to make rounds of 9cm/3½in. Cook for 1–2 minutes, or until the top of each pancake begins to show small bubbles, then turn over with a spatula and cook on the second side for 30 seconds more. Remove from the pan and repeat until all the pancake batter has been used.

3 Transfer the pancakes to plates, dust with icing sugar and serve warm.

225 Banana Scotch pancakes with chocolate sauce

PREPARATION TIME 5 minutes   **COOKING TIME** 15 minutes

1 recipe quantity Chocolate Scotch
  Pancake batter (see recipe 224)
2 bananas, mashed
butter, melted, for cooking pancakes

icing sugar, sifted, for dusting
1 recipe quantity Rich Chocolate
  Sauce (see page 204)

1 In a large bowl, mix the prepared pancake batter with the bananas until well combined, using a wooden spoon.

2 Heat a non-stick frying pan over a medium heat and brush with melted butter. Pour in the batter to make rounds of 9cm/3½in. Cook for 1–2 minutes, or until the top of each pancake begins to show small bubbles, then turn over with a spatula and cook on the second side for 30 seconds more. Remove from the pan and repeat until all the pancake batter has been used.

3 Transfer the pancakes to plates, dust with icing sugar and serve warm with the rich chocolate sauce.

226 Chocolate & blueberry Scotch pancakes

PREPARATION TIME 5 minutes   **COOKING TIME** 15 minutes

1 recipe quantity Chocolate Scotch
  Pancake batter (see recipe 224)
150g/5½ oz/1 cup blueberries

50g/1¾oz dark chocolate,
  broken into very small pieces
butter, melted, for cooking pancakes
icing sugar, sifted, for dusting

1 In a large bowl, mix the prepared pancake batter with the blueberries and chocolate until well combined, using a wooden spoon.

2 Heat a non-stick frying pan over a medium heat and brush with melted butter. Pour in the batter to make rounds of 9cm/3½in. Cook for 1–2 minutes, or until the top of each pancake begins to show small bubbles, then turn over with a spatula and cook on the second side for 30 seconds more. Remove from the pan and repeat until all the pancake batter has been used.

3 Transfer the pancakes to plates, dust with icing sugar and serve warm.

227 Chocolate crêpes

PREPARATION TIME 20 minutes plus 30 minutes' standing **COOKING TIME** 20 minutes
MAKES approximately 12 crêpes

150g/5¹/₂oz/1 cup plus 2 tbsp
  plain flour
2 tbsp cocoa powder, sifted
2 tsp caster sugar
1 egg, lightly beaten

300ml/10¹/₂fl oz/1¹/₄ cups milk
25g/1oz butter, melted,
  plus extra for cooking crêpes
icing sugar, sifted, for dusting

1 In a large bowl, combine the flour, cocoa and sugar, stirring with a wooden spoon. In a clean bowl, beat together the egg, milk and melted butter, using a hand whisk. Make a well in the middle of the flour mixture and pour in half the liquid mixture. Mix well with a wooden spoon, adding the remaining liquid as required so that the batter resembles thin cream. Allow the batter to stand for 30 minutes before using, and add a little extra milk if required.
2 Place a crêpe pan over a low heat and brush with a little melted butter. Pour in just enough batter to coat the base of the pan, then swirl it around and pour off any excess. Leave the batter to cook until the edges of the crêpe dry and begin to lift (approximately 50–55 seconds), then turn the crêpe over using a metal spatula. Cook for 30 seconds more, then remove from the pan and repeat until all the crêpe batter has been used.
3 Transfer the crêpes to plates, dust with icing sugar and serve warm.

228 Chocolate crêpes with chestnut cream

PREPARATION TIME 20 minutes

200g/7oz tinned, unsweetened
  chestnut purée
250ml/9fl oz/1 cup double cream
1 tsp cinnamon
2 tbsp caster sugar

1 recipe quantity Chocolate Crêpes,
  freshly cooked (see recipe 227)
1 recipe quantity Double Chocolate
  Sauce (see page 204)

1 In a large bowl, beat the chestnut purée until smooth, using an electric hand mixer. Stir in the cream, cinnamon and sugar, then spread each warm crêpe with the chestnut cream and fold into quarters.
2 Place 3 chocolate crêpes on each plate, top with the double chocolate sauce and serve immediately.

229 Chocolate crêpe gâteau

PREPARATION TIME 20 minutes, plus chilling **SERVES** 4–6

1 recipe quantity Chocolate Crêpes,
  cooked (see recipe 227)
1 recipe quantity Creamy Thick
  Chocolate Custard (see page 12)

100g/3¹/₂oz dark or milk chocolate,
  grated
1 recipe quantity Rich Chocolate
  Sauce (see page 204) or Espresso
  Chocolate Sauce (see page 205)

1 Layer the crêpes, creamy thick chocolate custard and grated chocolate on a serving plate, beginning and ending with a crêpe layer. Refrigerate for 1 hour.
2 Using a large, sharp knife, cut the crêpe gateau into wedges and serve with the rich chocolate sauce or espresso chocolate sauce.

230 Chocolate & strawberry liqueur crêpes

PREPARATION TIME 20 minutes   **COOKING TIME** 15–20 minutes

25g/1oz butter, plus extra
  for greasing
1 recipe quantity Chocolate Pastry
  Cream (see page 12)
1 tbsp double cream

1 recipe quantity Chocolate Crêpes,
  cooked (see page 145)
3 tbsp icing sugar
300g/10½oz/2 cups strawberries,
  hulled and cut in half
2 tbsp strawberry liqueur

1   Preheat the oven to 180°C/350°F/gas 4. Grease an ovenproof dish (large enough
    to hold the overlapping crêpes) with butter.
2   In a large bowl, mix the chocolate pastry cream with the cream. Lay out the
    crêpes on the work surface and divide the cream filling mixture equally among
    them. Fold each crêpe in half, and then in half again, to form a neat triangle.
    Arrange in the prepared dish.
3   In a non-stick saucepan, melt the butter with the icing sugar over a medium
    heat. Add the strawberries and the liqueur, and heat just until the strawberries
    are coated with the syrup but are still firm to the touch. Spoon this mixture over
    the prepared crêpes.
4   Cover the dish with foil, and bake the crêpes in the hot oven for 10–15 minutes,
    or until heated through. Remove from the oven and serve immediately.

231 Chocolate crêpes with orange, white chocolate & ricotta

PREPARATION TIME 15 minutes   **COOKING TIME** 10–15 minutes

butter, for greasing
100g/3½oz/¾ cup plus 1 tbsp
  sultanas
375g/13oz ricotta cheese
4 tbsp icing sugar
1 tbsp orange liqueur
zest of 1 orange, grated

50g/1¾oz white chocolate,
  melted and left to cool
1 recipe quantity Chocolate Crêpes,
  cooked (see page 145)
1 recipe quantity Double Chocolate
  Sauce (see page 204)

1   Preheat the oven to 180°C/350°F/gas 4. Grease an ovenproof dish (large enough
    to hold the overlapping crêpes) with butter.
2   To make the filling, place the sultanas in a small bowl and cover with boiling
    water for 10 minutes. Drain and set aside to cool. In a large bowl, mix the
    ricotta, sultanas, icing sugar, liqueur, orange zest and melted chocolate
    together until combined, using a wooden spoon.
3   Lay out the crêpes on the work surface and divide the filling mixture equally
    among them, spreading it to cover half of each crêpe. Fold each crêpe in half,
    and then in half again, to form a neat triangle. Place in the prepared dish.
    Repeat until all the crêpes and filling have been used.
4   Cover the dish with foil, and bake the crêpes in the hot oven for 10–15 minutes,
    or until heated through. Remove from the oven and serve with the double
    chocolate sauce.

232   Chocolate cherry crêpes

PREPARATION TIME 35 minutes   **COOKING TIME** 10–15 minutes

butter, for greasing
200g/7oz/1 cup pitted cherries
  (tinned), drained
1 recipe quantity Chocolate Pastry
  Cream (see page 12)

1 tbsp cherry liqueur
1 recipe quantity Chocolate Crêpes,
  cooked (see page 145)
100g/3¹/₂oz dark chocolate, grated
pouring cream, for serving (optional)

1   Preheat the oven to 180°C/350°F/gas 4. Grease an ovenproof dish (large enough to hold the overlapping crêpes) with butter.

2   To make the filling, cut the cherries in half with a sharp knife, place the cherry halves in a large bowl with the chocolate pastry cream and liqueur, and mix well, using a wooden spoon.

3   Lay out the crêpes on the work surface and divide the cherry filling mixture equally among them, spreading it to cover half of each crêpe. Fold each crêpe in half, and then in half again, to form a neat triangle. Place in the prepared dish. Repeat until all the crêpes and filling have been used.

4   Sprinkle over the grated chocolate, and bake the crêpes in the hot oven for 10–15 minutes, or until heated through. Remove the crêpes from the oven and serve warm with cream, if wanted.

233   Chocolate soufflé crêpes

PREPARATION TIME 25 minutes   **COOKING TIME** 13–15 minutes

butter, for greasing
250ml/9fl oz/1 cup milk
75g/2³/₄oz dark chocolate,
  broken into pieces
3 eggs, separated

6 tbsp caster sugar
4 tbsp plain flour
1 recipe quantity Chocolate Crêpes,
  cooked (see page 145)
icing sugar, sifted, for dusting

1   Preheat the oven to 220°C/425°F/gas 7. Grease 2 large baking dishes with butter.

2   In a small saucepan, heat the milk and chocolate together over a low heat until the chocolate has just melted. In a large bowl, mix the egg yolks, 4 tbsp of the sugar and the flour together, using a wooden spoon, then whisk in the warm chocolate milk, using an electric hand mixer. Return this custard mixture to the pan and continue cooking, stirring constantly, until thickened. Cook for 1 minute more, then remove from the heat and set aside to cool completely.

3   In a clean bowl, whisk the eggs whites until soft peaks form, using clean attachments for the electric hand mixer, then add the remaining sugar and whisk to stiff peaks. Gently fold the whisked whites into the cooled custard, using a metal spoon.

4   Lay out the crêpes on the work surface and spoon 2 tbsp of the filling mixture into the middle of each one. Spread it over each crêpe gently, then fold the crêpe in half. Using a spatula to help you, arrange 6 crêpes in a layer on each of the prepared baking dishes.

5   Bake the crêpes in the hot oven for 8–10 minutes, or until the filling is puffed. Remove from the oven, dust the crêpes with icing sugar and serve immediately.

234 Chocolate orange pots

PREPARATION TIME 15 minutes, plus chilling **MAKES** 4 pots

4 eggs, separated
125g/4¹/₂oz dark chocolate,
  melted and left to cool

2 tbsp double cream
zest of 1 orange, finely grated

1   In a large bowl, beat the yolks into the melted chocolate, using an electric hand mixer, then stir in the cream and orange zest. In a clean bowl, whisk the egg whites to soft peaks, using clean attachments for the electric hand mixer, then fold into the chocolate mixture, using a metal spoon.
2   Divide the mixture evenly between 4 dishes, then refrigerate for 2–3 hours before serving.

235 Fig & chocolate bread pudding

PREPARATION TIME 20 minutes plus 30 minutes' standing **COOKING TIME** 35–40 minutes

25g/1oz butter, softened,
  plus extra for greasing
1 small brioche loaf, cut into 8 slices
100g/3¹/₂oz soft dried figs, sliced
100g/3¹/₂oz dark chocolate, grated
4 eggs

125g/4¹/₂oz/¹/₂ cup plus 2 tsp
  caster sugar
250ml/9fl oz/1 cup milk
250ml/9fl oz/1 cup double cream
1 tsp vanilla essence

1   Preheat the oven to 150°C/300°F/gas 2. Grease a 1.5-litre/52fl oz/6-cup capacity ovenproof dish with butter.
2   Butter the brioche slices on one side and cut in half diagonally. Arrange half of the slices in the base of the prepared dish. Scatter over the figs and chocolate, then top with the remaining brioche slices. Beat the remaining ingredients together, using a hand whisk, and pour the resulting batter through a sieve over the top of the brioche slices. Leave to stand for 30 minutes.
3   Place the ovenproof dish in a bain marie (see page 10) and bake in a warm oven for 35–40 minutes, or until the pudding is just firm around the edges but still slightly wobbly in the middle. Remove from the oven and serve immediately.

236 Pear clafoutis with chocolate

PREPARATION TIME 25 minutes **COOKING TIME** 20–25 minutes

75g/2³/₄oz butter, softened,
  plus extra for greasing
100g/3¹/₂oz/¹/₃ cup plus 4 tsp
  caster sugar
2 eggs, lightly beaten
125g/4¹/₂oz/1 cup self-raising flour
75g/2³/₄oz/³/₄ cup ground almonds

125ml/4fl oz/¹/₂ cup milk
100g/3¹/₂oz dark chocolate, melted
  and left to cool
3 pears, ripe but not soft, peeled,
  quartered and cored
pouring cream, to serve (optional)

1   Preheat the oven to 180°C/350°F/gas 4. Grease a 1.5-litre/52fl oz/6-cup capacity ovenproof dish with butter.
2   In a large bowl, cream the butter and sugar together, using an electric hand mixer, then beat in the eggs, a little at a time. Combine the flour and ground almonds and fold into the butter mixture with the milk and melted chocolate to make a batter. Scatter the pears in the bottom of the baking dish and pour over the batter mixture.
3   Bake in the hot oven for 20–25 minutes; the middle should still be soft. Remove from the oven and leave the clafoutis to cool slightly, before serving with cream, if wanted.

237 Mocha pots with ricotta & coffee liqueur

PREPARATION TIME 25 minutes, plus chilling   **COOKING TIME** 5 minutes

275ml/9¹/₂fl oz/1 cup plus 2 tbsp
  double cream
50g/1³/₄oz dark chocolate,
  broken into pieces
350g/12oz ricotta cheese

100g/3¹/₂oz/³/₄ cup plus 1 tbsp
  icing sugar
2 tbsp coffee liqueur
1 tbsp coffee beans, freshly ground

1   In a small saucepan, heat 150ml/5fl oz/²/₃ cup of the cream over a low heat until just simmering, then remove from the heat and add the chocolate. Stir until smooth, using a metal spoon, and pour into a clean bowl to cool.
2   Place the ricotta, icing sugar, liqueur and coffee beans in the bowl of a food processor and process until smooth. Add the remaining cream and process briefly until all the ingredients are just combined.
3   Divide the ricotta mixture evenly between 4 glasses. Spoon 1 tbsp of the chocolate mixture on top of the ricotta mixture in each glass and refrigerate for 30–40 minutes until just firm.

238 Chocolate apple pudding

PREPARATION TIME 25 minutes **COOKING TIME** 55–60 minutes

butter, for greasing
6 cooking apples, peeled, cored
  and sliced
175g/6oz/³/₄ cup caster sugar
1 cinnamon stick

4 eggs, separated
125g/4¹/₂oz dark chocolate,
  melted and left to cool
300ml/10¹/₂fl oz/1¹/₄ cups double
  cream, whipped to soft peaks

1 Preheat the oven to 180°C/350°F/gas 4. Grease a 1.5-litre/52fl oz/6-cup capacity
   ovenproof ceramic dish with butter.
2 Place the prepared apples in a medium-sized saucepan with 100g/3 oz/¹/₃ cup
   plus 4 tsp of the sugar and the cinnamon stick, and pour in just enough water to
   come one-third of the way up the apples. Bring to the boil, then lower the heat
   and simmer for 20 minutes, or until soft. Drain off any excess liquid, discard the
   cinnamon stick and pour the apple into the prepared dish.
3 In a large bowl, stir the egg yolks into the melted chocolate, then fold in the
   cream with a metal spoon. Whisk the egg whites to soft peaks, using an electric
   hand mixer, then gradually whisk in the extra sugar until thick and glossy.
   Gently fold into the chocolate cream, then spread the mixture over the apple
   layer in the prepared dish.
4 Bake in the hot oven for 35–40 minutes, or until slightly puffed and dark brown.
   Remove from the oven and serve immediately.

239 Chocolate panettone & raisin puddings

PREPARATION TIME 40 minutes plus 30 minutes' standing   **COOKING TIME** 30–35 minutes

butter, for greasing
100g/3¹/₂oz/³/₄ cup plus 1 tbsp
  sultanas
1 tbsp dark rum
¹/₄ small panettone, or 4 slices
  of brioche
3 eggs

100g/3¹/₂oz/¹/₃ cup plus 4 tsp
  caster sugar
1 tsp vanilla essence
100g/3¹/₂oz dark chocolate,
  melted and left to cool
125ml/4fl oz/¹/₂ cup milk
200ml/7fl oz/³/₄ cup double cream

1 Preheat the oven to 150°C/300°F/gas 2. Grease 4 x 200ml/7fl oz/³/₄-cup capacity
   ovenproof dishes with butter.
2 Place the sultanas and rum in a small bowl, and heat in the microwave for
   1 minute. Set aside for 10 minutes. Cut the panettone or brioche slices into
   small cubes, using a sharp knife, and divide evenly between the 4 dishes.
   Sprinkle over the sultanas. In a large bowl, beat together the eggs, sugar,
   vanilla essence, melted chocolate, milk and cream, using a hand whisk, and
   pour evenly over the dishes. Leave to stand for 30 minutes.
3 Bake the puddings in a bain marie (see page 10) in the warm oven for 30–35
   minutes until set but still a little wobbly in the middle. Remove from the oven
   and set aside to cool for 10 minutes before turning out of the dishes to serve.

240 Pain-au-chocolat pudding

PREPARATION TIME 15 minutes **COOKING TIME** 40–45 minutes

6 mini or 3 large pains au chocolat
5 eggs
1 tsp vanilla essence

100g/3¹/₂oz/¹/₃ cup plus 4 tsp
   caster sugar
1.5 litres/52fl oz/6 cups milk
pouring cream, for serving (optional)

1   Preheat the oven to 150°C/300°F/gas 2. Cut the pains au chocolat into slices approximately 5mm/ ¹/₄in thick, and place them in the base of a 2-litre/70fl oz/ 8-cup capacity ovenproof dish approximately 23cm/9in in diameter.

2   In a large bowl, beat the eggs together with the vanilla essence and sugar, using a hand whisk, and then whisk in the milk.

3   Place the dish in a bain marie (see page 10) and bake in the warm oven for 40–45 minutes, or until the sides are firm but the middle is still slightly wobbly.

4   Remove the dish from the oven and leave to cool for 5 minutes before serving. Serve with cream, if wanted.

241　Chocolate crèmes caramels

PREPARATION TIME 15 minutes, plus chilling　COOKING TIME 35–42 minutes

200g/7oz/³/₄ cup plus 2 tbsp
　caster sugar
400ml/14fl oz/1²/₃ cups milk

3 eggs, lightly beaten
100g/3¹/₂oz dark chocolate,
　melted and left to cool

1　Preheat the oven to 150°C/300°F/gas 2. Place 4 x 200ml/7fl oz/³/₄-cup capacity ovenproof ramekins in the oven to warm.
2　Place half of the sugar with 125ml/4fl oz/¹/₂ cup water in a saucepan over a low heat, swirling until the sugar is dissolved. Turn up the heat, and boil until the mixture begins to brown around the edges. Swirl again, and continue cooking until the sugar becomes an even caramel colour. Divide the sugar mixture evenly between the warm ramekins, and set aside.
3　In a large bowl, beat the remaining sugar together with the milk, eggs and melted chocolate, using a hand whisk, and pour the mixture through a sieve into the ramekins.
4　Place the ramekins in a bain marie (see page 10) and bake in the warm oven for 25–30 minutes, or until the sides are firm but the middles are still wobbly. Remove the ramekins from the water using tongs and set aside to cool for 30 minutes.
5　Refrigerate the caramels for 30 minutes, then remove from the refrigerator. Run a sharp knife around the edges of the caramels to loosen them from the ramekins, then turn out on to plates.

242　White chocolate crèmes brûlées

PREPARATION TIME 15 minutes, plus chilling　COOKING TIME 40–45 minutes

5 egg yolks
130g/4¹/₂oz/¹/₂ cup plus 1 tbsp
　caster sugar
500ml/17fl oz/2 cups double cream

125g/4¹/₂oz white chocolate,
　broken into pieces
¹/₂ tsp vanilla essence

1　Preheat the oven to 130°C/250°F/gas ¹/₂.
2　In a large bowl, beat the egg yolks and 100g/3¹/₂oz/¹/₃ cup plus 4 tsp of the sugar together, using a hand whisk. In a small saucepan, heat the cream and chocolate together over a low heat until the chocolate has just melted. Remove the chocolate mixture from the heat and whisk until smooth, then whisk it into the egg yolk mixture with the vanilla essence until well combined.
3　Divide the mixture evenly between 4 x 150ml/5fl oz/¹/₃-cup capacity ovenproof ramekins. Place the ramekins in a bain marie (see page 10) and bake in the warm oven for 35–40 minutes, or until the custards are just set.
4　Remove the dish from the oven and take the ramekins out of the dish using tongs, then leave to cool for 30 minutes before refrigerating overnight.
5　Remove from the refrigerator. Sprinkle the remaining sugar over the tops of the custards and place under a very hot grill until the sugar melts and caramelizes (or use a domestic blowtorch). Serve immediately.

243 Chocolate crèmes brûlées

PREPARATION TIME 15 minutes, plus chilling   **COOKING TIME** 40–45 minutes

600ml/21fl oz/2½ cups double cream
75g/2¾oz dark chocolate,
   broken into pieces
1 tsp vanilla essence

6 egg yolks
3 tbsp caster sugar
85g/3oz/⅓ cup soft brown sugar

1   Preheat the oven to 130°C/250°F/gas ½.
2   In a small saucepan, heat the cream and chocolate together over a low heat
until the chocolate has just melted. In a large bowl, beat the vanilla essence,
egg yolks and caster sugar together, using a hand whisk, then whisk in the
heated cream mixture, combining well.
3   Divide the mixture evenly between 4 x 150ml/5fl oz/⅓-cup capacity ovenproof
ramekins or other pots. Place the ramekins in a bain marie (see page 10) and
bake in the warm oven for 35–40 minutes, or until the custards are just set.
4   Remove the dish from the oven and take the ramekins out of the dish using
tongs, then leave to cool for 30 minutes before refrigerating overnight.
5   Remove from the refrigerator. Sprinkle the brown sugar over the tops of the
custards and place under a very hot grill until the sugar melts and caramelizes
(or use a domestic blowtorch). Serve immediately.

244 Baked chocolate custard

PREPARATION TIME 10 minutes   **COOKING TIME** 45–50 minutes

875ml/30fl oz/3¹/₂ cups milk
100g/3¹/₂oz dark chocolate,
  broken into pieces
4 eggs

150g/5¹/₂oz/²/₃ cup caster sugar
1 tbsp cocoa powder
1 tsp vanilla essence

1   Preheat the oven to 150°C/300°F/gas 2.
2   In a large saucepan, heat the milk and chocolate together over a low heat until
    the chocolate starts to melt. Remove from the heat and whisk until smooth. In
    a large bowl, beat the eggs, sugar, cocoa and vanilla essence together, using
    a hand whisk, then whisk in the chocolate mixture. Pour through a sieve into
    a 1-litre/35fl oz/4-cup capacity ovenproof ceramic dish.
3   Place the dish in a bain marie (see page 10) and bake in the warm oven for
    40–45 minutes, or until the custard edges are just firm but the middle stays
    wobbly. Remove from the oven and leave to cool for 10 minutes before serving.

245 Chocolate sticky pudding & caramel sauce

PREPARATION TIME 20 minutes   **COOKING TIME** 20–25 minutes

75g/2³/₄oz butter, softened,
  plus extra for greasing
150g/5¹/₂oz/³/₄ cup plus 1 tbsp
  soft brown sugar
2 eggs, lightly beaten

75g/2³/₄oz dark chocolate, melted
  and left to cool
150g/5¹/₂oz/1 cup plus 2 tbsp
  self-raising flour
1 recipe quantity Chocolate
  Caramel Sauce (see page 204)

1   Preheat the oven to 170°C/325°F/gas 3. Grease a 1-litre/35fl oz/4-cup capacity
    ovenproof dish with butter.
2   In a large bowl, cream the butter and sugar together with a wooden spoon, and
    add the eggs a little at a time, beating well between additions. Stir in the melted
    chocolate and flour, and pour the mixture into the prepared dish.
3   Bake in the hot oven for 20–25 minutes, or until the pudding has risen and is just
    set in the middle. Remove from the oven and serve with chocolate caramel sauce.

246 Mocha pudding cakes

PREPARATION TIME 25 minutes   **COOKING TIME** 20–30 minutes

90g/3¹/₄oz butter, softened,
  plus extra for greasing
125g/4¹/₂oz/¹/₂ cup plus 2 tsp
  caster sugar
2 eggs, separated
3 tbsp cocoa powder

75g/2³/₄oz/¹/₂ cup plus 1 tbsp
  plain flour
2 tsp instant coffee granules
1 tsp vanilla essence
125ml/4fl oz/¹/₂ cup milk

1   Preheat the oven to 180°C/350°F/gas 4. Grease 4 x 175ml/6fl oz/scant ³/₄-cup
    capacity ovenproof ramekins with butter.
2   In a large bowl, beat the butter and 100g/3¹/₂oz/¹/₃ cup plus 4 tsp of the sugar
    together, using an electric hand mixer, then add the egg yolks. Add the cocoa,
    flour, coffee, vanilla essence and milk, stirring with a wooden spoon until just
    combined. In a clean bowl, whisk the egg whites to soft peaks, using clean
    attachments for the electric hand mixer, then gradually whisk in the remaining
    sugar. Fold the resulting meringue gently into the chocolate mixture, and pour
    evenly between the ramekins.
3   Place the pudding cakes in a bain marie (see page 10) and bake in the hot oven
    for 20–30 minutes, or until they are slightly puffed and look dry. Remove from
    the oven and leave the cakes to cool before serving.

247 Chocolate self-saucing pudding

PREPARATION TIME 15 minutes   **COOKING TIME** 20–25 minutes

75g/2¾oz butter,
  plus extra for greasing
150g/5½oz/1 cup plus 2 tbsp
  self-raising flour
2 tbsp cocoa powder
100g/3½oz/⅓ cup plus 4 tsp
  caster sugar
125ml/4fl oz/½ cup milk

1 tsp vanilla essence
1 egg, lightly beaten

FOR THE TOPPING
100g/3½oz/½ cup soft brown sugar
2 tbsp cocoa powder

1 Preheat the oven to 180°C/350°F/gas 4. Grease a 1.5-litre/52fl oz/6-cup capacity ovenproof dish with butter.
2 In a medium-sized bowl, combine the flour, cocoa and sugar. In a small saucepan, heat the butter, milk and vanilla essence over a low heat until the butter has just melted, then set aside to cool for 5 minutes. Whisk in the egg, using a hand whisk, then stir all of the liquid ingredients into the dry ingredients to combine. Pour the mixture into the prepared ovenproof dish.
3 For the topping, combine the brown sugar with the cocoa in a bowl, then sprinkle over the chocolate mixture in the dish. Pour over 300ml/10½fl oz/1¼ cups boiling water. Bake in the hot oven for 15–20 minutes, or until the pudding is firm but still slightly soft in the middle.
4 Remove from the oven and leave to cool for 5 minutes before serving.

248 Chocolate rice pudding

PREPARATION TIME 10 minutes   **COOKING TIME** 30–35 minutes

150g/5½oz/⅔ cup short-grain rice
2 tbsp caster sugar
1 tsp vanilla essence
500ml/17fl oz/2 cups milk
200ml/7fl oz/¾ cup double cream

75g/2¾oz dark chocolate,
  broken into pieces

1 Rinse the rice well under cold water and place in a medium-sized saucepan with the remaining ingredients. Bring to the boil, stirring well, then reduce to a low simmer for 25–30 minutes, or until most of the liquid has been absorbed and the rice is tender, stirring often to prevent it from sticking.
2 Serve warm or at room temperature.

249 White chocolate rice pudding

PREPARATION TIME 15 minutes   **COOKING TIME** 30–35 minutes

500ml/17fl oz/2 cups milk
200ml/7fl oz/¾ cup double cream
1 tsp nutmeg
zest of 1 large orange, finely grated

150g/5½oz/⅔ cup short-grain rice
1 tbsp caster sugar
100g/3½oz white chocolate, broken
  into small pieces

1 Place the milk, cream, nutmeg and orange zest in a large saucepan over a low heat, and bring to the boil.
2 Rinse the rice well under cold water and add to the milk mixture along with the sugar. Return to the boil, stirring well, then reduce to a low simmer for 25–30 minutes, or until the rice is tender, stirring often to prevent it from sticking.
3 Stir in the chocolate until it melts. Serve warm or at room temperature.

250 White chocolate & coconut rice pudding

PREPARATION TIME 10 minutes   **COOKING TIME** 30–35 minutes

100g/3½oz/½ cup short grain rice
400ml/14fl oz/1⅔ cups coconut milk
3 tbsp plus 1 tsp caster sugar

1 tsp vanilla essence
100g/3½oz white chocolate, melted
1 tsp nutmeg

1   Rinse the rice well under cold water. Place the rice, coconut milk and 250ml/
    9fl oz/1 cup water in a medium-sized saucepan and bring to the boil. Reduce to
    a low simmer for 25–30 minutes, or until most of the liquid has been absorbed
    and the rice is tender, stirring often to prevent it from sticking.
2   Remove from the heat and stir in the sugar, vanilla essence, melted chocolate
    and nutmeg. Serve warm or at room temperature.

251 Simple chilled chocolate puddings

PREPARATION TIME 15 minutes, plus chilling   **COOKING TIME** 5 minutes

400ml/14 fl oz/1⅔ cups
  double cream
200g/7oz dark chocolate,
  broken into pieces
75g/2¾oz butter, chopped

2 tbsp caster sugar
1 tsp vanilla essence
whipped cream, for serving
drinking chocolate, for dusting

1   Heat the cream, chocolate, butter and sugar in a medium-sized saucepan until
    just boiling, then remove from the heat and stir until smooth. Add the vanilla
    essence. Divide evenly between 4 x 200ml/7fl oz/¾-cup capacity ramekins.
2   Leave until cool then refrigerate for 2 hours or overnight. Top with the whipped
    cream and dust with the drinking chocolate just before serving.

252 Steamed banana pudding with chocolate

PREPARATION TIME 20 minutes   **COOKING TIME** 1¾ hours   **SERVES** 4–6

125g/4½oz butter, softened,
  plus extra for greasing
100g/3½oz/⅓ cup plus 4 tsp
  caster sugar
2 eggs, lightly beaten
300g/10½oz/2⅓ cups
  self-raising flour

2 tbsp cocoa powder
3 tbsp milk
1 tsp vanilla essence
1 banana, thinly sliced
100g/3½oz white chocolate chips

1   Grease a 1.25-litre/44fl oz/5-cup capacity pudding basin with butter. In a large
    bowl, beat the butter and sugar together until light and creamy, using an
    electric hand mixer. Beat in the eggs a little at a time until well combined. Fold
    in the flour, cocoa, milk, vanilla essence, banana and chocolate chips.
2   Spoon into the prepared basin and cover with a double layer of foil secured with
    string. Place the basin in a large saucepan and fill with water to come halfway
    up the side of the basin. Bring the water to the boil, turn down to a simmer and
    steam the pudding for 1¾ hours, adding extra boiling water as required.
3   Remove the basin from the saucepan and leave to cool for 10 minutes then turn
    the pudding out on to a serving plate.

253 Steamed chocolate pudding

PREPARATION TIME 20 minutes   **COOKING TIME** 1¾ hours   **SERVES** 4–6

100g/3½oz butter, softened,
  plus extra for greasing
100g/3½oz/⅓ cup plus 4 tsp
  caster sugar
2 eggs, lightly beaten
100g/3½oz/¾ cup plus 1 tbsp
  self-raising flour

2 tbsp cocoa powder
100g/3½oz dark chocolate, melted
2 tbsp milk
1 recipe quantity Rich Chocolate
  Sauce (see page 204) or Espresso
  Chocolate Sauce (see page 205)

1   Grease a 1.25-litre/44fl oz/5-cup capacity pudding basin with butter. In a large
    bowl, beat the butter and sugar together until light and creamy, using an
    electric hand mixer, then add the eggs a little at a time until smooth. Sift the
    flour and cocoa together, and fold into the mixture with the chocolate and milk.
2   Spoon into the prepared basin and cover with a double layer of foil secured with
    string. Place the basin in a large saucepan and fill with water to come halfway
    up the side of the basin. Bring the water to the boil, turn down to a simmer and
    steam the pudding for 1¾ hours, adding extra boiling water as required.
3   Remove the basin from the saucepan and leave to cool for 10 minutes then turn
    the pudding out on to a serving plate. Serve with one of the chocolate sauces.

254 Lemon & white chocolate pudding

PREPARATION TIME 25 minutes   **COOKING TIME** 18–20 minutes

100g/3¹/₂oz butter, softened,
plus extra for greasing
175g/6oz/³/₄ cup caster sugar
75g/2¹/₄oz white chocolate,
finely chopped

juice and finely grated zest of
2 lemons
4 eggs, separated
4 tbsp plain flour
150ml/5fl oz/²/₃ cup milk
icing sugar, sifted, for dusting

1   Preheat the oven to 180°C/350°F/gas 4. Grease a 2-litre/70fl oz/8-cup capacity ovenproof dish (29 x 21 x 5cm/12 x 8 x 2¹/₂in) with butter.
2   In a large bowl, mix the butter and sugar until light and creamy, using an electric hand mixer. Stir in the white chocolate, lemon zest and egg yolks and mix well. Gently mix in the flour and milk, then stir in the lemon juice. (The juice may cause the mixture to curdle slightly, but do not worry.) In a clean bowl, whisk the egg whites to soft peaks, using clean attachments for the electric hand mixer, and fold into the pudding mixture, using a metal spoon. Pour the mixture into the prepared ovenproof dish.
3   Bake in the hot oven for 18–20 minutes, or until lightly browned. Remove from the oven and leave to cool for 5 minutes, then dust with icing sugar and serve.

255 Chocolate puddings with rum sauce

PREPARATION TIME 75 minutes plus resting   **COOKING TIME** 35–40 minutes

60g/2¹/₄oz butter, softened,
plus extra for greasing
4 tbsp caster sugar
4 tbsp plain flour
75g/2³/₄oz dark chocolate,
broken into pieces
125ml/4fl oz/¹/₂ cup milk
3 eggs, separated

RUM SAUCE
3 tbsp plus 1 tsp caster sugar
60ml/2fl oz/¹/₄ cup rum
1 egg yolk
125ml/4fl oz/¹/₂ cup double cream,
whipped to soft peaks

1   Preheat the oven to 190°C/375°F/gas 5. Grease 4 x 375ml/13fl oz/1¹/₂-cup capacity moulds with butter. Start to prepare the rum sauce. In a small bowl, combine the sugar and rum, and stir well. Leave to stand for 30 minutes.
2   To make the puddings, in a large bowl, cream the butter and sugar together with a wooden spoon, then stir in the flour. In a small saucepan, heat the chocolate with the milk over a low heat until just melted. Pour the warm chocolate milk over the butter mixture, stirring well, then tip the mixture into the saucepan, return to the heat, and cook until the mixture begins to thicken. Remove the pan from the heat and add the egg yolks, stirring constantly, using a wooden spoon.
3   In a large bowl, whisk the egg whites until stiff, but not dry, using an electric hand mixer, and gently fold into the chocolate mixture. Pour the mixture evenly into the prepared moulds. Place the moulds in a bain marie (see page 10) and bake in the hot oven for 30–35 minutes, or until just firm.
4   While the puddings are baking, return to the sauce. In a clean bowl, beat the egg yolk until creamy, add the rum mixture, and rest for a further 30 minutes. Fold in the whipped cream and refrigerate for 5–10 minutes.
5   Remove the puddings from the oven and leave to cool for 5 minutes before un-moulding on to plates. Serve topped with the chilled sauce.

256 Chocolate amaretti pears

PREPARATION TIME 25 minutes **COOKING TIME** 15–20 minutes

75g/2³/₄oz butter, melted,
  plus extra for greasing
150g/5¹/₂oz amaretti biscuits
75g/2³/₄oz dark chocolate,
  melted and left to cool

1 egg yolk
4 ripe pears
1 recipe quantity Chocolate &
  Amaretto Sauce (see page 204)

1   Preheat the oven to 200°C/400°F/gas 6. Grease an ovenproof dish (large enough to hold the pears) with butter.
2   Crush the biscuits in a food processor, and mix with the melted butter, melted chocolate and egg yolk. Cut the pears in half lengthways, and scoop out the seeds using a sharp knife. Spoon the prepared biscuit filling into each pear cavity, press down firmly, then spread enough filling over the surface of each pear to cover it completely.
3   Place the pears in the prepared dish and bake in the hot oven for 15–20 minutes, until the pears are soft and the filling is dark brown. Remove from the oven and serve immediately with the chocolate and amaretto sauce.

257 Chocolate & banana fritters

PREPARATION TIME 20 minutes **COOKING TIME** 20–28 minutes

200g/7oz/1¹/₂ cups plus 4 tsp
  self-raising flour
2 tbsp cocoa powder
3 tbsp plus 1 tsp caster sugar,
  plus extra for sprinkling
1 egg

250ml/9fl oz/1 cup milk
vegetable oil. for deep-frying
4 ripe, firm bananas, peeled and
  cut into thirds
1 recipe quantity Rich Chocolate
  Sauce (see page 204)

1   In a large bowl, sift the flour and cocoa together, then add the sugar. In a clean bowl, whisk the egg and milk together, using a hand whisk, then add to the flour mixture, stirring well with a wooden spoon to form a smooth batter.
2   Heat the oil in a wide frying pan until a cube of bread turns brown within 30 seconds of being placed in it. Dip the bananas into the batter, then deep-fry in batches of 3 pieces for 5–7 minutes until golden brown. Remove the bananas from the pan, drain on absorbent paper and sprinkle with a little extra sugar.
3   Serve the banana fritters immediately with the chocolate sauce.

258 Fruit kebabs with chocolate fruit & nut sauce

PREPARATION TIME 15 minutes

1 small pineapple, peeled and
   cut into chunks
300g/10¹/₂oz/2 cups strawberries,
   hulled

1 ripe mango, cut into chunks
200g/7oz/1 cup seedless grapes
1 recipe quantity Chocolate
   Fruit & Nut Sauce (see page 206)

1 Thread the fruit alternately on to 8 wooden skewers, dividing the pieces evenly between the skewers.

2 Serve with the chocolate fruit & nut sauce.

259 Baked bananas with chocolate rum sauce

PREPARATION TIME 10 minutes   **COOKING TIME** 17–20 minutes

butter, for greasing
4 ripe, firm bananas, peeled and
   halved lengthways
200ml/7fl oz/³/₄ cup double cream

4 tbsp soft brown sugar
2 tbsp cocoa powder
1 recipe quantity Chocolate Rum
   Sauce (see page 206)

1 Preheat the oven to 180°C/350°F/gas 4. Grease an ovenproof ceramic dish (large enough to hold the bananas) with butter.

2 Arrange the bananas in the prepared dish. In a small saucepan, whisk the cream, sugar and cocoa together over a low heat until hot, then pour over the bananas.

3 Bake in the hot oven for 12–15 minutes, or until the bananas are soft. Remove from the oven and serve the bananas warm, with chocolate rum sauce.

260 Berries with white chocolate sauce

PREPARATION TIME 10 minutes   **COOKING TIME** 5 minutes

50g/2oz butter, chopped
4 tbsp caster sugar
1 tbsp strawberry liqueur

450g/1lb/3 cups mixed berries
1 recipe quantity White
   Chocolate Sauce (see page 206)

1 In a non-stick frying pan, melt the butter with the sugar over a medium heat, then add the liqueur. Turn the heat to low and stir in the berries with a wooden spoon. Cook for 3–4 minutes, or until the berries are just beginning to soften.

2 Divide the berries between 4 dishes and top with the white chocolate sauce.

261 Roast figs with chocolate sauce

PREPARATION TIME 10 minutes   **COOKING TIME** 15–20 minutes

75g/2¾oz butter, plus
  extra for greasing
8 large figs
2 tbsp caster sugar

250ml/9fl oz/1 cup double cream,
  whipped to soft peaks
1 recipe quantity Rich Chocolate
  Sauce (see page 204)

1   Preheat the oven to 180°C/350°F/gas 4. Grease an ovenproof dish (large enough to hold the figs) with butter.

2   Cut a cross in the top of each fig, taking care to keep the fig in one piece. Divide the butter into 8 pieces, and place one piece inside each fig. Place the figs in the prepared dish and sprinkle over the caster sugar.

3   Bake in the hot oven for 15–20 minutes, or until the figs are soft but still hold their shape. Remove from the oven and set the baked figs aside in the dish to cool for 10 minutes.

4   Divide the figs between 4 plates, top with a spoonful of cream, and pour over the rich chocolate sauce.

CHAPTER 4

Ices

I have never tasted anything so wonderful as freshly churned ice cream. If you have ever thought about making your own, then now is the time, as chocolate and ice cream are the perfect combination. You will need an ice-cream maker, which come in a range of models from hand-churned to battery-operated and electric. If you really want to splash out, an electric self-frigerating ice-cream machine is simple to use, and, while it is an investment, I guarantee that it will not remain idle on your bench for long. Homemade ice cream is refreshingly free of preservatives and colourings and so it has a shorter shelf life (around 7–10 days) than the commercial variety, but, in my experience, it never lasts that long anyway! The natural qualities of homemade ice cream also mean that it tends to freeze to a harder consistency than the commercial varieties and therefore needs to be removed from the freezer and placed in the refrigerator for around 30 minutes before you want to serve it. However, the very best way to eat fresh ice cream, if not always the most practical, is straight from the churn. Scoop it into a chilled bowl and enjoy!

262 Rich chocolate ice cream

PREPARATION TIME 20 minutes, plus chilling and churning **COOKING TIME** 5 minutes
MAKES 1 litre/35fl oz/4 cups

300ml/10½fl oz/1¼ cups milk
300ml/10½fl oz/1¼ cups
  double cream
350g/12oz dark or milk chocolate,
  broken into pieces

4 egg yolks
100g/3½fl oz/⅓ cup plus 4 tsp
  caster sugar

1   In a small saucepan, heat the milk, cream and chocolate together over a low heat until the chocolate has just melted. Remove the pan from the heat and stir with a wooden spoon until smooth.
2   In a large bowl, beat the egg yolks and sugar together, using a hand whisk, then pour in the hot chocolate mixture, whisking constantly. Return the mixture to the saucepan and heat, stirring constantly with a wooden spoon, until the mixture just begins to thicken and lightly coats the back of the spoon. Do not allow the mixture to boil, as it will curdle.
3   Remove from the heat, pour into a clean bowl and leave to cool completely. Refrigerate for 3 hours or overnight, then churn in an ice-cream machine according to the manufacturer's instructions.

263 Chocolate & banana ice cream

PREPARATION TIME 15 minutes, plus chilling and churning   **MAKES** 1 litre/35fl oz/4 cups

3 ripe bananas
100g/3½oz/⅓ cup plus 4 tsp
  caster sugar
300ml/10½fl oz/1¼ cups milk
500ml/17fl oz/2 cups double cream

1 egg, lightly beaten
200g/7oz dark chocolate, melted
  and cooled

1   Pulse the bananas with the sugar in the bowl of a food processor, then add the milk, cream, egg and melted chocolate. Process until just combined.
2   Refrigerate for 3 hours or overnight, then churn in an ice-cream machine according to the manufacturer's instructions.

264 Turkish delight ice cream

PREPARATION TIME 20 minutes, plus chilling and churning   **COOKING TIME** 5 minutes
MAKES 1 litre/35fl oz/4 cups

300ml/10½fl oz/1¼ cups milk
500ml/17fl oz/2 cups double cream
200g/7oz dark chocolate,
  broken into pieces
100g/3½oz/⅓ cup plus 4 tsp
  caster sugar

4 egg yolks
1 tbsp cornflour
200g/7oz Turkish delight
  (any variety), chopped
1 tbsp rosewater (optional)

1   In a medium-sized saucepan, heat the milk, cream and chocolate together over a low heat until the chocolate has just melted.
2   In a large bowl, beat the sugar and egg yolks together, using a hand whisk, then pour in the chocolate mixture, whisking constantly. Return the mixture to the pan and heat, stirring constantly with a wooden spoon, until the mixture just begins to thicken and just coats the back of the spoon. Do not let it boil, as it will curdle.
3   Remove from the heat, pour into a clean bowl and leave to cool completely. Refrigerate for 3 hours or overnight. Stir in the chopped Turkish delight and rosewater, if using, then churn in an ice-cream machine according to the manufacturer's instructions.

265 Chocolate, raisin & amaretto ice cream

PREPARATION TIME 25 minutes, plus chilling and churning **COOKING TIME** 5 minutes
MAKES 1 litre/35fl oz/4 cups

60g/2¼oz/½ cup raisins
1½ tsp amaretto liqueur
100g/3½oz/⅓ cup plus 4 tsp
  caster sugar
250ml/9fl oz/1 cup milk

400ml/14fl oz/1⅔ cups double cream
2 tsp vanilla essence
100g/3½oz dark chocolate, grated

1 Place the raisins and liqueur in a small bowl and microwave for 30 seconds.
   Set aside to cool completely.
2 In a medium-sized saucepan, heat the sugar and milk together over a low
   heat until the sugar has dissolved. Remove from the heat and add the cream.
   Pour into a clean bowl and leave to cool completely. Refrigerate for 3 hours
   or overnight.
3 When cold, stir in the marinated raisins, vanilla essence and chocolate, then
   churn in an ice-cream machine according to the manufacturer's instructions.

266 White chocolate ice cream

PREPARATION TIME 20 minutes, plus chilling and churning **COOKING TIME** 5 minutes
MAKES 1 litre/35fl oz/4 cups

250ml/9fl oz/1 cup double cream
125ml/4fl oz/½ cup milk
175g/6oz white chocolate,
  broken into pieces

1 tsp vanilla essence
2 eggs
100g/3½oz/⅓ cup plus 4 tsp
  caster sugar

1 In a medium-sized saucepan, heat the cream, milk, chocolate and vanilla
   essence over a low heat until the chocolate has just melted.
2 In a large bowl, beat the eggs and sugar together, using a hand whisk, then
   pour in the hot chocolate mixture, whisking constantly. Return the mixture
   to the saucepan and heat, stirring constantly with a wooden spoon, until the
   mixture just begins to thicken and lightly coats the back of the spoon. Do not
   allow the mixture to boil, as it will curdle.
3 Remove from the heat, pour into a clean bowl and leave to cool completely.
   Refrigerate for 3 hours or overnight, then churn in an ice-cream machine
   according to the manufacturer's instructions.

267 Strawberry & white chocolate cheesecake ice cream

PREPARATION TIME 15 minutes, plus chilling and churning
MAKES 1 litre/35fl oz/4 cups

200g/7oz cream cheese, softened
150g/5½oz/⅔ cup caster sugar
250ml/9fl oz/1 cup double cream
250ml/9fl oz/1 cup sour cream

150g/5½oz/1 cup strawberries,
  chopped
125g/4½oz white chocolate,
  melted and left to cool

1 In a large bowl, beat the cream cheese and sugar together until soft, using
   an electric hand mixer. Whisk in the cream and sour cream, then stir in the
   strawberries and melted chocolate until just combined.
2 Refrigerate for 3 hours or overnight, then churn in an ice-cream machine
   according to the manufacturer's instructions.

268 Caramel & chocolate ice cream

PREPARATION TIME 20 minutes, plus chilling and churning   **COOKING TIME** 5 minutes
MAKES 1 litre/35fl oz/4 cups

400ml/14fl oz/1²/₃ cups milk
300ml/10¹/₂fl oz/1¹/₄ cups
  double cream
200g/7oz dark chocolate,
  broken into pieces

100g/3¹/₂oz/¹/₃ cup plus 4 tsp
  caster sugar
3 egg yolks
1 tbsp cornflour
2 tbsp dulce de leche or
  similar caramel paste

1 In a medium-sized saucepan, heat the milk, cream and chocolate over a low heat until the chocolate has just melted.

2 In a large bowl, beat the sugar, egg yolks and cornflour together, using a hand whisk, then pour in the hot chocolate mixture, whisking constantly. Return the mixture to the saucepan and heat, stirring constantly with a wooden spoon, until the mixture just begins to thicken and lightly coats the back of the spoon. Do not allow the mixture to boil, as it will curdle.

3 Remove from the heat and stir in the dulce de leche until smooth, then pour into a clean bowl and leave to cool completely. Refrigerate for 3 hours or overnight, then churn in an ice-cream machine according to the manufacturer's instructions.

269 Mocha ice cream

PREPARATION TIME 25 minutes, plus chilling and churning   **COOKING TIME** 5 minutes
MAKES 1 litre/35fl oz/4 cups

250ml/9fl oz/1 cup milk
250ml/9fl oz/1 cup double cream
3 tsp instant coffee granules
6 egg yolks

100g/3¹/₂oz/¹/₂ cup plus 2 tsp
  soft brown sugar
200g/7oz dark chocolate,
  melted and left to cool

1 In a small pan, heat the milk, cream and coffee over a low heat until just warm.

2 In a large bowl, beat the egg yolks and sugar together, using a hand whisk, then pour in the hot coffee mixture, whisking constantly. Return the mixture to the pan and heat, stirring constantly with a wooden spoon, until it begins to thicken and coats the back of the spoon. Do not allow the mixture to boil, as it will curdle.

3 Remove from the heat, pour into a clean bowl and leave to cool slightly before whisking in the melted chocolate, then leave to cool completely. Refrigerate for 3 hours or overnight, then churn in an ice-cream machine according to the manufacturer's instructions.

270 Roasted macadamia & chocolate ice cream

PREPARATION TIME 30 minutes, plus chilling and churning   **COOKING TIME** 5 minutes
MAKES 1 litre/35fl oz/4 cups

50g/1³/₄oz butter
100g/3¹/₂oz/²/₃ cup macadamia nuts,
  chopped
2 tbsp soft brown sugar
375ml/13fl oz/1¹/₂ cups milk

375ml/13fl oz/1¹/₂ cups double cream
2 tbsp maple syrup
125g/4¹/₂oz dark chocolate,
  melted and left to cool

1 In a non-stick frying pan, heat the butter until melted, then stir in the chopped macadamia nuts. Sprinkle over the sugar, then cook over a medium heat for 3–4 minutes, or until the nuts brown lightly.

2 In a large bowl, beat together the milk, cream, maple syrup and melted chocolate, then stir in the sugared nuts. Refrigerate for 3 hours or overnight, then churn in an ice-cream machine according to the manufacturer's instructions.

271 Ginger & chocolate ice cream

PREPARATION TIME 25 minutes, plus chilling and churning   **COOKING TIME** 5 minutes
MAKES 1 litre/35fl oz/4 cups

250ml/9fl oz/1 cup milk
100g/3¹/₂oz dark chocolate,
   broken into pieces
3 egg yolks

100g/3¹/₂oz/¹/₃ cup plus 4 tsp
   caster sugar
500ml/17fl oz/2 cups double cream
100g/3¹/₂oz stem ginger, chopped
1 tbsp syrup from stem ginger jar

1   In a small saucepan, heat the milk and chocolate together over a low heat until just melted.

2   In a large bowl, beat the egg yolks and sugar together, using a hand whisk, then pour in the hot chocolate mixture, whisking constantly. Return the mixture to the saucepan and heat, stirring constantly with a wooden spoon, until the mixture just begins to thicken and lightly coats the back of the spoon. Do not allow the mixture to boil, as it will curdle.

3   Remove from the heat, pour into a clean bowl and leave to cool completely, then stir in the cream, ginger and ginger syrup. Refrigerate for 3 hours or overnight, then churn in an ice-cream machine according to the manufacturer's instructions.

272 Chocolate ice-cream & ginger biscuit sandwiches

PREPARATION TIME 40 minutes, plus chilling   **COOKING TIME** 12–15 minutes

100g/3½oz butter, softened,
plus extra for greasing
100g/3½oz/¾ cup plus 1 tbsp
icing sugar
2 egg yolks
150g/5½oz/1 cup plus 2 tbsp
plain flour

4 tsp ground ginger
2 tbsp cocoa powder
1 recipe quantity Rich Chocolate
Ice Cream (see page 104)
icing sugar, sifted, for dusting
(optional)

1   Preheat the oven to 180°C/350°F/gas 4. Grease a baking tray with butter.
2   In a large bowl, beat the butter and sugar together until pale and light, using
    an electric hand mixer, then beat in the egg yolks. In a clean bowl, mix the flour,
    ginger and cocoa together and gently stir into the butter mixture to form a
    dough. Wrap the dough in plastic film, flatten slightly and refrigerate for
    45 minutes, or until the dough is firm but not hard.
3   Roll the dough out on a lightly floured surface to about 5mm/¼in thick,
    and cut out 8 biscuit rounds using a large cookie cutter. Place the rounds
    on the prepared baking tray, prick them with a fork and bake in the hot
    oven for 12–15 minutes, or until the biscuits are firm and lightly golden.
4   Remove from the oven, and leave the biscuits on the tray to cool completely.
    Sandwich pairs of biscuits together with the chocolate ice cream. Dust with
    icing sugar, if wanted.

273 Honeycomb & chocolate ice cream

PREPARATION TIME 20 minutes, plus chilling and churning   **COOKING TIME** 5 minutes
MAKES 1 litre/35fl oz/4 cups

300ml/10½fl oz/1¼ cups milk
500ml/17fl oz/2 cups double cream
200g/7oz dark chocolate,
broken into pieces
5 tbsp caster sugar
4 egg yolks
1 tbsp cornflour

2 tbsp clear honey
100g/3½oz chocolate-coated
honeycomb pieces, finely chopped
1 tsp vanilla essence
1 recipe quantity Chocolate Caramel
Sauce (see page 204)

1   In a medium-sized saucepan, heat the milk, cream and chocolate together
    over a low heat until the chocolate has just melted.
2   In a large bowl, beat the sugar, egg yolks and cornflour together, using a hand
    whisk, then pour in the hot chocolate mixture, whisking constantly. Return the
    mixture to the saucepan and heat, stirring constantly with a wooden spoon, until
    the mixture just begins to thicken and lightly coats the back of the spoon.
    Do not allow the mixture to boil, as it will curdle.
3   Remove from the heat and and whisk in the honey, then pour into a clean bowl
    and leave to cool completely. Refrigerate for 3 hours or overnight. Remove from
    the refrigerator and stir in the chopped honeycomb and vanilla essence just
    before churning in an ice-cream machine according to the manufacturer's
    instructions. Serve with chocolate caramel sauce.

274 Chocolate nougat ice cream

PREPARATION TIME 20 minutes, plus chilling and churning   **COOKING TIME** 5 minutes
MAKES 1 litre/35fl oz/4 cups

300ml/10½fl oz/1¼ cups milk
200g/7oz dark chocolate,
   broken into pieces
4 egg yolks
100g/3½ oz/⅓ cup plus
   4 tsp caster sugar
300ml/10½fl oz/1¼ cups
   double cream

100g/3½oz soft nougat,
   finely chopped
1 tsp vanilla essence

1   In a small saucepan, heat the milk and chocolate together over a low heat
     until the chocolate has just melted.
2   In a large bowl, beat the egg yolks and sugar together, using a hand whisk,
     then whisk in the warm chocolate milk. Return the mixture to the pan and heat,
     stirring constantly with a wooden spoon, until the mixture just begins to thicken
     and lightly coats the back of the spoon. Do not allow the mixture to boil, as
     it will curdle.
3   Remove from the heat, pour into a clean bowl and leave to cool completely.
     Refrigerate for 3 hours or overnight. Remove from the refrigerator and stir
     in the cream, nougat and vanilla essence, then churn in an ice-cream machine
     according to the manufacturer's instructions.

275 Chocolate ice cream with Irish Cream

PREPARATION TIME 20 minutes, plus chilling and churning   **COOKING TIME** 5 minutes
MAKES 1 litre/35fl oz/4 cups

300ml/10½fl oz/1¼ cups milk
500ml/17fl oz/2 cups double cream
150g/5½oz dark chocolate,
   broken into pieces
100g/3½oz/⅓ cup plus 4 tsp
   caster sugar

4 egg yolks
1 tbsp cornflour
4 meringue shells, roughly crushed
8 tbsp Irish Cream liqueur
1 recipe quantity Espresso Chocolate
   Sauce (see page 205)

1   In a medium-sized saucepan, heat the milk, cream and chocolate together
     over a low heat until the chocolate has just melted.
2   In a large bowl, beat the sugar, egg yolks and cornflour together, using a hand
     whisk, then whisk in the warm chocolate milk. Return the mixture to the pan
     and heat, stirring constantly with a wooden spoon, until the mixture just begins
     to thicken and lightly coats the back of the spoon. Do not allow the mixture to
     boil, as it will curdle.
3   Remove from the heat, pour into a clean bowl and leave to cool completely.
     Refrigerate for 3 hours or overnight. Remove from the refrigerator and stir in
     the crushed meringue shells and half the liqueur, then churn in an ice-cream
     machine according to the manufacturer's instructions. Serve the ice cream
     with the remaining liqueur poured over the top, accompanied by the espresso
     chocolate sauce.

276 Mint chocolate-chip ice cream

PREPARATION TIME 20 minutes, plus chilling and churning   **COOKING TIME** 5 minutes
MAKES 1 litre/35fl oz/4 cups

375ml/13fl oz/1¹/₂ cups milk
125g/4¹/₂oz/¹/₂ cup plus 2 tsp
 caster sugar
375ml/13fl oz/1¹/₂ cups double cream

175g/6oz dark chocolate, grated
2 tsp peppermint essence
2–3 drops green colouring (optional)

1   In a medium-sized saucepan, heat the milk and sugar together over a medium
    heat until the sugar has dissolved. Pour into a clean bowl and add the cream.
    Leave the mixture to cool completely before stirring in the chocolate,
    peppermint essence and green colouring, if using.
2   Refrigerate for 3 hours or overnight, then churn in an ice-cream machine
    according to the manufacturer's instructions.

277 Chocolate mint sorbet

PREPARATION TIME 15 minutes, plus chilling and churning   **COOKING TIME** 5 minutes
MAKES 1 litre/35fl oz/4 cups

150g/2³/₄oz/²/₃ cup caster sugar
1 tbsp cocoa powder

125g/4¹/₂oz dark chocolate,
 broken into pieces
3 drops peppermint essence

1   In a large saucepan, heat 750ml/26fl oz/3 cups water and the sugar together
    over a medium heat until the sugar dissolves, stirring frequently. In a large
    bowl, combine the cocoa and chocolate and pour over the hot sugar mixture.
    Leave to stand for 2 minutes, then whisk until smooth, using a hand whisk.
    Stir in the peppermint essence and set aside to cool completely.
2   Refrigerate for 2 hours or overnight, then churn in an ice-cream machine
    according to the manufacturer's instructions.

278 Chocolate semifreddo with Marsala

PREPARATION TIME 25 minutes, plus freezing   **SERVES** 4–6

750ml/26fl oz/3 cups double cream
350g/12oz/1¹/₂ cups caster sugar
6 egg yolks
1 tsp vanilla essence
2 tbsp Marsala wine

200g/7oz dark chocolate, melted,
 plus 5 tbsp grated
1 recipe quantity Rich Chocolate
 Sauce (see page 204)

1   Line a 24 x 12cm/9 x 4¹/₂in loaf tin (ideally silicone) with plastic film so that it
    hangs over the edges of the tin.
2   In a large bowl, whisk the cream and half the sugar together until the cream
    forms soft peaks, using an electric hand mixer. In a clean bowl, beat the egg
    yolks, vanilla essence, Marsala wine and the remaining sugar together until the
    mixture is thick and pale, using the electric hand mixer, then stir in the melted
    chocolate. Fold the cream and the chocolate mixtures together, using a metal
    spoon, then stir in the grated chocolate.
3   Pour the mixture into the prepared loaf tin, covering the top with the plastic
    film to make a well-enclosed parcel, and freeze for 8 hours or overnight.
4   Take the semifreddo out of the freezer, turn out from the tin on to a serving
    plate and remove the plastic film. Serve with the rich chocolate sauce.

279　Chocolate sorbet

PREPARATION TIME 30 minutes, plus chilling and churning　**COOKING TIME** 25 minutes
MAKES 1 litre/35fl oz/4 cups

250g/9oz/1 cup plus 4 tsp
　caster sugar

150g/5½oz cocoa powder, sifted
2 tsp vanilla essence

1　In a large saucepan, mix together the sugar and 900ml/33fl oz/3¾ cups water over a medium heat, stirring well until the sugar has dissolved. Whisk in the cocoa, using a hand whisk. Bring to the boil, then reduce the heat and simmer for 20 minutes over a low heat, stirring occasionally. Remove from the heat, pour into a clean bowl and add the vanilla essence, then leave to cool completely.
2　Refrigerate for 2 hours or overnight, then churn in an ice-cream machine according to the manufacturer's instructions.

280 Chocolate & nougat semifreddo

PREPARATION TIME 25 minutes, plus freezing   **SERVES** 4–6

750ml/26fl oz/3 cups double cream
300g/10¹/₂oz/1¹/₃ cups caster sugar
6 egg yolks
1 tbsp amaretto liqueur
125g/4¹/₂oz/1 cup raspberries,
 lightly crushed, plus extra, whole,
 for serving (optional)

100g/3¹/₂oz soft nougat, chopped
100g/3¹/₂oz/²/₃ cup almonds, roasted
 and chopped
125g/4¹/₂oz dark chocolate, grated
1 recipe quantity Traditional Hot
 Fudge Sauce (see page 208)

1   Line a 24 x 12cm/9 x 4¹/₂in loaf tin (ideally silicone) with plastic film so that it
    hangs over the edges of the tin.
2   In a large bowl, whisk together the cream and half the sugar until soft peaks
    form, using an electric hand mixer. In a clean bowl, whisk the yolks, liqueur and
    remaining sugar until the mixture is thick and pale. Fold the yolk mixture into
    the whipped cream, then fold in the raspberries, soft nougat, almonds and
    grated chocolate.
3   Pour the mixture into the prepared loaf tin, covering the top with the
    overhanging plastic film to make a well-enclosed parcel. Freeze for 8 hours
    or overnight.
4   Take the semifreddo out of the freezer, turn out from the tin on to a serving
    plate and remove the plastic film. Serve with the extra raspberries, if wanted,
    and the traditional hot fudge sauce.

281 Chocolate semifreddo

PREPARATION TIME 25 minutes, plus freezing   **SERVES** 4–6

2 eggs, separated
100g/3¹/₂oz/¹/₃ cup plus 4 tsp
 caster sugar
125g/4¹/₂oz dark chocolate,
 melted and left to cool
1 tbsp frangelico liqueur

pinch salt
375ml/13fl oz/1¹/₂ cups double
 cream, whipped to soft peaks
1 recipe quantity Espresso Chocolate
 Sauce (see page 205)

1   Line a 24 x 12cm/9 x 4¹/₂in loaf tin (ideally silicone) with plastic film so that
    it hangs over the edges of the tin.
2   In a large bowl, beat the egg yolks and sugar together until thick and pale,
    using an electric hand mixer, then stir in the chocolate and liqueur. In a clean
    bowl, whisk the egg whites with the salt until stiff.
3   Fold the cream and the egg whites into the chocolate mixture, using a metal
    spoon, and pour into the prepared tin, covering the top with the overhanging
    plastic film to make a well-enclosed parcel. Freeze for 8 hours or overnight.
4   Take the semifreddo out of the freezer, turn out from the tin on to a serving
    plate and remove the plastic film.

282 Frozen espresso mousse with chocolate sauce

PREPARATION TIME 30 minutes, plus freezing

4 egg yolks
100g/3¹/₂oz/¹/₃ cup plus 4 tsp
  caster sugar
125ml/4fl oz/¹/₂ cup strong,
  black hot coffee
2 tbsp coffee liqueur

250ml/9fl oz/1 cup double cream,
  whipped to soft peaks
1 recipe quantity Rich Chocolate
  Sauce (see page 204)

1   In a large bowl, beat the egg yolks and sugar together until pale, using an
    electric hand mixer. Slowly pour the hot coffee into the yolk mixture, whisking
    constantly, and continue whisking until the mixture is very thick. Using a metal
    spoon, fold in the liqueur and cream until just combined.
2   Divide the mixture evenly between 4 x 200ml/7fl oz/³/₄-cup freezerproof ceramic
    dishes and freeze for 3 hours or overnight.
3   Take the dishes out of the freezer, dip them briefly in warm water, run a knife
    around the edges and turn the mousses out on to plates. Serve with the rich
    chocolate sauce poured over the top.

283 Coffee parfait with chocolate sauce

PREPARATION TIME 15 minutes, plus freezing   **SERVES** 4–6

125ml/4fl oz/¹/₂ cup strong,
  black hot coffee
4 tbsp caster sugar
450g/16oz can condensed milk

250ml/9fl oz/1 cup double cream,
  whipped to soft peaks
1 recipe quantity Traditional Hot
  Fudge Sauce (see page 206)

1   In a small bowl, mix the hot coffee and the sugar together until the sugar has
    dissolved, stirring with a metal spoon. Set aside to cool completely. In a large
    bowl, beat together the condensed milk and the cooled coffee mixture, using an
    electric hand mixer.
2   Fold the whipped cream into the coffee milk. Divide the mixture evenly between
    4–6 freezerproof ceramic dishes and freeze for 3 hours or overnight.
3   Take the parfaits out of the freezer and serve with the traditional hot fudge sauce.

284 White chocolate & raspberry parfait

PREPARATION TIME 25 minutes, plus freezing   **COOKING TIME** 5 minutes

125ml/4fl oz/¹/₂ cup double cream
125g/4¹/₂oz white chocolate,
   broken into pieces
2 egg whites
100g/3¹/₂oz/¹/₃ cup plus 4 tsp
   caster sugar

125g/4¹/₂oz/1 cup raspberries,
   lightly crushed, plus extra, whole,
   for serving
1 tbsp strawberry or
   raspberry liqueur

1   In a small saucepan, heat the cream and chocolate together over a low heat
    until just melted, then set aside to cool. In a large bowl, whisk the egg whites
    until soft peaks form, using an electric hand mixer, then gradually add the
    sugar until the mixture is thick and shiny. Fold in the chocolate cream,
    raspberries and liqueur, and divide evenly between 4 x 200ml/7fl oz/³/₄-cup
    moulds. Freeze the parfaits for 3 hours or overnight.
2   Remove the parfaits from the freezer, turn out on to individual plates and
    serve with the extra raspberries.

285 Chocolate affogatto

PREPARATION TIME 5 minutes

8 scoops Rich Chocolate Ice Cream
(see page 164) or good-quality
bought ice cream

4 tbsp hot espresso coffee
4 tbsp Frangelico liqueur

1 Place 2 scoops of ice cream into each of 4 glasses.
2 Pour 1 tbsp of the hot espresso and 1 tbsp of the liqueur over each helping
and serve immediately.

286 Quick honeycomb & chocolate ice cream

PREPARATION TIME 10 minutes   **MAKES** 1 litre/35fl oz/4 cups

750ml/26fl oz/3 cups homemade
or good-quality bought vanilla
ice cream, slightly softened
150g/5^1/$_2$oz chocolate-coated
honeycomb pieces, chopped
150g/5^1/$_2$oz dark chocolate, grated

1 recipe quantity Rich Chocolate
Sauce (see page 204)

1 In a large bowl, mix together the softened ice cream, chopped honeycomb
pieces and grated chocolate, using a wooden spoon.
2 Serve with the rich chocolate sauce.

287 Crushed candied ice cream

PREPARATION TIME 10 minutes   **MAKES** 1 litre/35fl oz/4 cups

200g/7oz/1 cup multi-coloured
candy-coated chocolates
3 tbsp chocolate sauce

1 recipe quantity Rich Chocolate Ice
Cream (see page 164) or same
quantity good-quality bought ice
cream, softened

1 Place the candy-coated chocolates in the bowl of a food processor and process
until they are broken into small pieces. In a large bowl, fold the chocolate sauce
and candy pieces into the softened ice cream (leaving it streaky), using
a wooden spoon.
2 Serve immediately.

288 Chocolate marshmallow ice cream

PREPARATION TIME 20 minutes, plus chilling and churning   **COOKING TIME** 5 minutes
MAKES 1 litre/35fl oz/4 cups

500ml/17fl oz/2 cups milk
100g/3^1/$_2$oz dark chocolate,
broken into pieces

40 marshmallows
1 tsp vanilla essence
250ml/9fl oz/1 cup double cream

1 In a large saucepan, heat the milk, chocolate and marshmallows together
over a low heat, stirring with a wooden spoon until the chocolate has just
melted. Stir in the vanilla essence, add the cream and transfer the mixture to a
clean bowl. Set aside to cool completely, then refrigerate for 3 hours or overnight.
2 Churn in an ice-cream machine according to the manufacturer's instructions.

289 Frozen Mississippi mud pie

PREPARATION TIME 35 minutes, plus chilling and churning **COOKING TIME** 5 minutes
MAKES 1 x 23cm/9in pie

1 recipe quantity Chocolate
  Crumb Crust (see page 13)
600ml/21fl oz/2½ cups Rich
  Chocolate Ice Cream (see page 164)
  or good-quality bought ice cream,
  slightly softened
600ml/21fl oz/2½ cups good-quality
  bought or ready-made coffee ice
  cream, slightly softened

175g/6oz dark chocolate,
  broken into pieces
2 tbsp double cream
1 tbsp golden syrup
1 tsp vanilla essence
chocolate curls, for decorating

1   Press the chocolate crumb crust into the bottom and sides of a fluted, loose-
    bottomed 23cm/9in flan tin, 3–4cm/1½in deep, then freeze for 30 minutes.
2   Spoon the chocolate ice cream over the crumb crust base, spreading it evenly,
    then layer with the coffee ice cream. Return to the freezer for 1 hour.
3   In a medium-sized saucepan, heat the chocolate, cream, golden syrup and
    vanilla essence together over a low heat until the chocolate has just melted.
    Remove from the heat and stir until smooth, using a wooden spoon. Set aside
    to cool for 15 minutes, then pour over the ice-cream mixture. Return to the
    freezer for a further 30 minutes or until firm.
4   Decorate the pie with chocolate curls before serving.

290 Frozen zabaglione with chocolate sauce

PREPARATION TIME 25 minutes, plus freezing **COOKING TIME** 15 minutes

4 egg yolks
100g/3½oz/⅓ cup plus 4 tsp
  caster sugar
250ml/9fl oz/1 cup double cream

4 tbsp Marsala wine
1 recipe quantity Rich Chocolate
  Sauce (see page 204)
2 tbsp flaked almonds, toasted

1   Place the egg yolks and sugar in a medium-sized bowl set over a pan of just
    simmering water (taking care not to let the bowl touch the water or the yolks
    will curdle), and beat together until thick. Remove from the heat and whisk for
    a few more minutes as the mixture cools. Pour into a clean bowl.
2   In a second clean bowl, whisk the cream and Marsala wine together until soft
    peaks form, using an electric hand mixer, then fold into the egg mixture, using
    a metal spoon. Divide the mixture evenly between 4 x 150ml/5½oz/⅔-cup
    freezerproof dishes and freeze for 3 hours or overnight.
3   When ready to serve, remove from the freezer, dip each dish briefly into hot
    water, then turn out on to individual plates. Pour over the rich chocolate sauce
    and sprinkle with flaked almonds.

291 Tiramisu ice-cream cake

PREPARATION TIME 40 minutes, plus chilling **COOKING TIME** 5 minutes
MAKES 1 x 23cm/9in cake

200g/7oz/³/₄ cup plus 2 tbsp
   caster sugar
375ml/13fl oz/1¹/₂ cups strong coffee
2 tbsp Marsala wine
1 x 23cm/9in sponge cake
6 tbsp chocolate, grated

500ml/17fl oz/2 cups good-quality
   bought or ready-made coffee ice
   cream, slightly softened
500ml/17fl oz/2 cups Rich Chocolate
   Ice Cream (see page 164) or
   good-quality bought ice cream,
   slightly softened

1   In a small saucepan, heat the sugar and 150ml/5fl oz/²/₃ cup water over a medium heat until the sugar has dissolved, stirring frequently with a metal spoon. Remove from the heat, pour into a clean bowl and add the coffee and Marsala wine. Set aside to cool completely.

2   Line a 23cm/9in spring-form cake tin with baking paper. Cut the sponge horizontally to create two layers and place the bottom layer into the prepared tin. Using a pastry brush, spread half of the cooled coffee syrup over the bottom layer of sponge and sprinkle over half the grated chocolate.

3   In a large bowl, whisk the coffee ice cream until it is spreadable, using an electric hand mixer, then spread it over the bottom layer of sponge, using a palette knife. Sprinkle over the remaining grated chocolate and place the remaining sponge layer on top. Using a pastry brush, brush the top sponge layer with the rest of the coffee syrup. In a large bowl, whisk the chocolate ice cream until it is spreadable, then use a palette knife to spread over the top sponge layer.

4   Place the ice-cream cake in the freezer for 30 minutes, or until firm. Remove from the freezer and serve immediately.

292 Chocolate baked Alaska

PREPARATION TIME 10 minutes **COOKING TIME** 4–5 minutes **SERVES** 6

1 recipe quantity Chocolate Fudge
   Brownies, baked in a 20cm/8in
   round or square tin (see page 98)
3 egg whites
125g/4¹/₂oz/¹/₂ cup plus
   2 tsp caster sugar
pinch cream of tartar

500ml/17fl oz/2 cups good-quality
   bought or ready-made vanilla ice
   cream, slightly softened
500ml/17fl oz/2 cups Rich Chocolate
   Ice Cream (see page 164) or
   good-quality bought ice cream,
   slightly softened

1   Place the brownie (uncut) on a kitchen foil-lined baking tray. Preheat the oven to 230°C/455°F/gas 8.

2   In a large bowl, whisk the egg whites to stiff peaks, using an electric hand mixer, then whisk in the sugar and cream of tartar until the meringue is thick and shiny. Scoop the vanilla and chocolate ice creams on to the top of the baked brownie, alternating the flavours. Spread the meringue over the sides and top of the ice-cream cake, so that the ice cream is completely covered, and bake in the very hot oven for 4–5 minutes until the meringue is lightly browned.

3   Remove the baked Alaska from the oven and serve immediately.

293 Chocolate pear sundae with roasted almonds

PREPARATION TIME 20 minutes **COOKING TIME** 5 minutes

100g/3¹/₂oz/¹/₃ cup plus 4 tsp
  caster sugar
4 ripe pears
8 scoops Ginger & Chocolate
  Ice Cream (see page 167),
  slightly softened

1 recipe quantity Double Chocolate
  Sauce (see page 204)
200g/7oz/1¹/₂ cups flaked
  almonds, roasted

1 In a small saucepan, heat the sugar and 100ml/3¹/₂fl oz/¹/₃ cup water together over a medium heat until the sugar has dissolved, stirring frequently with a metal spoon.
2 Peel the pears and cut in half vertically, keeping the stalks intact if possible. Remove the seeds and core, using a melon baller to create a neat shape. Toss the halved pears in the sugar syrup until lightly coated.
3 Divide the pears between 4 serving dishes. Place 2 scoops of ice cream on each dish and spoon over the double chocolate sauce. Sprinkle with flaked almonds.

294 Grilled pineapple, macadamia & chocolate sundaes

PREPARATION TIME 15 minutes **COOKING TIME** 5 minutes

1 small, ripe pineapple, peeled
100g/3¹/₂oz/¹/₃ cup plus 2 tsp
  soft brown sugar
2 tbsp dark rum
8 scoops Rich Chocolate Ice Cream
  (see page 164) or good-quality
  bought ice cream, slightly softened

1 recipe quantity Chocolate Rum
  Sauce (see page 206)
85g/3oz/¹/₂ cup macadamia nuts,
  roasted and chopped
4 ice-cream wafers (optional)

1 Cut the pineapple into quarters and remove the core, then slice into 1cm/¹/₂in slices. Place the slices in a large bowl with the brown sugar and dark rum and toss until well combined.
2 Place the pineapple slices on an oven tray under a hot grill for a few minutes until the pineapple has warmed slightly and has a light glaze.
3 Divide the grilled pineapple slices between 4 plates and top each one with 2 scoops of chocolate ice cream and the chocolate rum sauce. Sprinkle with chopped macadamia nuts and serve with ice-cream wafers, if using.

295 Peach & amaretto sundae with chocolate

PREPARATION TIME 30 minutes, plus cooling   **COOKING TIME** 15–17 minutes

150g/5¹/₂oz/²/₃ cup caster sugar
4 ripe, firm, yellow peaches
8 scoops Rich Chocolate Ice Cream
   (see page 164) or good-quality
   bought ice cream, slightly softened

1 recipe quantity Rich Chocolate
   Sauce (see page 204)
100g/3¹/₂oz amaretto biscuits,
   crushed

1   In a small saucepan, heat the sugar and 250ml/9fl oz/1 cup water together over
    a medium heat until the sugar has dissolved, stirring frequently with a metal
    spoon. Bring to a simmer, then add the peaches and cook for 8–10 minutes
    until just tender. Remove the peaches from the syrup using a slotted spoon and
    set aside in a bowl to cool completely, then peel, cut in half horizontally and
    remove the stones.
2   Return the syrup to the heat and bring to the boil, then simmer until the syrup
    has reduced by half. Pour into a bowl and leave to cool.
3   Divide the peach halves equally between 4 dishes and spoon over some of the
    syrup. Place a scoop of chocolate ice cream on each peach half, top with some
    rich chocolate sauce and sprinkle over the crushed amaretto biscuits.

296 Chocolate sorbet with pineapple carpaccio

PREPARATION TIME 15 minutes, plus chilling

1 small, ripe pineapple, peeled
juice of 1 orange

8 scoops Chocolate Sorbet
   (see page 171) or good-quality
   bought sorbet
3 tbsp mint leaves, finely chopped

1　Cut the pineapple in half lengthways and remove the core. Using a very sharp knife, cut the pineapple into wafer thin slices. Place the pineapple slices in a bowl and refrigerate for 30 minutes.
2　Divide the pineapple evenly between 4 plates and drizzle over the orange juice. Top each plate with 2 scoops of chocolate sorbet and sprinkle over the mint.

297 Marsala strawberries layered with chocolate ice cream

PREPARATION TIME 40 minutes, plus marinating

300g/10¹/₂oz/2 cups strawberries,
   sliced
4 tbsp Marsala wine
2 tbsp icing sugar
4 scoops Rich Chocolate Ice Cream
   (see page 164) or good-quality
   bought ice cream

1 recipe quantity Chocolate Chantilly
   Cream (see page 208)
100g/3oz dark chocolate,
   melted and left to cool

1　In a large bowl, mix together the strawberries, Marsala wine and icing sugar, stirring well to combine. Leave to marinate for 30 minutes.
2　Place a scoop of the chocolate ice cream into each of 4 bowls and divide the strawberry mixture equally over the ice cream. Place a spoonful of chocolate chantilly cream on top of each scoop. Drizzle the ice cream with melted chocolate just before serving.

298 Mulled berries with chocolate ice cream

PREPARATION TIME 20 minutes　**COOKING TIME** 8 minutes

280g/10oz/2 cups mixed berries
250ml/9fl oz/1 cup red wine
100g/3¹/₂oz/¹/₃ cup plus 4 tsp
   caster sugar
zest and juice of 1 orange

1 cinnamon stick
2 cloves
8 scoops Rich Chocolate Ice Cream
   (see page 164) or good-quality
   bought ice cream

1　Place the berries in a bowl – slicing the strawberries and pitting the cherries, if using.
2　In a medium-sized saucepan, heat the red wine, sugar, orange zest and juice, cinnamon stick and cloves until boiling. Lower the heat and simmer for 5 minutes, then remove from the heat. Leave to cool for 15 minutes, then pour the mulled wine mixture over the berries.
3　Place 2 scoops of ice cream in each of 4 tall glasses, and pour over the warm berries along with some of the liquid. Serve immediately.

299 Frozen chocolate yogurt

PREPARATION TIME 20 minutes, plus chilling and churning   **COOKING TIME** 5 minutes
MAKES 1 litre/35fl oz/4 cups

100g/3¹/₂oz/¹/₃ cup plus 4 tsp
   caster sugar
1 tbsp cornflour
375ml/13fl oz/1¹/₂ cups milk
1 egg, lightly beaten

125ml/4fl oz/¹/₂ cup chocolate sauce
1 tbsp honey
375ml/13fl oz/1¹/₂ cups plain or
   vanilla-flavoured yogurt
1 tsp vanilla essence

1   In a small bowl, mix the sugar and cornflour to a paste using a little of the milk.
    Place the remaining milk in a small saucepan over a low heat and, using a hand
    whisk, whisk in the cornflour mixture and the egg. Continue to heat, stirring
    constantly with a wooden spoon, until the mixture thickens and coats the back
    of the spoon. Pour the mixture into a clean bowl and stir in the chocolate syrup
    and honey. Set aside until cold, then refrigerate for 3 hours.
2   Whisk in the yogurt and vanilla essence, using a hand whisk, then churn in an
    ice-cream machine according to the manufacturer's instructions.

CHAPTER 5

Chocolates
& drinks

Handmade chocolates and treats make a very special way to enjoy chocolate at any time of day. An assortment of truffles passed around after dinner will make your friends and family feel truly indulged. Alternatively, a selection of truffles, fudge squares and chocolate-dipped fruits presented in a decorative box makes a perfect gift.

Bear in mind that handmade chocolates are best kept in a cool, dry place if you are intending to keep them for a while. If the weather is warm, you might like to keep them in the fridge; however, the moisture may cause them to develop a 'bloom'. Although this doesn't look so nice, if you do find that your chocolates have developed a bloom, don't despair – it will do very little damage to the flavour and texture of the chocolates.

To round off this chapter I have included a number of chocolate drinks, from Spiced Hot Chocolate and White Hot Chocolate to warm up cold winter months, to a refreshingly chilled Divine Iced Mint Chocolate for hot summer days.

300 Cranberry & port chocolate truffles

PREPARATION TIME 25 minutes, plus chilling   **COOKING TIME** 5 minutes   **MAKES** 30 truffles

200g/7oz dark chocolate,
  broken into pieces
60ml/2fl oz/¼ cup double cream
2 tbsp port

4 tbsp dried cranberries,
  chopped
250g/9oz white chocolate,
  melted and left to cool

1   In a small saucepan, combine the chocolate and cream over a low heat until the chocolate has just melted, stirring frequently with a wooden spoon. Remove from the heat and stir until smooth, then add the port and dried cranberries. Pour into a clean bowl and leave to cool completely, then refrigerate for approximately 30 minutes until firm.

2   Roll teaspoonfuls of the mixture in the melted white chocolate to form balls, put on a baking tray lined with baking paper and refrigerate for 1 hour until firm.

301 Double chocolate truffles

PREPARATION TIME 25 minutes, plus chilling   **COOKING TIME** 5 minutes   **MAKES** 20 truffles

150g/5½oz dark chocolate,
  broken into pieces
4 tbsp double cream

2 tbsp liqueur of your choice
  (e.g. Kahlua, Grand Marnier)
2 tbsp cocoa powder, sifted

1   In a small saucepan, combine the chocolate and cream over a low heat until the chocolate has just melted, stirring frequently with a wooden spoon. Remove from the heat and add your chosen liqueur. Pour the mixture into a clean bowl and leave to cool completely, then refrigerate for approximately 30 minutes until firm.

2   Roll teaspoonfuls of the mixture into small balls and toss in the cocoa to coat. Place the cocoa-coated balls on a baking tray lined with baking paper and refrigerate for 1 hour until firm.

302 Peanut butter & milk chocolate truffles

PREPARATION TIME 30 minutes, plus chilling   **COOKING TIME** 5 minutes   **MAKES** 30 truffles

200g/7oz milk chocolate,
  broken into pieces
100ml/3½fl oz/⅓ cup double cream

3 tbsp crunchy peanut butter
100g/3½oz/⅔ cup roasted
  peanuts, crushed

1   In a small saucepan, combine the chocolate and cream over a low heat until the chocolate has just melted, stirring frequently with a wooden spoon. Remove from the heat, add the peanut butter and stir until smooth. Pour into a clean bowl and leave to cool completely, then refrigerate for approximately 30 minutes until firm.

2   Roll rounded teaspoonfuls of the mixture in the crushed peanuts, then place on a baking tray lined with baking paper and refrigerate for 1 hour until firm.

303 Chocolate rum truffles

PREPARATION TIME 20 minutes, plus chilling **COOKING TIME** 5 minutes **MAKES** 18 truffles

150g/5$\frac{1}{2}$oz dark chocolate,
   broken into pieces
4 tbsp double cream

3 tbsp rum
200g/7oz/1 cup chocolate sprinkles

1 In a small saucepan, combine the chocolate and cream over a low heat until the chocolate has just melted, stirring frequently with a wooden spoon. Remove from the heat and add the rum. Pour into a clean bowl and leave to cool completely, then refrigerate for approximately 30 minutes until firm.
2 Roll teaspoonfuls of the mixture into balls and toss in the chocolate sprinkles to coat. Place on a baking tray lined with baking paper and refrigerate for 1 hour until firm.

304 Chocolate & orange truffles

PREPARATION TIME 20 minutes, plus chilling **COOKING TIME** 5 minutes **MAKES** 18 truffles

150g/5$\frac{1}{2}$oz dark chocolate,
   broken into pieces
4 tbsp double cream

3 tbsp orange liqueur
zest of 1 orange, finely grated
icing sugar, sifted, for coating

1 In a small saucepan, combine the chocolate and cream over a low heat until the chocolate has just melted, stirring frequently with a wooden spoon. Remove from the heat and stir in the liqueur and orange zest, using a wooden spoon. Pour into a clean bowl and leave to cool completely, then refrigerate for approximately 30 minutes until firm.
2 Roll teaspoonfuls of the mixture into balls and coat with icing sugar. Place on a baking tray lined with baking paper and refrigerate for 1 hour until firm.

305 Candied citrus peel

PREPARATION TIME 30 minutes **COOKING TIME** 20 minutes **MAKES** 24 pieces

3 ripe lemons or oranges
5 tbsp granulated sugar

100g/3$\frac{1}{2}$oz dark chocolate,
   melted and left to cool

1 Remove the peel from the fruit, using a wide-bladed vegetable peeler. Using a sharp knife, cut away any remaining white pith (this will be bitter), and cut the rind into strips approximately 1cm/$\frac{1}{2}$in wide. Place the strips in a small saucepan, cover with water, then bring to the boil. Drain immediately in a colander, then refresh under cold water.
2 In a small saucepan, heat the sugar and 125ml/4fl oz/$\frac{1}{2}$ cup water over a medium heat until the sugar has dissolved, then add the blanched rind. Continue to cook over a medium heat for approximately 15 minutes until the liquid has evaporated and the peel is bright-coloured and shiny. Remove the peel from the water using a slotted spoon and spread on baking paper to cool.
3 Pour the melted chocolate into a bowl, dip each piece of candied citrus peel in the chocolate and leave on baking paper to set.

306 White chocolate, citrus & coconut truffles

PREPARATION TIME 25 minutes, plus chilling   **COOKING TIME** 5 minutes   **MAKES** 30 truffles

100ml/3½fl oz/⅓ cup coconut cream
350g/12oz white chocolate,
 broken into pieces
2 tsp lemon zest, finely grated

2 tsp lime zest, finely grated
2 tbsp coconut rum liqueur
90g/3¼ oz/1 cup desiccated coconut

1   In a small saucepan, combine the coconut cream and chocolate together over
   a low heat until just melted, stirring frequently with a wooden spoon. Remove
   from the heat, and stir until smooth. Pour into a clean bowl and leave to cool,
   then stir in the lemon and lime zests and liqueur. Refrigerate for approximately
   30 minutes until firm.
2   Roll teaspoonfuls of the mixture in the desiccated coconut to form balls. Place
   on a baking tray lined with baking paper and refrigerate for 1 hour until firm.

307 Chocolate biscuit truffles

PREPARATION TIME 20 minutes, plus chilling   **MAKES** 36 truffles

300g/10½oz digestive biscuits, finely crushed
2 tbsp cocoa powder

250ml/9fl oz/1 cup condensed milk
90g/3¼oz/1 cup desiccated coconut

1   In a large bowl, mix the crushed biscuits, cocoa and condensed milk together until well combined.
2   Roll teaspoonfuls of the mixture into balls and toss in the coconut to coat. Place on a baking tray lined with baking paper and refrigerate for 1–2 hours until firm.

308 Gingernut & chocolate truffles

PREPARATION TIME 25 minutes, plus chilling   **MAKES** 30 truffles

300g/10½oz gingernut biscuits, finely crushed
3 tbsp cocoa powder
2 pieces stem ginger, finely chopped

250ml/9fl oz/1 cup condensed milk
90g/3¼oz/1 cup desiccated coconut

1   In a large bowl, mix together the biscuits, cocoa, stem ginger and condensed milk until well combined.
2   Using slightly wet hands, roll heaped teaspoonfuls of the mixture into balls and roll in the coconut to coat. Place on a baking tray lined with baking paper and refrigerate for 1 hour until firm.

309 Roasted macadamia & ginger white chocolate drops

PREPARATION TIME 15 minutes, plus chilling   **COOKING TIME** 5 minutes
MAKES 18 truffles

200g/7oz white chocolate, broken into pieces

160g/5½oz/1 cup whole macadamia nuts, roasted
3 pieces stem ginger, finely chopped

1   In a small saucepan, melt the chocolate over a low heat, stirring until smooth. Add the nuts and ginger, and stir to combine, using a wooden spoon.
2   Place teaspoonfuls of the mixture on a baking tray lined with baking paper to create neat drops, then refrigerate for approximately 30 minutes until firm.

310 Roasted almond drops

PREPARATION TIME 15 minutes, plus chilling   **COOKING TIME** 5 minutes
MAKES 18 drops

200g/7oz dark or milk chocolate,
   broken into pieces

250g/9oz/2 cups slivered
   almonds, toasted

1   In a small saucepan, melt the chocolate over a low heat, stirring until smooth.
   Remove from the heat and stir in the toasted almonds until well combined.
2   Leave to cool for 5 minutes, then place teaspoonfuls of the mixture on a
   baking tray lined with baking paper and refrigerate for approximately
   30 minutes until firm.

311 Cranberry & raisin chocolate drops

PREPARATION TIME 15 minutes, plus chilling **COOKING TIME** 5 minutes **MAKES** 14 drops

150g/5½oz white chocolate,
  broken into pieces

100g/3½oz/¾ cup plus 1 tbsp
  dried cranberries
4 tbsp raisins

1 In a small saucepan, melt the chocolate over a low heat, stirring until smooth.
   Stir in the cranberries and raisins to combine, and leave to cool slightly.
2 Place teaspoonfuls of the mixture on a baking tray lined with baking paper
   to create neat drops, then refrigerate for approximately 30 minutes until firm.

312 Mint chocolate fudge

PREPARATION TIME 30 minutes, plus chilling **COOKING TIME** 5 minutes **MAKES** 16 squares

350g/12oz dark chocolate,
  broken into pieces
397g/14oz tin condensed milk

175g/6oz/1⅓ cups plus 4 tbsp
  icing sugar
2 tsp vanilla essence
1 tbsp peppermint essence

1 Line a shallow 23cm/9in square cake tin with baking paper.
2 In a small saucepan, combine the chocolate and condensed milk over a low
   heat until just melted. Remove from the heat and stir until smooth, using
   a wooden spoon, then stir in the sugar and both essences.
3 Pour the fudge mixture into the prepared tin and leave to cool completely, then
   refrigerate for approximately 30 minutes until firm. Turn out of the tin using the
   paper to help you, before cutting the fudge into squares, using a sharp knife.

313 Chocolate marshmallow fudge

PREPARATION TIME 20 minutes, plus chilling **COOKING TIME** 15 minutes **MAKES** 16 squares

75g/2¾oz butter
300g/10½oz/1⅓ cups caster sugar
150ml/5fl oz/⅔ cup milk

175g/6oz dark chocolate,
  broken into pieces
175g/6oz marshmallows
1 tsp vanilla essence

1 Line a 23cm/9in square, shallow-sided cake tin with baking paper.
2 In a small saucepan, heat the butter, sugar and milk together, stirring
   occasionally with a wooden spoon, and bring to the boil. Lower the heat and
   simmer for approximately 10 minutes, stirring constantly with a wooden spoon,
   until a small amount of the mixture dropped into a glass of cold water forms a
   soft ball. Stir in the chocolate until melted, then add the marshmallows and
   vanilla essence.
3 Pour the fudge mixture into the prepared tin, smoothing the top with a palette
   knife. Leave the fudge to cool completely at room temperature. Turn out of the
   tin, using the paper to help you, before cutting into squares with a sharp knife.

314 Chocolate hazelnut fudge

PREPARATION TIME 30 minutes   **COOKING TIME** 10 minutes   **MAKES** 16 squares

150ml/5fl oz/²/₃ cup
  evaporated milk
350g/12oz/1¹/₂ cups caster sugar

50g/1³/₄oz/¹/₃ cup hazelnuts,
  roasted and roughly chopped
350g/12oz milk chocolate,
  broken into pieces

1   Line a shallow 23cm/9in square cake tin with baking paper.
2   In a saucepan, bring the milk and sugar to the boil, stirring occasionally with
    a wooden spoon. Lower the heat and simmer for 5 minutes, stirring frequently.
    Remove the pan from the heat and add the hazelnuts and chocolate, stirring
    constantly until the chocolate has melted.
3   Pour the fudge mixture into the prepared tin, smoothing the top with a palette
    knife. Leave in the tin until completely set, then turn out from the tin, using
    the paper to help you and cut into 2.5cm/1in squares, using a sharp knife.

315 Cappuccino slims

PREPARATION TIME 15 minutes, plus chilling   **COOKING TIME** 5 minutes   **MAKES** 16 squares

200/7oz dark chocolate,
  broken into pieces
1 tsp instant coffee granules
1 tbsp coffee liqueur

150g/5¹/₂oz white chocolate,
  broken into pieces
2 tsp cocoa powder, sifted

1   Line a shallow 23cm/9in square cake tin with baking paper, letting the edges
    overhang the sides of the tin.
2   In a small saucepan, heat the dark chocolate over a low heat until just melted,
    then remove from the heat and stir until smooth, using a wooden spoon. Stir in
    the coffee and liqueur. Spread the mixture over the base of the prepared tin
    using a palette knife, and refrigerate for approximately 30 minutes until firm.
3   In a small saucepan, heat the white chocolate over a low heat until melted,
    then spread it over the dark chocolate mixture using a palette knife. Dust the
    top with cocoa.
4   Refrigerate for 30 minutes, then remove from the refrigerator and turn out from
    the tin, using the paper to help you, before cutting into squares with a knife that
    has been dipped in hot water first to warm it.

316 Mint slims

PREPARATION TIME 10 minutes, plus chilling   **COOKING TIME** 5 minutes   **MAKES** 16 squares

200g/7oz dark or milk chocolate,
  broken into pieces
2 tsp peppermint essence

150g/5¹/₂oz mint-flavoured
  chocolate, roughly chopped

1   Line a shallow 23cm/9in square cake tin with baking paper, letting the edges
    overhang the sides of the tin.
2   In a small saucepan, heat the chocolate over a low heat until just melted,
    remove the pan from the heat and stir until smooth, using a wooden spoon.
    Stir in the peppermint essence, and leave to cool for 10 minutes.
3   Stir in the chopped mint chocolate. Pour the mixture into the prepared tin
    and refrigerate for approximately 30 minutes until firm. Remove from the
    refrigerator and turn out from the tin, using the paper to help you, then cut
    into squares with a knife that has been dipped in hot water first to warm it.

317 Chocolate-dipped dried fruits

PREPARATION TIME 15 minutes, plus chilling   **COOKING TIME** 5 minutes
MAKES 24 chocolates

250g/9oz dark chocolate,
  broken into pieces

24 pieces dried fruit, including
  apricots, pear and pineapple

1   In a small saucepan, heat the chocolate over a low heat until just melted,
    then remove from the heat and stir until smooth.
2   Wipe the dried fruit with paper towels, and dip each piece in the melted
    chocolate to cover halfway. (If the chocolate runs off without making a nice
    coating, leave it to cool for a few minutes, then try again.)
3   Place the dipped fruit on a baking tray lined with baking paper, and refrigerate
    for approximately 30 minutes until the chocolate has set.

318 Marshmallow Lamingtons

PREPARATION TIME 30 minutes

200g/7oz white marshmallows
250g/9oz dark chocolate, melted
and left to cool

180g/6oz/2 cups desiccated coconut

1 Pierce a marshmallow with a long skewer and dip into the melted chocolate. Put the coconut in a large bowl and roll the marshmallow in it until well coated. Remove from the coconut and put on a baking tray lined with baking paper to set.
2 Repeat until all the marshmallows are coated.

319 Chocolate popcorn

PREPARATION TIME 20 minutes   **COOKING TIME** 5 minutes   **MAKES** 1 large bowl

1 tbsp vegetable oil
50g/1³/₄oz/¹/₄ cup popcorn kernels

200g/7oz dark chocolate, melted

1 In a large saucepan, heat the oil for a few moments, then add the popcorn kernels and place the lid on the pan. Leave for 1–2 minutes until all the kernels have popped (shake the pan after the first minute), and then pour the popcorn into a large bowl to cool slightly.
2 Pour over the melted chocolate. Stir to coat well, and then spread the chocolate-coated popcorn over a baking tray lined with baking paper to set.

320 Chocolate hedgehog

PREPARATION TIME 25 minutes, plus chilling   **COOKING TIME** 5 minutes   **MAKES** 16 squares

250g/8oz butter, chopped
250g/8oz/1 cup plus 4 tsp
caster sugar
3 tbsp cocoa powder
1 egg, lightly beaten
300g/10¹/₂oz digestive biscuits,
roughly crushed

115g/3¹/₂oz/1 cup walnuts, chopped
150g/5¹/₂oz milk chocolate,
melted and left to cool
1 recipe quantity Dark Chocolate
Ganache (see page 209)

1 Line a 20 x 30cm/8 x12in cake tin with baking paper, leaving enough to come up the sides slightly.
2 In a small saucepan, melt the butter over a low heat, remove from the heat and leave to cool. When cool, add the sugar, cocoa and egg, and beat together, using a hand whisk.
3 In a large bowl, mix together the biscuits and walnuts, then add the melted chocolate and butter mixture, stirring well with a wooden spoon to combine. Pour the mixture into the prepared tin and spread it evenly over the base. Cool, then refrigerate for approximately 30 minutes until firm, then ice with the dark chocolate ganache and leave to set.
4 Remove from the tin, using the paper to help you, and cut into squares with a sharp knife.

321 White chocolate & raspberry brittle

PREPARATION TIME 15 minutes   **COOKING TIME** 5 minutes   **MAKES** 16 squares

150g/5¹/₂oz white chocolate,
  broken into pieces

60g/2¹/₄oz/¹/₂ cup raspberries,
  puréed

1 Line a 23cm/9in square shallow-sided cake tin with baking paper,
   leaving some overlapping the edges.
2 In a small saucepan, heat the chocolate over a low heat until just melted.
   Remove from the heat and stir until smooth, using a wooden spoon. Spread
   the melted chocolate over the base of the prepared tin using a palette knife.
3 Drizzle the raspberry purée over the top of the chocolate mixture with a spoon,
   then swirl through the white chocolate with a skewer to create a marbled effect.
4 Leave the brittle in a cool place until firm. (Refrigerate only if it is a warm day.)
   Remove from the tin, using the paper to help you, before cutting into squares.

322 White chocolate & nut treats

PREPARATION TIME 15 minutes, plus chilling   **MAKES** 24 treats

200g/7oz white chocolate, melted
50g/1³/₄oz/¹/₂ cup flaked almonds,
  lightly toasted

100g/3¹/₂oz/1³/₄ cups flaked coconut

1 In a medium-sized bowl, mix all the ingredients together, then place teaspoonfuls
   of the mixture on a baking tray lined with baking paper.
2 Refrigerate for approximately 30 minutes until firm.

323 White chocolate & pistachio log

PREPARATION TIME 15 minutes, plus chilling   **COOKING TIME** 5 minutes
MAKES 1 log

200g/7oz white chocolate,
  broken into pieces
75g/2³/₄oz butter
50g/1³/₄oz/¹/₃ cup pistachio nuts,
  roughly chopped

50g/1³/₄oz/¹/₃ cup hazelnuts,
  roasted and roughly chopped
50g/1³/₄oz/¹/₂ cup desiccated
  coconut, lightly toasted
100g/3¹/₂oz pink Turkish delight,
  cut into cubes

1 In a small saucepan, melt the white chocolate and butter together over a very
   low heat, remove from the heat and set aside until cool but still liquid.
2 In a bowl, mix together the nuts, coconut and Turkish delight until well
   combined, using a wooden spoon, then add the cooled chocolate mixture and
   stir well.
3 Spoon the mixture into the middle of a piece of plastic film, roll over a flat surface
   to form a log shape, then twist the ends of the film together. Refrigerate for
   approximately 30 minutes until firm.
4 Remove from the fridge, take off the plastic film and cut the log into slices.

324   Marzipan-stuffed chocolate prunes

PREPARATION TIME 25 minutes, plus setting   **MAKES** 20 chocolate prunes

75g/2³/₄oz marzipan
20 large pitted prunes

150g/5¹/₂oz dark chocolate,
   melted and left to cool

1   Knead the marzipan until soft, then take small balls of it and stuff them inside the prunes.
2   Dip each prune into the melted chocolate to coat half, and place on a baking tray lined with baking paper. Set aside at room temperature to set.

325   Chocolate panforte

PREPARATION TIME 25 minutes   **COOKING TIME** 15 minutes   **MAKES** 24 slices

butter, for greasing
175g/6oz/1¹/₄ cups roasted
   hazelnuts, chopped
175g/6oz/1 cup plus 2 tbsp roasted
   almonds, chopped
175g/6oz/1³/₄ cups roasted walnuts,
   chopped
175g/6oz/1 cup dried figs, chopped
175g/6oz/1 cup dried apricots,
   chopped

175g/6oz/³/₄ cup dried prunes,
   chopped
125g/4¹/₂oz/1 cup plain flour
2 tbsp cocoa powder,
   plus extra, sifted, for dusting
1 tsp nutmeg, grated
¹/₂ tsp ground cloves
¹/₂ tsp cinnamon
150g/5¹/₂oz/²/₃ cup caster sugar
150ml/5fl oz/²/₃ cup clear honey

1   Preheat the oven to 180°C/350°F/gas 4. Grease a 25cm/10in spring-form cake tin with butter, and line with baking paper.
2   In a large bowl, combine the nuts, dried fruits, flour, cocoa and spices. In a small saucepan, heat the sugar and honey together over a low heat until boiling, stirring constantly with a wooden spoon. Reduce the heat and simmer for 1 minute, then pour the honey syrup over the fruit and nut mixture, stirring well to combine. (The mixture will be very thick.)
3   Spoon the mixture into the prepared tin, and smooth the surface with slightly wet hands. Bake in the hot oven for 15 minutes. While still warm, run a sharp knife around the edges of the panforte to release it from the tin.
4   Leave the panforte to cool completely in the tin, before cutting into thin slices, using a sharp knife. Dust with cocoa before serving.

326   Chocolate-coated coffee beans

PREPARATION TIME 10 minutes, plus chilling   **COOKING TIME** 5 minutes
MAKES 125g/4¹/₂oz/1¹/₄ cups

50g/1³/₄oz/²/₃ cup large, good-quality
   coffee beans, roasted

75g/2³/₄oz dark chocolate,
   broken into pieces

1   Wipe the coffee beans with a paper towel, and set aside.
2   In a small saucepan, heat the chocolate over a low heat until just melted, then remove from the heat and stir until smooth. Leave to cool for 5 minutes.
3   Toss the coffee beans in the melted chocolate and stir well to coat, then remove the beans with a fork, draining off any excess chocolate, and arrange the chocolate-coated beans on a baking tray lined with baking paper. Refrigerate for approximately 30 minutes until firm.

327 Chocolate florentines

PREPARATION TIME 35 minutes   **COOKING TIME** 6–8 minutes   **MAKES** 24 florentines

50g/1¾oz butter, plus extra
  for greasing
3 tbsp plus 1 tsp caster sugar
2 tsp clear honey
50g/1¾oz/½ cup flaked almonds

50g/1¾oz/¼ cup red glacé cherries,
  chopped
50g/1¾oz/⅓ cup sultanas
150g/5½oz milk chocolate,
  melted and cooled

1   Preheat the oven to 180°C/350°F/gas 4. Line 2 large baking trays with
    baking paper.
2   In a small saucepan, melt the butter, sugar and honey together over a low heat
    until melted. Remove the pan from the heat. In a large bowl, mix together the
    almonds, glacé cherries and sultanas, then pour the butter mixture into the
    bowl, stirring well with a wooden spoon to combine. Place tablespoonfuls of the
    mixture on the baking tray, leaving 5cm/2in between them for room to spread,
    and press down lightly to flatten the mixture into rounds.
3   Bake in the hot oven for 6–8 minutes, or until lightly golden. Remove the trays
    from the oven, allow the florentines to cool for 5 minutes, then transfer them
    to a wire rack to cool completely.
4   When cold, turn the biscuits over (the backs will be smooth), and spread with
    melted chocolate. Once the chocolate has cooled slightly, make lines using a
    fork or wavy icing spreader. Leave on the baking tray until the chocolate is set.

328 Chocolate gingernut squares

PREPARATION TIME 25 minutes, plus chilling   **COOKING TIME** 5 minutes   **MAKES** 16 squares

400g/14oz dark chocolate,
  broken into pieces
125g/4¹/₂ oz butter, chopped
397g/14oz can condensed milk
5 pieces stem ginger,
  finely chopped
250g/9oz gingernut biscuits, crushed

75g/2³/₄oz/³/₄ cup desiccated
  coconut, toasted, plus 3 tbsp
  for sprinkling

1 Line a shallow 23cm/9in square cake tin with kitchen foil, leaving enough at the edges to overhang the sides.
2 In a small saucepan, heat the chocolate and butter together until just melted, then remove from the heat and stir until smooth. Stir in the remaining ingredients, and spoon into the prepared tin. Sprinkle with the extra coconut.
3 Refrigerate the chocolate gingernut mixture until firm. Remove from the fridge and turn out of the tin, using the foil to help you, then cut into squares with a sharp knife.

329 Chocolate & almond truffle squares

PREPARATION TIME 35 minutes, plus chilling   **COOKING TIME** 5 minutes
MAKES 16 squares

450g/1lb dark chocolate,
  broken into pieces
125ml/4fl oz/¹/₂ cup double cream

3 tbsp amaretto liqueur
50g/1³/₄oz/¹/₃ cup roasted
  almonds, roughly chopped

1 Line a shallow 20cm/8in square cake tin with kitchen foil.
2 In a small saucepan, heat 350g/12oz of the chocolate with the cream over a low heat until just melted. Remove the pan from the heat and stir until smooth, using a wooden spoon. Stir in the amaretto, then leave the mixture to one side.
3 In a clean pan, melt the remaining chocolate separately over a low heat. Spread half of the melted chocolate over the base of the prepared tin.
4 Refrigerate the chocolate base until firm, then top with the truffle mixture and sprinkle with the chopped almonds. Drizzle the remaining melted chocolate over the truffle mixture in a decorative pattern. Refrigerate for approximately 30 minutes until firm, then turn out using the foil to help you, before cutting into squares with a sharp knife.

330 Chocolate raisin clusters

PREPARATION TIME 15 minutes, plus chilling   **MAKES** 14

150g/5¹/₂oz milk, dark or white
  chocolate, melted and left to cool
100g/3¹/₂oz/³/₄ cup raisins

50g/1³/₄oz/¹/₃ cup roasted almonds,
  roughly chopped

1 In a large bowl, mix together the melted chocolate, raisins and almonds, and leave to cool slightly.
2 Place rounded tablespoonfuls of the chocolate and raisin mixture on a baking tray lined with baking paper. Refrigerate for approximately 30 minutes until set.

331 Best-ever hot chocolate

PREPARATION TIME 15 minutes   **COOKING TIME** 5 minutes

250ml/9fl oz/1 cup milk
250ml/9fl oz/1 cup double cream
2 tbsp caster sugar

125g/4½oz dark chocolate,
 broken into pieces
cocoa powder, sifted for dusting
 (optional)

1   Heat the milk and half the cream in a saucepan until just boiling. Remove from
    the heat and beat in the sugar and chocolate, using an electric hand mixer.
2   Divide the chocolate milk equally between 4 small cups (the mixture is very rich).
    Whip the remaining cream until it forms soft peaks, using an electric hand mixer,
    then place a tablespoonful on each cup and dust with cocoa powder, if using.
    Serve immediately.

332 Spiced hot chocolate

PREPARATION TIME 10 minutes, plus standing **COOKING TIME** 5 minutes

1 litre/35fl oz/4 cups milk
4 tbsp soft brown sugar
6 cardamom pods, crushed
6 cloves
1 cinnamon stick
1 star anise, lightly crushed

½ tsp whole coriander seeds
½ tsp ground nutmeg
¼ tsp red pepper flakes
3 tbsp cocoa powder
½ tsp vanilla essence

1 In a medium-sized saucepan, combine together the milk, sugar, cardamom, cloves, cinnamon, star anise, coriander seeds, nutmeg and red pepper flakes over a medium heat until hot. Remove the pan from the heat, whisk in the cocoa, using a hand whisk, then leave to stand for 20 minutes.

2 Sieve the spiced milk into a clean saucepan and reheat until just boiling. Add the vanilla essence, then divide the chocolate drink equally between 4 cups.

333 Cinnamon hot chocolate

PREPARATION TIME 10 minutes **COOKING TIME** 5 minutes

1 litre/35fl oz/4 cups milk
4 tbsp caster sugar
4 tbsp cocoa powder
¼ tsp cinnamon
½ tsp vanilla essence

2 tbsp dark chocolate chips
4 tbsp Chocolate Chantilly Cream
(see page 208)
2 tbsp grated dark chocolate

1 In a medium-sized saucepan, heat the milk until it just begins to simmer. Remove the pan from the heat and whisk in the sugar, cocoa, cinnamon and vanilla essence, using a hand whisk.

2 Divide the chocolate chips between 4 tall heatproof glasses or mugs and top with the hot chocolate milk. Place a tablespoonful of the chocolate chantilly cream on top of each glass, and decorate with the grated chocolate.

334 Bitter-sweet hot chocolate

PREPARATION TIME 5 minutes **COOKING TIME** 5 minutes

600ml/21fl oz/2½ cups milk
4 tsp cocoa powder
4 tbsp dark chocolate chips

4 tsp brandy or rum
4 tbsp Chocolate Chantilly Cream
(see page 208)

1 In a medium-sized saucepan, heat the milk until it just comes to the simmer. Remove the pan from the heat and whisk in the cocoa, chocolate chips and brandy or rum.

2 Divide the chocolate milk equally between 4 small heatproof glasses or mugs, and top each glass with a tablespoonful of the chocolate chantilly cream.

335 White hot chocolate

PREPARATION TIME 5 minutes **COOKING TIME** 5 minutes

1.75 litres/62fl oz/7 cups milk
175g/6oz white chocolate,
　broken into pieces
1 tsp vanilla essence

125ml/4floz/^{1}/$_2$ cup double cream,
　whipped to soft peaks
cinnamon, for sprinkling

1　In a medium-sized saucepan, heat the milk and chocolate over a low heat until the chocolate has just melted, stirring with a wooden spoon. Remove the pan from the heat and add the vanilla essence.
2　Divide the chocolate milk equally between 4 cups. Top each cup with a tablespoonful of whipped cream, then sprinkle over a little cinnamon.

336 Rich mint hot chocolate

PREPARATION TIME 5 minutes **COOKING TIME** 5 minutes

300ml/10^1/$_2$ fl oz/1^1/$_4$ cups milk
425ml/15 fl oz/1^3/$_4$ cups
　double cream

200g/7oz dark chocolate, grated,
　plus 3 tbsp for sprinkling
4 tsp caster sugar (optional)
5 tbsp peppermint liqueur

1　In a medium-sized saucepan, heat the milk, 300ml/10^1/$_2$fl oz/1^1/$_4$ cups of the cream and the chocolate over a low heat until hot, stirring with a wooden spoon. Remove the pan from the heat, add the sugar to taste and stir in the liqueur.
2　Whip the remaining cream to soft peaks using an electric hand mixer.
3　Divide the drink equally between 4 heatproof glasses or mugs and top each glass with a tablespoonful of whipped cream and a little grated chocolate.

337 Hot chocolate with orange

PREPARATION TIME 5 minutes **COOKING TIME** 5 minutes

500ml/17fl oz/2 cups milk
peel from 1 orange, cut into strips
200g/7oz dark chocolate,
　broken into pieces

2 tsp instant coffee granules
3 tbsp orange liqueur

1　In a medium-sized saucepan, heat the milk and orange peel together until just boiling. Remove from the heat, strain the liquid through a sieve to remove the peel, then whisk in the chocolate and coffee, using an electric hand mixer.
2　Divide the liqueur between 4 tall heatproof glasses or mugs, then top with the chocolate mixture.

338 Nutty chocolate coffee

PREPARATION TIME 5 minutes   **COOKING TIME** 5 minutes

1 litre/35fl oz/4 cups milk
4 tsp cocoa powder
4 tsp instant coffee granules
4 tbsp caster sugar

4 tbsp hazelnut liqueur
125ml/4floz/¹/₂ cup double cream,
  whipped to soft peaks
pinch cinnamon, to sprinkle

1   In a medium-sized saucepan, heat the milk until just boiling. Remove
    from the heat and whisk in the cocoa, coffee, sugar and liqueur.
2   Strain the mixture into a clean jug and divide equally between 4 cups.
    Top each cup with a tablespoonful of the whipped cream, then sprinkle
    over the cinnamon.

339 Chocolate Irish coffee

PREPARATION TIME 10 minutes

3 tbsp cocoa powder
875ml/30fl oz/3¹/₂ cups freshly
  brewed coffee
4 tsp caster sugar

2 tbsp Irish whisky
4 tbsp Chocolate Chantilly Cream
  (see page 208)
3 tbsp grated dark chocolate

1   Place the cocoa in a bowl and blend to a paste with 125ml/4fl oz/¹/₂ cup of
    the coffee. Whisk in the remaining coffee, the sugar and whisky, using a
    hand whisk.
2   Divide the coffee mixture evenly between 4 heatproof glasses. Top each glass
    with a tablespoonful of chocolate chantilly cream, then sprinkle with the grated
    dark chocolate.

340 Chocolate milkshakes

PREPARATION TIME 5 minutes

500m/17fl oz/2 cups cold milk
1 tsp vanilla essence
4 tbsp chocolate sauce

8 tbsp Rich Chocolate Ice Cream
  (see page 164) or good-quality
  bought ice cream

1   Combine all of the ingredients in a blender and process until well combined.
2   Divide the milkshake mixture equally between 4 glasses.

341 Iced mocha shake

PREPARATION TIME 20 minutes, plus chilling

875ml/30fl oz/3¹/₂ cups
  hot, strong coffee
3 tbsp cocoa powder
2 tbsp caster sugar

4 scoops Rich Chocolate Ice Cream
  (see page 164) or good-quality
  bought ice cream
125ml/4floz/¹/₂ cup double cream,
  whipped to soft peaks
4 tbsp grated dark chocolate

1   Pour the coffee into a large bowl. In a small bowl, mix the cocoa to a paste with
    2 tablespoonfuls of the coffee. Whisk the paste back into the remaining coffee,
    with the sugar, using a hand whisk, then stir well with a wooden spoon until the
    sugar is dissolved. Leave to cool completely, then refrigerate for 30 minutes.
2   Place a scoop of chocolate ice cream in the bottom of each of 4 tall glasses.
    Pour over the coffee, dividing it equally between the glasses. Spoon a generous
    tablespoonful of the whipped cream over the top of each glass, then sprinkle
    with grated chocolate. Serve immediately.

342 Divine iced mint chocolate

PREPARATION TIME 15 minutes

75g/2³/₄oz dark or milk chocolate,
  melted and left to cool
400ml/14fl oz/1²/₃ cups cold milk
150ml/5fl oz/²/₃ cup natural or
  vanilla-flavoured yogurt

6 mint leaves, plus extra
  to decorate
4 scoops Rich Chocolate Ice Cream
  (see page 164) or good-quality
  bought ice cream

1 Place the chocolate, milk, yogurt and mint in a blender; combine until smooth.
2 Divide the milk mixture equally between 4 tall glasses and top with a scoop of
   chocolate ice cream. Decorate with mint leaves and serve immediately.

CHAPTER 6

Sauces,
Frostings
& Icings

These recipes deserve a chapter devoted just to them

as you will use them time and time again. While a number

of the recipes throughout the book suggest a sauce, frosting

or icing, feel free to mix and match them to your needs.

All of the recipes are very simple to make and will transform

a favourite recipe into a something special. This chapter

includes a deliciously indulgent Double Chocolate Sauce,

a Chocolate Caramel Sauce and a wickedly mouthwatering

Chocolate & Amaretto Sauce, all of which can be used with

an assortment of the recipes or simply poured over a bowl of

fresh strawberries or a bowl of vanilla ice cream. Try making

two or three sauces and surrounding them with a selection

of freshly cut fruit and let your family and friends dip their

fruit into the sauce of their choice: a simple, but absolutely

delicious way to end a meal. Chocolate Fudge Frosting, White

Chocolate Frosting or Chocolate Cream Cheese Frosting will

transform your favourite cake or slice, so don't restrict them

just to the recipes in this book. Experiment and enjoy!

343 Rich chocolate sauce

PREPARATION TIME 10 minutes   **COOKING TIME** 5 minutes   **MAKES** 375ml/13fl oz/1½ cups

250ml/9fl oz/1 cup double cream
150g/5½oz dark chocolate,
　　broken into pieces

1 tbsp chocolate liqueur (optional)
1 tbsp icing sugar
1 tsp vanilla essence

1　In a small saucepan, combine the cream and chocolate over a low heat, stirring with a wooden spoon until smooth. Remove the pan from the heat.
2　Stir in the liqueur, if using, sugar and vanilla essence. Serve warm.

344 Double chocolate sauce

PREPARATION TIME 10 minutes   **COOKING TIME** 5 minutes   **MAKES** 250ml/9fl oz/1 cup

125ml/4fl oz/½ cup double cream
100g/3½oz dark chocolate,
　　broken into pieces

25g/1oz milk chocolate,
　　broken into pieces

1　In a small saucepan, heat the cream until just boiling. Remove the pan from the heat.
2　Add both chocolates, stirring with a wooden spoon until they have melted, and serve warm.

345 Chocolate caramel sauce

PREPARATION TIME 15 minutes   **COOKING TIME** 5 minutes   **MAKES** 375ml/13fl oz/1½ cups

200g/7oz dark chocolate,
　　broken into pieces
250ml/9fl oz/1 cup double cream

2 tbsp dulce de leche or similar
　　caramel paste
1 tsp vanilla essence

1　In a small saucepan, combine the chocolate and cream over a low heat until the chocolate has just melted. Remove the pan from the heat.
2　Add the dulce de leche and vanilla essence, stirring until smooth. Set aside to cool for 10 minutes before serving.

346 Chocolate & amaretto sauce

PREPARATION TIME 10 minutes   **COOKING TIME** 5 minutes   **MAKES** 375ml/13fl oz/1½ cups

250ml/9fl oz/1 cup double cream
150g/5½oz dark or milk chocolate,
　　broken into pieces

2 tbsp amaretto liqueur
1 tsp vanilla essence

1　In a small saucepan, combine the cream and chocolate over a low heat until the chocolate has melted, stirring with a wooden spoon until smooth. Remove the pan from the heat.
2　Stir in the amaretto and vanilla essence and set aside to cool for 10 minutes before serving.

347 Espresso chocolate sauce

PREPARATION TIME 10 minutes   **COOKING TIME** 5 minutes   **MAKES** 375ml/13fl oz/1½ cups

250ml/9fl oz/1 cup double cream
150g/5½oz dark chocolate,
   broken into pieces

60ml/2fl oz/¼ cup hot, strong
   espresso coffee
1 tbsp coffee liqueur

1   In a small saucepan, combine the cream and chocolate over a low heat until the chocolate has just melted. Remove the pan from the heat.
2   Add the coffee and liqueur and set aside to cool for 10 minutes before serving.

348 Chocolate fruit & nut sauce

PREPARATION TIME 20 minutes   **COOKING TIME** 5 minutes   **MAKES** 375ml/13fl oz/1½ cups

100g/3½oz/¾ cup plus 1 tbsp raisins
100g/3½oz/¾ cup plus 1 tbsp
 dried cranberries
2 tbsp orange liqueur
250ml/9fl oz/1 cup double cream

150g/5½oz milk or dark chocolate,
 broken into pieces
100g/3½oz/⅔ cup roasted almonds,
 roughly chopped

1   Place the raisins and cranberries in a small, microwaveable bowl with the liqueur. Heat in the microwave for 1 minute, then remove and leave to soak for 10 minutes.
2   In a small saucepan, combine the cream and chocolate over a low heat until the chocolate has just melted. Remove from the heat and stir with a wooden spoon until smooth.
3   Stir in the almonds and soaked fruits, and serve immediately.

349 White chocolate sauce

PREPARATION TIME 10 minutes   **COOKING TIME** 5 minutes   **MAKES** 375ml/13fl oz/1½ cups

250ml/9fl oz/1 cup double cream
125g/4½oz white chocolate,
 broken into pieces

1 tsp vanilla essence

1   In a small saucepan, combine the cream and chocolate over a low heat until the chocolate has just melted. Add the vanilla essence and stir until smooth, using a wooden spoon.
2   Remove the pan from the heat and serve warm.

350 Traditional hot fudge sauce

PREPARATION TIME 10 minutes   **COOKING TIME** 5 minutes   **MAKES** 375ml/13fl oz/1½ cups

100g/3½oz dark or milk chocolate,
 broken into pieces
50g/1¾oz butter, chopped

150g/5½oz/¾ cup plus 1 tbsp
 soft brown sugar
1 tsp vanilla essence
125ml/4fl oz/½ cup double cream

1   Place all of the ingredients in a saucepan over a low heat, stirring well, until the mixture just comes to the boil – the chocolate should be melted and the sauce smooth.
2   Remove the pan from the heat and serve warm.

351 Chocolate rum sauce

PREPARATION TIME 10 minutes   **COOKING TIME** 5 minutes   **MAKES** 300ml/10½fl oz/1¼ cups

250ml/9fl oz/1 cup double cream
2 tsp granulated sugar

100g/3½oz dark chocolate,
 broken into pieces
2 tbsp dark rum

1   In a small saucepan, heat the cream, sugar and chocolate together over a low heat until the chocolate has melted, stirring with a wooden spoon until smooth.
2   Remove the pan from the heat, stir in the rum and serve warm.

352 Chocolate Marsala cream

PREPARATION TIME 10 minutes   **MAKES** 250ml/9fl oz/1 cup

250ml/9fl oz/1 cup double cream
1 tbsp icing sugar

1 tbsp Marsala wine
cocoa powder, sifted, to dust

1   In a large bowl, combine the cream, icing sugar and Marsala wine and whip
    to soft peaks, using an electric hand mixer.
2   Dust the top of the cream with cocoa just before serving.

353 Chocolate chantilly cream

PREPARATION TIME 15 minutes   **MAKES** 250ml/9fl oz/1 cup

250ml/9fl oz/1 cup double cream
2 tbsp icing sugar

100g/3½oz dark or milk chocolate,
   melted and left to cool

1   In a large bowl, whip the cream and icing sugar together to form soft peaks,
    using an electric hand mixer.
2   Gently fold in the melted chocolate until just combined, before using.

354 Chocolate mascarpone cream

PREPARATION TIME 10 minutes, plus chilling   **MAKES** 250ml/9fl oz/1 cup

125g/4½oz milk chocolate,
   melted and left to cool

1 tsp vanilla essence
125g/4oz mascarpone cheese

1   In a large bowl, whisk all the ingredients together, using an electric hand mixer.
2   Refrigerate for 30 minutes before using.

355 Chocolate buttercream

PREPARATION TIME 15 minutes, plus chilling   **MAKES** 375ml/13fl oz/1½ cups

175g/6oz butter
200g/7oz/1 cup plus 1 tbsp
   soft brown sugar
1 egg yolk

1 tbsp milk
1 tbsp cocoa powder
100g/3½oz dark chocolate,
   melted and left to cool

1   In a large bowl, beat the butter and sugar together until light and fluffy, using
    an electric hand mixer. Add the remaining ingredients and continue beating
    until thick and light.
2   Refrigerate for 30 minutes before using.

356 Mocha buttercream

PREPARATION TIME 45 minutes, plus cooling and chilling   **COOKING TIME** 5 minutes
MAKES 500ml/17fl oz/2 cups

175ml/6fl oz/scant ¾ cup milk
100g/3½oz dark chocolate,
   broken into pieces
4 tsp instant coffee granules
1 tsp vanilla essence

3 egg yolks
100g/3½oz butter, softened
200g/7oz/1½ cups plus 4 tsp
   icing sugar

1   In a large saucepan, combine the milk, chocolate, coffee and vanilla essence
    over a low heat until the chocolate has just melted, then remove the pan from
    the heat. Beat the yolks in a bowl and whisk in the chocolate mixture. Return
    the mixture to the pan and cook, stirring constantly with a wooden spoon, until
    the mixture begins to thicken and coats the back of the spoon. Do not allow to
    boil. Pour the mixture into a bowl and set aside to cool for 30 minutes.
2   In a clean bowl, whisk the butter until light and creamy, using an electric hand
    mixer, then add the chocolate mixture with the icing sugar. Continue to whisk
    until thick and glossy. Refrigerate for 30 minutes before using.

357 Dark chocolate ganache

PREPARATION TIME 5 minutes, plus cooling **COOKING TIME** 5 minutes
MAKES 250ml/9fl oz/1 cup

175g/6oz dark chocolate,
  broken into pieces

25g/1oz butter
125ml/4fl oz/¹/₂ cup double cream

1 In a small saucepan, combine all of the ingredients over a low heat, and stir
until the chocolate and butter have melted. Remove the pan from the heat.
2 Pour into a clean bowl and leave to cool for around 20 minutes, or until the
mixture begins to thicken. Use as a filling or topping in your chosen cake
recipe, or serve warm as a sauce.

358 White chocolate ganache

PREPARATION TIME 10 minutes, plus cooling **COOKING TIME** 5 minutes
MAKES 250ml/9fl oz/1 cup

125ml/4fl oz/½ cup crème fraîche

125g/4½oz white chocolate, broken into pieces

1 In a small saucepan, heat the crème fraîche over a low heat. Remove the pan from the heat and add the white chocolate. Stir gently until the chocolate has melted, using a wooden spoon, then continue stirring for a few more minutes until smooth.
2 Set aside to cool for 30 minutes, or until the ganache has thickened slightly.

359 White chocolate frosting

PREPARATION TIME 10 minutes, plus cooling and chilling **COOKING TIME** 5 minutes
MAKES 375ml/13fl oz/1½ cups

100g/3½oz white chocolate, broken into pieces

250ml/9fl oz/1 cup double cream
250g/9oz mascarpone cheese

1 In a small saucepan, combine the chocolate and 150ml/5fl oz/⅔ cup of the cream over a low heat until the chocolate has just melted. Remove the pan from the heat, and stir until smooth. Pour the mixture into a clean bowl and leave to cool for 30 minutes, stirring occasionally, then refrigerate for approximately 1 hour.
2 In a large bowl, stir the mascarpone until smooth, using a wooden spoon. Add the chocolate mixture and as much of the remaining cream as required to make a spreading consistency.

360 Chocolate sour cream frosting

PREPARATION TIME 15 minutes **COOKING TIME** 5 minutes **MAKES** 375ml/13fl oz/1½ cups

150g/5½oz dark chocolate, broken into pieces
25g/1oz butter

125ml/4fl oz/½ cup sour cream
1 tsp vanilla essence
375g/13oz/3 cups icing sugar, sifted

1 In a small saucepan, combine the chocolate and butter over a low heat until just melted.
2 Remove the pan from the heat and leave to cool for 10 minutes, then add the sour cream and vanilla essence. Stir the icing sugar into the chocolate mixture, using a wooden spoon. Continue stirring until the mixture thickens. Add a little hot water if the icing becomes too thick to spread.

361   Chocolate cream cheese frosting

PREPARATION TIME 10 minutes   **MAKES** 375ml/13fl oz/1½ cups

250g/9oz cream cheese, softened
100g/3½oz dark chocolate,
  melted and left to cool

15g/½oz butter, softened
1 tsp vanilla essence
250g/9oz/2 cups icing sugar, sifted

1   In a large bowl, beat the cream cheese until light, using an electric hand mixer.
2   Add the melted chocolate, butter, vanilla essence and icing sugar, and continue beating until creamy and thickened.

362   Chocolate fudge frosting

PREPARATION TIME 15 minutes   **COOKING TIME** 5 minutes   **MAKES** 375ml/13fl oz/1½ cups

75g/2¾oz dark chocolate, broken into pieces
75g/2¾oz butter, chopped
250g/9oz/2 cups icing sugar

2 tbsp cocoa powder
5 tbsp milk
1 tsp vanilla essence

1   In a small saucepan, heat the chocolate and butter over a low heat until just melted. In a medium-sized bowl, mix the icing sugar and cocoa together, and pour the melted chocolate over. Add the milk and vanilla essence, and stir to combine well.

2   Put the bowl containing the mixture into a larger bowl containing a little iced water and beat the mixture with a wooden spoon until it is thick enough to spread and hold its shape.

363   Chocolate rum frosting

PREPARATION TIME 15 minutes   **COOKING TIME** 5 minutes   **MAKES** 375ml/13fl oz/1½ cups

100g/3½oz dark chocolate, broken into pieces
25g/1oz butter, chopped
300g/10½oz/2⅓ cups icing sugar

100ml/3½fl oz/⅓ cup double cream
2 tbsp dark or light rum
1 tsp vanilla essence

1   In a small saucepan, combine the chocolate and butter together over a low heat, and stir until smooth.

2   Place the icing sugar in a large bowl and, using a wooden spoon, mix in the chocolate mixture, cream, rum and vanilla essence. Whisk until thick, using an electric hand mixer.

364   Creamy chocolate icing

PREPARATION TIME 10 minutes   **MAKES** 250ml/9fl oz/1 cup

225g/8oz/1¾ cups icing sugar
3 tbsp cocoa powder

25g/1oz butter, melted
4–5 tbsp milk

1   Sift the icing sugar and cocoa into a bowl.

2   Stir in the butter and enough of the milk to make a creamy consistency.

365   Shiny chocolate icing

PREPARATION TIME 15 minutes   **MAKES** 250ml/9fl oz/1 cup

400g/14oz/3 cups icing sugar
2 tbsp cocoa powder

15g/^{1}/$_2$oz butter, softened

1   Place the icing sugar and cocoa in a bowl and make a small well in the middle.
     Place the butter in the well and pour over 2^1/$_2$ tbsp boiling water. Stir until
     the butter has melted, then continue stirring until the icing is of spreading
     consistency, adding about another 2^1/$_2$ tbsp water as required.
2   Use immediately.

Index

A

almonds: chocolate &
  almond marble cake 84
chocolate & almond
  truffle squares 196
chocolate & almond
  tuiles 125
chocolate almond
  squares 117
chocolate pear sundae with
  toasted almonds 170
chocolate-almond friands
  with raspberries 96
roasted almond drops 188

B

bananas: baked bananas with
  chocolate rum sauce 160
banana & chocolate loaf
  cake with liqueur 72
banana & white chocolate
  muffins 130
banana Scotch pancakes
  with chocolate sauce 144
chocolate & banana
  fritters 159
chocolate & banana
  ice cream 164
chocolate banana bread 71
chocolate-banana
  mascarpone cheesecake 20
chocolate banana
  swirl cake 72
steamed banana pudding
  with chocolate 156
bavarois: chocolate &
  coconut bavarois 29
chocolate nut bavarois 27
dark chocolate
  orange bavarois 28
mocha bavarois 28
white chocolate bavarois
  with blueberries 29
berries with white
  chocolate sauce 160
biscuits:
  chewy chocolate biscuits 103
  chocolate & almond tuiles 125
  chocolate & hazelnut
    biscuits 107
  chocolate & peanut butter
    biscuits 107
  chocolate & pistachio
    biscuits 109
  chocolate Anzac biscuits 106
  chocolate ice-cream & ginger
    biscuit sandwiches 168
  chocolate melting
    moments 104
  chocolate soufflé biscuits 108
  chocolate-chip biscotti 110
  dark chocolate & coffee
    biscuits 106
  double chocolate biscotti
    with hazelnuts 110
  double chocolate biscuits 103
  macadamia & chocolate
    wafers 125
  orange chocolate-chip
    biscuits 108
blondies 102
brandy snaps with
  chocolate cream 36
bread pudding, fig &
  chocolate 148
brownies:
  brown sugar brownies 101
  cakey chocolate brownies 100
  cappuccino brownies 100
  cashew & chocolate-chip
    brownies 98
  chocolate brownie
    cookies 114
  chocolate cream cheese
    brownies 97
  chocolate fudge brownies
    98
  cream liqueur brownies 97
  dark & white chocolate
    brownies 99
  rocky road brownies 101
buttercream: chocolate
  buttercream 208

mocha buttercream 208
butterscotch & chocolate
  slice 123

C

cakes: all-in-one chocolate
  & sour cream cake 73
apple chocolate cake 89
banana & chocolate
  loaf cake with liqueur 72
bourbon chocolate cake 76
butterfly cakes with
  chocolate cream 94
chocolate & almond marble
  cake 84
chocolate & orange loaf
  cake 84
chocolate almond
  squares 117
chocolate angel food cake 79
chocolate banana
  swirl cake 72
chocolate beer cake 78
chocolate brownie cake 86
chocolate bundt cake 73
chocolate cake with
  Marsala 70
chocolate chestnut cake 68
chocolate courgette loaf
  cake 81
chocolate cream roll with
  strawberries 87
chocolate ginger cake 90
chocolate lava cakes 62
chocolate mousse cake 58
chocolate pear cake 80
chocolate polenta cake 81
chocolate raisin cake 80
chocolate ricotta cake 78
crunchy chocolate-topped
  squares 118
devil's food cake 76
easy fudge cake 77
flourless chocolate &
  citrus cake 74
Italian chocolate
  custard cake 58
lemon & chocolate drizzle
  loaf cake 83
Mississippi mud cake 70
mocha pudding cakes 154
nutty chocolate, rum & fig
  cake 85
orange loaf cake with
  chocolate chips 85
peanut butter chocolate
  cake 86
pear, pistachio & chocolate
  loaf cake 75
simple chocolate &
  raspberry jam cake 74
sinful chocolate cake 62
sour cream chocolate
  cake 77
sticky chocolate cake 63
upside-down apple &
  chocolate cakes 94
white chocolate cake 83
white chocolate, ginger &
  apricot loaf cake 90
white chocolate mousse
  cake 61
white chocolate Sauternes
  cake 82
cashew & chocolate-chip
  brownies 98
cheesecakes: chilled
  chocolate cheesecake 16
chocolate & vanilla ripple
  cheesecake 18
chocolate hazelnut
  cheesecake 17
chocolate mascarpone
  cheesecake 20
chocolate sour cream
  cheesecake 17
chocolate-banana
  mascarpone cheesecake
  20
mini white chocolate
  cheesecakes 19
mocha marble cheesecake
  16
raspberry ripple white
  chocolate cheesecake 18
strawberry & white chocolate
  cheesecake ice cream 165

white chocolate & blueberry
  cheesecake 21
white chocolate
  cheesecake 21
chocolate banana bread 71
chocolate crumb crust 13
chocolate-dipped
  dried fruit 191
chocolate hedgehog 192
chocolate truffle dessert 35
coconut: chocolate & coconut
  bavarois 29
chocolate & coconut
  cherry slice 119
chocolate & coconut
  cream fondue 56
chocolate & coconut rough
  slice 119
chocolate-chip & coconut
  muffins 129
chocolate coconut drops 128
chocolate coconut slice 122
coconut & white chocolate
  panna cottas 31
marshmallow Lamingtons
  192
white chocolate & coconut
  rice pudding 156
white chocolate, citrus &
  coconut truffles 186
white chocolate, coconut &
  blueberry friands 96
white chocolate, lime &
  coconut cup cakes 93
coffee: cappuccino slims 190
chocolate affogato 175
chocolate Irish coffee 200
chocolate-coated coffee
  beans 194
coffee parfait with chocolate
  sauce 175
coffee, chocolate & praline
  mousse 32
dark chocolate & coffee
  biscuits 106
espresso chocolate sauce
  205
frozen espresso mousse with
  chocolate sauce 173
iced mocha shake 200
Irish coffee meringues with
  chocolate 50
mocha buttercream 208
nutty chocolate coffee 200
cookies: chocolate brownie
  cookies 114
chocolate-chip pecan
  cookies 111
chocolate pine nut
  cookies 113
crispy chocolate chip
  cookies 111
spiced chocolate cookies 114
truffle dough cookies 112
white & dark truffle dough
  cookies 113
cranberry & raisin chocolate
  drops 189
cream: chocolate Chantilly
  cream 208
chocolate mascarpone
  cream 208
crèmes brûlées: chocolate
  crèmes brûlées 153
white chocolate crèmes
  brûlées 152
crèmes caramels,
  chocolate 152
crêpes see pancakes & crêpes
cup cakes:
  chocolate cup cakes 91
  chocolate surprise cup
    cakes 92
  dark & white chocolate cup
    cakes 92
  white chocolate cup cakes 93
  white chocolate, lime &
    coconut cup cakes 93
custard:
  baked chocolate custard 154
  chocolate custard mille-
    feuilles 26
  creamy thick chocolate 12

D

dark chocolate marquise 35
devil's food cake 76

E F

éclairs, chocolate 22
flapjacks, chocolate 124
florentines, chocolate 195
fondues: chocolate & coconut
   cream fondue 56
   chocolate fondue 56
   chocolate liqueur fondue 57
   marbled chocolate fondue 56
friands: chocolate-almond
   friands with raspberries 96
   white chocolate, coconut &
   blueberry friands 96
frostings: chocolate cream
   cheese frosting 211
   chocolate fudge frosting 212
   chocolate rum frosting 212
   chocolate sour cream
   frosting 210
   white chocolate frosting 210
fruit kebabs with chocolate
   fruit & nut sauce 160
fudge: chocolate hazelnut
   fudge 190
   chocolate marshmallow
   fudge 189
   mint chocolate fudge 189

G

ganache: dark chocolate
   ganache 209
   white chocolate ganache 210
ginger: chocolate ginger
   cake 90
   chocolate gingernut
   squares 196
   chocolate ice-cream & ginger
   biscuit sandwiches 168
   ginger & chocolate
   ice cream 167
   gingernut & chocolate
   truffles187
   roasted macadamia & ginger
   white chocolate drops 187
   white chocolate, ginger &
   apricot loaf cake 90
grasshopper pie 25

H

hazelnuts: chocolate &
   hazelnut biscuits 107
   chocolate hazelnut
   cheesecake 17
   chocolate hazelnut fudge 190
   chocolate hazelnut
   meringues 49
   chocolate hazelnut torte 69
   double chocolate biscotti
   with hazelnuts 110
   hazelnut thumbprints 115
   nutty white chocolate
   shortbread 116
   strawberry, hazelnut &
   chocolate shortcakes 22
hot chocolate: best-ever hot
   chocolate 197
   bitter-sweet hot chocolate 198
   cinnamon hot chocolate 198
   hot chocolate with orange 199
   nutty chocolate coffee 200
   rich mint hot chocolate 199
   spiced hot chocolate 198
   white hot chocolate 199

I

ice creams: caramel &
   chocolate ice cream 166
   chocolate & banana
   ice cream 164
   chocolate baked Alaska 177
   chocolate ice-cream & ginger
   biscuit sandwiches 168
   chocolate ice cream with
   Irish Cream 169
   chocolate marshmallow
   ice cream 175
   chocolate nougat
   ice cream 169
   chocolate pear sundae with
   toasted almonds 178
   chocolate, raisin & amaretto
   ice cream 165
   crushed candied ice cream 175
   ginger & chocolate
   ice cream 167
   grilled pineapple, macadamia
   & chocolate sundaes 178

honeycomb & chocolate
   ice cream 168
Marsala strawberries layered
   with chocolate ice cream 180
mint chocolate-chip
   ice cream 170
mocha ice cream 166
mulled berries with chocolate
   ice cream 180
peach & amaretti sundae
   with chocolate 179
quick honeycomb & chocolate
   ice cream 175
rich chocolate ice cream 164
roasted macadamia &
   chocolate ice cream 166
strawberry & white chocolate
   cheesecake ice cream 165
tiramisu ice-cream cake 177
Turkish delight ice cream 164
white chocolate ice cream 165
icings: creamy chocolate
   icing 212
   shiny chocolate icing 213

L

Lamingtons: chocolate
   Lamingtons 88
   double chocolate
   Lamingtons 88
   marshmallow Lamingtons 192
   white chocolate Lamingtons 89
lemons:
   candied citrus peel 185
   chocolate-crusted lemon
   tart 136
   lemon & chocolate drizzle
   loaf cake 83
   lemon & white chocolate
   pudding 159
   lemon roulade with chocolate
   drizzle 64
   tangy lemon & chocolate
   tarts 139
   white chocolate, citrus &
   coconut truffles 186

M

macadamia nuts: chocolate
   macadamia nut tart 25
   grilled pineapple, macadamia
   & chocolate sundaes 178
   macadamia & chocolate
   wafers 125
   roasted macadamia &
   chocolate ice cream 166
   roasted macadamia & ginger
   white chocolate drops 187
macaroons: chocolate cherry
   macaroons 105
   chocolate macaroons 104
madeleines, chocolate 95
meringues: chocolate &
   chestnut mess 37
   chocolate floating islands 51
   chocolate ganache
   meringues 50
   chocolate hazelnut
   meringues 49
   chocolate meringue kisses 51
   chocolate meringue tart 59
   chocolate meringue torte 44
   chocolate meringues with
   blackberries 48
   Irish coffee meringues with
   chocolate 50
   mini mallow meringues with
   chocolate cream 47
   passionfruit, white chocolate
   & strawberry meringue
   roulade 45
   poached meringues with
   chocolate sauce 49
   white chocolate & raspberry
   Eton mess 37
milkshakes:
   chocolate milkshakes 200
   divine iced mint
   chocolate 201
   iced mocha shake 200
mille-feuilles: chocolate
   custard mille-feuilles 26
   strawberry & chocolate
   mille-feuilles 26
mint slims 190
mocha pots with ricotta &
   coffee liqueur 149

mousses:
   cappuccino mousse 33
   chocolate liqueur mousse
   with raisins 33
   chocolate nougat mousse 32
   coffee, chocolate & praline
   mousse 32
   frozen espresso mousse with
   chocolate sauce 173
   mocha rum mousse 33
   quickest-ever chocolate
   mousse 31
   white chocolate &
   passionfruit mousse 32
   white chocolate mousse
   with raspberries 34
muffins: banana & white
   chocolate muffins 130
   chocolate cherry muffins 129
   chocolate-chip & coconut
   muffins 129
   chocolate donut
   mini-muffins 128
   double chocolate muffins 131
   flourless chocolate
   muffins 132
   white chocolate & blueberry
   muffins 130
   white chocolate & strawberry
   muffins 132

O

oranges:
   candied citrus peel 185
   chocolate & orange loaf
   cake 84
   chocolate & orange
   truffles 185
   chocolate crêpes with
   orange, white chocolate &
   ricotta 146
   chocolate orange pots 148
   hot chocolate with orange 198
   orange loaf cake with
   chocolate chips 85
   orange chocolate-chip
   biscuits 108

P

pancakes & crêpes:
   banana Scotch pancakes with
   chocolate sauce 144
   chocolate & blueberry Scotch
   pancakes 144
   chocolate & strawberry
   liqueur crêpes 146
   chocolate cherry crêpes 147
   chocolate crêpe gâteau 145
   chocolate crêpes 145
   chocolate crêpes with
   chestnut cream 145
   chocolate crêpes with
   orange, white chocolate &
   ricotta 146
   chocolate Scotch pancakes 144
   chocolate soufflé crêpes 147
panforte, chocolate 194
panna cottas: coconut & white
   chocolate panna cottas 31
   mocha panna cottas 31
   white chocolate
   panna cottas 30
parfaits: coffee parfait with
   chocolate sauce 173
   white chocolate & raspberry
   parfait 174
pastry:
   chocolate mud pastries 133
   chocolate shortcrust 13
   choux 13
   sweet shortcrust 13
pastry cream, chocolate 12
pavlovas: chocolate pavlova 46
   mini strawberry pavlovas
   with chocolate drizzle 47
   pavlova with white chocolate
   & passionfruit cream 46
peach & amaretti sundae
   with chocolate 179
pears:
   chocolate amaretti pears 159
   chocolate pear cake 80
   chocolate pear sundae with
   toasted almonds 178
   chocolate pear tart 134
   pear clafoutis with
   chocolate 148

pear, pistachio & chocolate loaf cake 75
pies: frozen Mississippi mud pie 176
grasshopper pie 25
popcorn, chocolate 192
pots: chocolate orange 148
white chocolate, blueberry & citrus 35
profiteroles: passionfruit profiteroles with white chocolate sauce 24
profiteroles with coffee cream & chocolate sauce 23
strawberry profiteroles with chocolate sauce 24
prunes: marzipan-stuffed chocolate prunes 194
puddings:
chocolate apple pudding 150
chocolate panettone & raisin puddings 150
chocolate puddings with rum sauce 158
chocolate self-saucing pudding 155
chocolate sticky pudding & caramel sauce 154
fig & chocolate bread pudding 148
lemon & white chocolate pudding 159
mocha pudding cakes 154
pain-au-chocolat puddings 151
simple chilled chocolate puddings 156
steamed banana pudding with chocolate 156
steamed chocolate pudding 157

R
raspberries: chilled chocolate & raspberry soufflé 55
chocolate & raspberry tart 135
chocolate-almond friands with raspberries 96
chocolate raspberry ganache torte 60
raspberry & chocolate meringue roulade 45
raspberry ripple white chocolate cheesecake 18
white chocolate & raspberry brittle 193
white chocolate & raspberry Eton mess 37
white chocolate & raspberry parfait 174
white chocolate mousse with raspberries 34
white chocolate roulade with raspberries 64
white chocolate tiramisu with raspberries 42
rice puddings:
chocolate rice pudding 155
white chocolate & coconut rice pudding 156
white chocolate rice pudding 155
roast figs with chocolate sauce 161
roulades: chocolate roulade with cinnamon cream 44
chocolate roulade with mixed berries & white chocolate cream 65
lemon roulade with chocolate drizzle 64
mocha roulade with chocolate mascarpone cream 65
passionfruit, white chocolate & strawberry meringue roulade 45
white chocolate roulade with raspberries 64

S
sauces:
caramel sauce 12
chocolate & amaretto sauce 204
chocolate caramel sauce 204
chocolate fruit & nut sauce 206
chocolate Marsala sauce 207
chocolate rum sauce 206
double chocolate sauce 204
espresso chocolate sauce 205
rich chocolate sauce 204
traditional hot fudge sauce 206
white chocolate sauce 206
scones:
chocolate chunk scones 126
chocolate scones 126
cranberry & white chocolate scones 127
semifreddos: chocolate & nougat semifreddo 172
chocolate semifreddo 172
chocolate semifreddo with Marsala 170
shortbread: chocolate shortbread 115
chocolate-dipped shortbread 116
nutty white chocolate shortbread 116
slices: butterscotch & chocolate slice 123
chocolate & coconut rough slice 119
chocolate & coconut cherry slice 119
chocolate coconut slice 122
chocolate peppermint slice 122
chocolate-chip & nut slice 120
crunchy chocolate crisp slice 118
mincemeat & chocolate slice 123
rocky road slice 120
white chocolate fruit & nut slice 121
sorbets:
chocolate mint sorbet 170
chocolate sorbet 171
chocolate sorbet with pineapple carpaccio 180
soufflés: chestnut & chocolate soufflés 54
chilled chocolate & raspberry soufflé 55
chilled dark mocha soufflés 54
chilled white chocolate & passionfruit soufflés 55
hot chocolate soufflés 52
hot mocha & rum soufflés 53
white chocolate soufflé pots 53
strawberries: chocolate & strawberry liqueur crêpes 146
chocolate cream roll with strawberries 87
individual berry & white chocolate trifle 40
Marsala strawberries layered with chocolate ice cream 180
mini strawberry pavlova with chocolate drizzle 47
passionfruit, white chocolate & strawberry meringue roulade 45
strawberries romanoff with white chocolate 36
strawberry & chocolate mille-feuilles 26
strawberry & white chocolate cheesecake ice cream 165
strawberry profiteroles with chocolate sauce 24
strawberry, hazelnut & chocolate shortcakes 22
white chocolate & strawberry muffins 132

sweets: cappucino slims 190
chocolate popcorn 192
chocolate-dipped dried fruit 191
mint slims 190
white chocolate & nut treats 193
white chocolate & raspberry brittle 193

T
tarts & tortes: chocolate & raspberry tart 135
chocolate Bakewell tart 140
chocolate berry torte 69
chocolate caramel tarts 133
chocolate celebration tarts 59
chocolate custard tart 137
chocolate hazelnut torte 69
chocolate macadamia nut tart 25
chocolate mascarpone tart 141
chocolate meringue tart 59
chocolate meringue torte 44
chocolate pear tart 134
chocolate pecan tart 141
chocolate raspberry ganache torte 60
chocolate tart with cardamom 136
chocolate-crusted lemon tart 136
chocolate-glazed peanut butter tart 140
double chocolate tart 138
Italian-style chocolate tart 138
mincemeat & chocolate tart 134
mocha truffle tart 60
tangy lemon & chocolate tarts 139
warm chocolate & nut torte 68
white chocolate & berry tarts 137
white chocolate & lime tart 61
tiramisu:
dark chocolate tiramisu 43
quick tiramisu with chocolate 42
tiramisu ice-cream cake 177
white chocolate tiramisu with raspberries 42
trifles: black cherry trifle 41
fig, chocolate & Marsala trifle 40
individual berry & white chocolate trifles 40
truffles: chocolate & almond truffle squares 196
chocolate & orange truffles 185
chocolate biscuit truffles 187
chocolate rum truffles 185
cranberry & port truffles 184
double chocolate truffles 184
gingernut & chocolate truffles 187
peanut butter & milk chocolate truffles 184
white chocolate, citrus & coconut truffles 186

W
white chocolate & pistachio log 193
white chocolate, blueberry & citrus pots 35

Y Z
yogurt, frozen chocolate 181
zabaglione: chilled chocolate zabaglione 39
chocolate zabaglione 38
frozen zabaglione with chocolate sauce 176
zucotto 39

Author's acknowledgements

My sincere thanks go to the entire team at Duncan Baird Publishers who helped in the creation of this book. My special thanks go to Grace Cheetham, my commissioning editor, and Alison Bolus, my food editor, for all of their patience, encouragement and good humour. Thank you also to home economist Bridget Sargeson and photographer William Lingwood, who created the beautiful images throughout the book.